LUST VIRUS

by

Ron J.

Libera, Simi Valley

Library of Congress Control Number: 2007902955

ISBN 978-0-9614831-2-8

Cover and book design by Hespenheide Design

The scene: A house on Family Avenue, Everytown, U.S.A.

It is 1:30 in the morning, and the attractive young wife, barefoot, in her nightgown, and holding her infant daughter in her arms, has awakened and is looking for her husband. As she approaches the den, she looks into the darkened room through the door, which is slightly ajar. Her husband is at the computer, utterly tranced-out on the monitor. She is repulsed by the look on his face, the wild lascivious flare of his eyes devouring what is on the screen. She is terrified. That is not her husband; it's a ravenous beast! Then, seeing the image he's watching, she reels as if struck by a savage kick to the stomach. She staggers back, gagging, crying out in horrified disbelief. The man turns, terror-stricken.

Both are caught in this shattering moment of truth. The dark force kept in bounds for so long has just ripped through the firmament of their lives like a shaft of furious lightning, exposing the Lie. How can she—how can anyone—comprehend what has turned her Dr. Jekyll husband into this rapacious Mr. Hyde? What *is* that force? What's behind that *Look*? What kind of sexuality is *this*?

News Item

A new plague has broken out on modern man and is now pandemic. It has already infected most of the males and has begun spreading to females. The virus-like entity is energized by an as yet unrecognized source of energy from within the male himself, creating a ravenous need for more and more of the person upon which to feed. The human immune system is powerless over this, the most virulent contagion the world has ever known. Science not only has no remedy, it doesn't know the plague exists.

PREFACE

Astronomers infer the existence of unseen planets by noting the aberrations they exert on the orbits of other planets. They know there must be something out there producing the gravitational pull causing the orbit's irregularity.

Most everyone knows there are aberrations in the orbit of today's sexuality. But what's the force pulling it out of kilter? A few hundred years ago, there was barely a wobble. By the turn of the 19th century, the unsteadiness was more noticeable. And by the time photography, advertising, consumerism, movies, and television were part of everyday life, the orbit of our sexuality was shimmying up a storm. By the sixties, it was really getting shaken up. And now, with all the dizzying new technologies and millions of hits per hour for Internet sex, we're breaking out of orbit and don't even know where we're headed.

So what is that invisible force causing the disturbance? Not sex, not porn; those are merely visible indicators of the aberration. What is it? We're faced here with something far more threatening than the cigarette-cancer connection, environmental pollution, or global warming—wake-up calls for our physical well-being. More threatening because our very humanity and personhood are at stake. Yet there's a strange acceptance of things as they are and denial of the disturbance, as we are giddily swept along on the exciting ride. Honest conversation is discouraged and even opposed. To open such a conversation is what this book is about.

Male lust has been around since the beginning of time. However, there's a *new lust* in the air. Appearing under the guise of sexuality, it is nonetheless anti-sexual, working against the real and propagating a false or *pseudo*-sexuality. It's a killer virus, infecting the very soul of today's sexualities across the board. And it has created a personal and social disease of mass epidemic proportions, where our attitudes, thinking, and behavior work against true sexuality and human relations.

The historical and cultural evidence, combined with data from my own personal recovery experience and that of others over the last thirty-three years, indicates that millions of today's males, however we may categorize ourselves, are really *pseudo*-sexuals. We have fallen victim to diseased thinking and behavior that work against our own sexuality. And, unaware of our infection, we become carriers of the virus propagating the disease, unwitting pawns advancing the pseudo-sexual revolution.

Though this plague affects all of us, this book addresses mostly male issues, derived from male data. The book should also be of intense interest to women who live and move in the same contagious air. They're the ones who are gut-wrenchingly affected by our failure at manhood and cry out, *"What's wrong?!"* This study should cast new light on the feminine dilemma and also help clarify the "orientation" quandary. Also, implications of the connection between lust and violence and lust and sexual violence are staggering.

We are confronted with the prospect of a new journey of discovery—deep within ourselves—one that points the way to remedy. Our humanity is at stake. For increasing numbers of us, our very survival is at stake. For those who can see and identify, there is incredible hope.

CONTENTS

PART IV
Other Forces Driving Pseudosexuality 183

PART V
Where Do We Go from Here? 205

APPENDIXES

INTRODUCTION

Lust is one of the most enduring words in the English language, dating back well before the year 888, as we see in the quote below.

Þa saede he se lust waere hehste good.

Aelfred, *Boethius*, 888

("He [the philosopher Epicurus] *said that lust is the highest good.")*

The *Oxford English Dictionary* lists some six distinct meanings in the history of the word lust up to 1928, when the first edition was published: pleasure; desire, appetite, relish; sensuous appetite or desire; lawless and passionate desire of or for some object; vigor, lustiness; and, the chief then-current use, sexual appetite or desire. By 1989, *Webster's* has added "intense or unbridled sexual desire." One cannot help wondering whether the intensification reflected in 1989—the beginning of the "slice-of-culture" period represented in this book—signifies a change that had taken place between 1928 and 1989. We will attempt to show that there is a change; something new is in the air.

It is very important to realize what we are *not* talking about in this book. We are not talking about whatever it is that produces the normal chemistry of love, romance, passion, and sex; for example: "the goofy grins and sweaty palms as men and women gazed deeply into each other's eyes." Those are the chemicals of attraction, attachment, and cuddling (*Time* February 15, 1993). These are natural phenomena that have been around forever, for which we are only now beginning to discover biochemical markers. Also, we are not talking about sex per se, and we are not talking about porn.

We are talking about lust. Not "hormones," lust. Lust in the context of the maelstrom of cultural forces shaping and driving our sexuality. What I shall call the new lust.

1

The Rise of Solitary Sex and the New Lust

One way to introduce this slippery concept—we might just as easily call it *modern* lust—is by looking at what UC Berkeley historian Thomas Laquer has called the new masturbation. "Modern masturbation," he says, "can be dated with a precision rare in cultural history."[1] The date given is 1712, but the intriguing thing is his use of the term "modern." I will attempt to show that the advent of what he is calling modern masturbation roughly coincides with the faint beginnings of what I am calling the new lust.

Masturbation, like lust, has been around for ages. So what is modern masturbation, when and how did it develop over time, why is it "new," and how does it tie in with the new lust and pseudosexuality? The year 1712 is cited as the transition to modern masturbation because it was about that time an anonymous pamphlet, now known to be written by a British surgeon, was published in London with the lurid title *Onania, or The Heinous Sin of Self Pollution, and all its Frightful Consequences, in both SEXES Considered, with Spiritual and Physical Advice to those who have already injured themselves by this abominable practice. And seasonable admonition to the Youth of the nation of Both SEXES.*

Before 1712, that is, roughly before the Enlightenment, sex with oneself was apparently no big deal, either medically or culturally. (The Enlightenment was the philosophical movement of the eighteenth century marked by "rejection of the traditional and reliance on rationality, characterized by innovations in social, religious, political, and educational ideas.") The *Onania* pamphlet thus revealed a fundamental shift in that consciousness, as its title suggests. So what was there about solitary sex back then that began to catch and hold the public interest, causing people to think differently about their relation to pleasure and sexuality? Why did masturbation move from "the distant moral horizon to the ethical foreground"?

It was the "particular combination of market capitalism, scientific and medical inquiry, and the print culture of the early eighteenth century" that combined to create solitary sexual activity as the threat it was perceived to be. The relatively new practice of silent, private reading, especially novels, played into the construction of the new masturbation and its perception as a problem because "the cultural energy of reading novels was the cultural energy of solitary sex."

Books and novels were "crucial in the creation of desire and its ethical management; and were predicated on solitude, fantasy, the free play of imagination, and *the capacity to dwell within the self*" (emphasis added).

So what was it in 1712 that was deemed so unnatural about solitary sex? The answer given is that it was intimately tied in with the very core of the emerging Enlightenment consciousness. Imagination, exploration, luxury, autonomy, sexuality—these were becoming central to the culture itself. And masturbation "relies on the imagination (rather than nature or reality), its practice is solitary and secret (rather than social or observable) and it arouses desires that can neither be satiated nor moderated (and thus overrides reason)." This is an unusually perceptive observation, sounding like insights a thoughtful recovering masturbator might have. It turns out that, apparently, the new masturbation was a by-product of the very changes the Enlightenment had brought about. It embodied both the qualities that the age idealized and the prospect of those very qualities being jeopardized. We will show that the new lust is a by-product of accelerating cultural changes since then that bring us to where we are today.

It's as though writers, beginning with the author of *Onania* and through the early twentieth century, were saying, What's going on here? This resorting to self-sex. What kind of impact is this having on our culture? It's all in the mind, for goodness sake. Sex with self is abetting this going deeper into inwardness. It's taking us *away* from human social intercourse, not to mention what's happening to the human condition itself! Are we losing something here? Where's this thing going? And what's happening to the self when masturbation is becoming central to the development of the new self? Powerful questions that need honest investigation.

"This . . . practice that had once signified so little would come to represent the psychic depths of boys and girls, men and women—as well as a danger to their relationships with their family, lovers, and the social order more generally—for the next three centuries [after 1712]." Apparently, the sense was that masturbation was "conquering the whole world of our sexuality." Thus, by 1712 the culture's evolving consciousness and growing questioning about solitary sex had apparently reached the point when someone, such as the physician-author of *Onania*, could air the topic in such starkly negative terms, reflecting the culture's mood.

Of course, sometime around the 1960s and 1970s this consciousness was shifting: solitary sex was again no big deal, at least in the media consciousness. Whether it is so in the personal consciousness today is another matter. One psychoanalyst, devoting a whole book to the subject, concluded "everyone masturbates, and everyone feels guilty about it."

That books and novels were "crucial in the creation of desire" tells us something about the impact of culture on sexuality. And what Laquer's cultural history of solitary sex is mirroring may well be the advent of modern lust. My guess is that the incidence of solitary sex was increasing as we were going deeper into the self. Civilization was not only offering new ways by which we could extend our inwardness, but also at the same time beginning to press in upon us. We had to seek new forms of relief and escape into that inwardness.

Thus, the Enlightenment is perhaps the precursor to those modern cultural forces we'll be looking at that have been shaping our sexualities. And we can see what will turn out to be the beginnings of the cultural origins of the new lust. In a way, we will be tracing the cultural "autobiography" of the lust virus as it has mutated into what it is today.

Shakespeare on Lust

It is significant that William Shakespeare (1564–1616) comes onto the scene at the leading edge of the Enlightenment we've just been talking about. A man before his time, he may be considered a force contributing to the Enlightenment. It is thus not a coincidence that he has given the world one of the most perceptive and compelling descriptions of lust ever put into words (*Sonnet* 129):

> *The expense of spirit in a waste of shame*
> *Is lust in action; and till action, lust*
> *Is perjured, murderous, bloody, full of blame,*
> *Savage, extreme, rude, cruel, not to trust;*
>
> *Enjoy'd no sooner but despised straight;*
> *Past reason hunted, and no sooner had,*

Past reason hated, as a swallowed bait,
On purpose laid to make the taker mad;

Mad in pursuit, and in possession so;
Had, having, and in quest to have, extreme;
A bliss in proof, and proved, a very woe;
Before, a joy proposed; behind, a dream.

> *All this the world well knows; yet none knows well*
> *To shun the heaven that leads men to this hell.*

The expense of spirit in a waste of shame. Lust exacts a price; we are diminished, and in a wasteland of shame. Shakespeare's use of the word "spirit" is significant. In lust, we're dealing with something deeper than the psyche—the *spiritual* component, the very core of personality, the very heart, our spirit, our deep inner self. This wasteland is the very core of our being.

Note the string of adjectives having connotations of violence that Shakespeare connects with lust: *murderous, bloody, savage, extreme, rude, cruel.* When lust is active, it's as though a negative force is unleashed that must have its way. A self-confessed luster relates how he was cruising for prostitutes once when none seemed to be around. Then, one appeared on a street corner. Suddenly, out of nowhere, other cars began careening around wildly in the heavy rush-hour traffic, trying to get to her first. He did an insane U-turn in the middle of the block across three other lanes of traffic on that main city thoroughfare to try and beat the others to her. His lust was not only murderous but suicidal! We shall see later that lust not only is the "expense" of spirit but also kills the spirit. Spiritual violence.

Lust *full of blame?* How true. Blame the lust object, the wife, the boss, God . . . . Any excuse will do—and must do—to justify another "drink." (A "drink" and "getting drunk" are terms used by recovering lusters to denote the visual act of imbibing an image or person that triggers lust, much as alcoholics get their "fix" by taking a drink of alcohol.)

Enjoy'd no sooner but despised straight. Enjoyed and despised? "It makes me feel so good, but so bad." It's crazy! The lust payoff is so intense and seductive we never learn, even when we wind up despising ourselves. Lust entails a deliberate suspension of disbelief, a distortion of our own reality.

Past reason hunted. The lust-oriented individual knows what this means; we hunt lust past reason itself. Temporary insanity. Then, *past reason hated.* Self-loathing. How could Shakespeare know the human heart so well that he sees the connection between lust and corroded self-esteem?

As a swallowed bait on purpose laid to make the taker mad. How diabolical lust seems to become, almost as though it's out there—or is it really in here?—baiting us. Shakespeare was no stranger to the forces acting upon and within the depths of the human spirit.

Mad in pursuit, and in possession so. Mad, yes, but we only realize the insanity after the act—that is, if we've had an attitude change. Shakespeare's reiteration of the madness theme in this sonnet calls our attention to the aspect of distortion, the perversion of reality inherent in lust. And that will become clearer as we move along. I myself was beginning to cross the bounds into the "extreme" while chasing sex on the streets. Only humans can do with and to sex what lust can do.

A bliss in proof, and proved a very woe / Before, a joy proposed; behind, a dream. We lusters never doubt that lust will bring bliss—it must! But if lust is so great, why the woe and fading bliss—fading as a dream, surreal, unreal, anti-real?

Finally, *All this the world well knows; yet none knows well / To shun the heaven that leads men to this hell.* Deliberate suspension or perversion of reality, again and again—a key theme in our discovery and analysis. This male playwright/poet had an incredible sense of the human condition. And if Shakespeare perceived lust as he did in his day, what would he say today?

Another very significant thing about this sonnet: In Shakespeare's portrait of lust there are indications that lust can possess and overpower the person. He can find himself under the grip of something he cannot shake, no matter how he may feel about what he's doing, even against his own will. Today we call this addiction. (Ref. Appendix 1, What *Is* Lust?)

As it turns out, Shakespeare's penetrating insights prophetically highlight key elements of the new lust and the lust-violence connection. Let's see what some young men at Duke University have to say; they provide a telling commentary on the new lust without ever using the term.

PART I

THE NEW LUST
AND
PSEUDOSEXUALITY

"SEX WITH THE UNREAL WOMAN"— THE BOYS AT DUKE

Remember . . . . Lust makes you stupid.

"Sylvia" cartoon by Nicole Hollander June 10, 1993

SHOE By Jeff MacNelly   January 25, 2000

The following are excerpts from an ABC News *20/20* program of January 29, 1993, entitled "Sex with the Unreal Woman," in which a group of young male and female students at Duke University was interviewed regarding the impact on their lives, relations, and sexuality of resorting to picture-women. These interviews represent a remarkable departure in probing the subjective aspect of sexual behavior. This approach has more value than many so-called scientific surveys that simply list how many of which category are doing what—the "count and catalog" approach. This peek into the pre-Internet genesis of the new lust, as it was developing in boys in the 1970s, will help reveal basic elements of its essential character. The credit for these frank insights must go to the young men and women themselves, who initiated their own inquiry, which was remarkable.

The men at Duke came together in the wake of the problems between the sexes that they were observing on campus—from date rape to just plain bad relationships—to see if there was any connection with the pictures they had seen and used sexually as kids. Two years prior to the interview, the group of young men began meeting on their own once a week to discuss what had gone wrong in their sexuality and relations. Their conversations with each other were intimate and painfully honest. It is amazing how a false sexuality (what I am calling *pseudo*-sexuality) can be seen evolving in these young men, strongly suggesting its connection with media, especially images. These students, as well as the interviewer, refer to material such as *Playboy*, *Penthouse*, and *Hustler* as "pornography."

Verbatim excerpts from the broadcast interview follow (courtesy of ABC News—*20/20*). My comments are in brackets.

> Barbara Walters, introducing the panel, asks, "Is it an innocent rite of passage or are these sexual images so powerful that they make a lasting impression?" Let's let the boys and girls speak for themselves. (Numbers refer to the order in which the students responded.)
>
> **3rd Student (male):** My little friend was over at my house, and my parents were gone, and we decided we're going to look for pornography. And he said, "Wait. They always hide your birthday presents. Where do they hide that?" And I was like, "In my mom's closet." And so we went in there, and there was this big box up on a shelf. And we opened it up and there were like tons and tons and tons of *Playboy*'s and *Penthouse*'s and things and, you know, it's just like porn bonanza.
>
> **4th Student (male):** We took them all out and cut them up and it was just like trading cards, and we would actually trade them. Like I remember I gave him like—like brunettes for a blonde or something like that. And this is second, third, or fourth grade. . .

5th Student (male): Then we divided them up and it was like, Yeah. You know, it was like, This is mine now, you know, These women are mine. My first sexual experience was, you know, dividing up women.

David Gutterman (student): A part of our culture is the permission that men have to look at women as sexual beings, as only sexual beings. . . . Pornography's going to teach you a lot. It's sex education. . . .We see here a woman in the workplace [referring to pictures viewed by the interviewer] . . . in her police uniform, and on the left and in all of the other photos of this woman in the magazine, it's this woman naked. . . . And the message . . . clearly is that no matter where this woman is or wherever women are, they're seen, at their core, as sexual bodies.

Interviewer (Lynn Sherr, ABC News): What did it teach you to look for?

Jason Schultz (student): The image of beauty—large breasts, thin waist, model-esque features. . . .

David Gutterman (student): Now it's right in this very touchy period of puberty where you're watching your body develop, and you're seeing or reading about what bodies are going to look like—tremendous, 12-inch penises, that men have perfect control over all the time—and you're anxious for that day to come. And when that day doesn't come, it's a big disappointment. . . .

3rd Student: It's like this is the thing adult men have, you know, and, "I don't know how to use it exactly." And you know, "When will I be a man and get to—get to have this stuff? [Notice the depersonalization of woman into *stuff to be had* and the presumed right to *take* (is that incipient violence?) This is typical for users of porn and symptomatic of the perversion of woman already beginning in these boys.]. . . .

6th Student(male): By junior high, it was kind of implicitly known that, you know, if you're borrowing it for the night, you know, you're going to take it home.

7th Student (male): So that's how I found out what you do with it, 'cause people joke. They say, "Oh, look at him, he's taking it home," and then they take it home the next night . . . . it became something to think about, think about using it to masturbate to. . . .

Interviewer (Sherr): Did you use pornography to masturbate the first time you ever had an orgasm?

Mr. Schultz (male student): Oh. Oh, yeah, and as touchy as it may be to say, a lot of the men, in fact, almost all the men I've talked to have similar experiences. . . .

8th Student (male): It's just a picture of a person. It doesn't mean anything. But when you're about to masturbate and you're thinking about masturbating, or you're thinking about everything in a sexual context, it takes on a power. . . . [It is that very "power" that is the essence of what we'll be looking at in this book.]

Catharine MacKinnon (Lawyer/Activist): The way it works is it gives the man who is consuming it the experience of using a woman. First of all, she is flat, she is inert, she does not talk back to him. She is not real. . . . [Note the word *consuming*, a remarkably accurate insight.] She is two-dimensional, an object for use. . . . it absolutely does condition him in his body. . . .

Mr. Gutterman (male): And the second level is, "Wow, I'm really interested in her in my English class," and what you fantasy you have with the blueprints that you have from *Penthouse Forum* are what you use to plug these women and girls from your classes, from your life, into these scenarios.

6th Student (male): You believed what you read in the magazine, so I don't ever remember it crossing my mind that that might not be the case.

1st Student (male): This taught me that women are, in a sense, easy, that all it takes is a little persuasive talking—you know, pushing the right buttons, almost—and she'll be ready to have sex.

Interviewer (Sherr): And what if the woman says no?

Mr. Gutterman (student): Women in pornography don't say no. Women in pornography never say no.

1st Student (male): And when they do, they don't mean it.

Mr. Gutterman (student): . . . They don't say no to your fantasies, because you control the woman on the page. . . .

6th Student (male): I feel like I spent the first like four or five relationships, serious relationships of my life, working through the difference between what I took as gospel truth—you know *Penthouse Forum* was it—and working out what real relationships were like. And when the emotional stuff came around and when I started falling in love, I fled. . . . [Note carefully this flight from woman.]

8th Student (male): When you're finished in pornography [read *after you've masturbated to it*], it goes back up on the shelf, and in real life, there's a person there, even after you ejaculate.

5th Student(male): And what's scary—I've caught myself sometimes like, when having sex, where I have to like—to get—to finally climax, to get over that edge, I've had to close my eyes and imagine the woman I'm with. I had to see an image within myself and see an image of the person I was with, not actually opening my eyes and looking at that person. [What he's really talking about is picture-lust-induced functional impotence. No wonder the Viagra revolution was just around the corner.]

5th Student (male): A friend of mine has the expression of "masturbating into a woman." That is—that is sort of like a logical conclusion of pornography or masturbating to pornography. When—when you're finally with a real person, you're not really with them. . . .

9th Student (female): As I have gone through puberty and looked through stacks of *Playboy* in my father's closet, I've, you know, also looked through the pages and looked [at] these standards of what I'm supposed to look like to be a desirable woman . . . seductive, alluring.

10th Student (female): . . . "I'm waiting for you. . . ." "This is how I look all the time and I'm here solely for you to look at me. . . ."

2nd Student (female): He started talking about, "You really like this, don't you?" And it was, "You want this, don't you?" It wasn't, "Do you want this?" . . . It was thrust upon me. "This is what you want, this is what you want." . . . . I saw him watch it. I mean, I was there with him when he was watching it and—he had me watch it.

11th Student (female): I had a boyfriend who would want to try different things . . . I'd say okay and then, "No, I don't like that. . . ." He's seen pornos, and the women liked it. . . . And I'm going, "No, no. Stop." . . . It was kind of like suffocating, actually truthfully. I felt like I was caught in a closed space, and I was saying, "No, no," and I couldn't get away, I couldn't move. And it was very—I felt entrapped and— . . . I was very scared. I kind of felt like I was losing control, you know, of the situation. And this was a person that I was in love with, which made it even, you know, more frightening.

Interviewer (Sherr): How did it affect your sexual relationships afterward?

11th Student (female): I kind of distanced myself from, you know, sex . . . it did cause problems. We— you know, we—I never wanted to have sex. You know, I—and I think pornography had a big deal to do with it. You know, I think that that was a— a big factor. [Flight from man?]

Interviewer (Sherr): . . . What do you do . . . to overcome the images, specifically, the stereotypes created by porn of how men should act?

Mr. Gutterman (student): . . . [B]reak silence from adult to child, break silence between men and, in particular, break silence between men and women about the impact that pornography has had on their lives. . . ."

A Look Back

Below is a brief excerpt from one of the picture-lust case studies in Appendix 4 describing the genesis and progression of picture-lust in someone who could well have been one of the boys at Duke, now forty-four and looking back from a standpoint of recovery.

1. *At what age did you experience images coupled with any kind of sexual thinking or behavior?* "Twelve or thirteen."
2. *Describe the scene of how that initial connection between pictures and sex (or sexual type thinking or activity) came about.* "On shelves at convenience stores. Detective magazine cover; inside more pictures of scantily clad women. Submissive women. Then more explicit magazines in the *Gent* and *Playboy* genre."
3. *Describe the image itself, what the picture shows.* "A woman posing, scantily clad, emphasizing breasts, large breasts, stockings, garters. I remember white stockings and garters, fishnets, bra and panties, women usually looking into the camera."
4. *What effect did viewing that image have inside of you? If you can, play back your feelings in slow motion so we can see the progression of feelings and impact. Another way of asking this is, What was the picture (or pose) communicating to you?* "I was particularly aroused when the woman was looking at the camera; this communicated that she was posing for me. Looking into her eyes gave me a sense of connection with a real person and a feeling she wanted to arouse me."
5. *With the picture there in front of you, what did you do?* "Usually ended in masturbation. When I didn't have pictures handy I would close my eyes and act out to memory of them or picture a real person."
6. *Did your use of images escalate? How? Did your inner reactions and feelings change over time as you continued to resort to picture sex? Please describe.* "Yes. Began stealing magazines from stores. Acting out to pictures more often. [My] stash grew. Took my favorite pictures with me even on family vacations. Discovered hardcore pornography, films, pictures. My inner reactions, feelings: Developed more of a fantasy world. Depended more on pictures, fantasy to deal with loneliness.
7. *Did you reach a point when you would say that you had crossed the line into addiction? At what age?* "Yes. Fourteen to fifteen."
8. *Did you experience any turning point(s) in your history of picture-sex where something new was going on, either in the content of the images themselves, your behavior, or your thinking? Was there some specific*

incident connected with this, such as a special picture or experience? Describe the picture and/or incident. "I had been addicted to hardcore pornography films for years. Oral sex images where the woman was looking at the camera (making me feel I was participant) were my choice. Also, every new perversion I witnessed on film made vivid extreme imprint (golden showers, bestiality, S&M), hooking me in. I remember in my early twenties reading a foreign-film pornography catalog, when I experienced a hard drool and a rush from head to toe, like something had overtaken me. This was a very real moment that I can reflect on and realize I was totally enthralled by the addiction overpowering me like a drug . . . ."

It is encouraging to note that as of this writing, the above man, still single, has been sexually abstinent for over nine years, has progressively experienced release from the lust obsession, and is beginning to date and learn to relate to women in a joyous new freedom.

. . .

Barbara Walters' opening question in the interview was, "Is it an innocent rite of passage or are these sexual images so powerful that they make a lasting impression?" The boys at Duke had already answered that question by having discovered on their own that resorting to those images damaged their sexuality and interpersonal relations. This *20/20* segment was titled "Sex With the Unreal Woman." What kind of force is mediated through picture-sex that can so pervert normal sexuality that, as one of the boys said, "when you're finally with a real person, you're not really with them?" (The term "mediated" is used in the sense of "how the media shapes your world and the way you live in it," as in *Mediated*, a book with that subtitle.) If we can identify the force mediated through picture-sex, we will have come a long way toward seeing what is at the root of the new lust and how it is mediated through images.

But first, let's trace the "lustification" of the female image in recent media history. This should help explain the tremendous impact of picture-woman on today's sexuality and reveal telltale signs of the lust virus at work.

THE LUSTIFICATION OF PICTURE-WOMEN

"LUST is up this year."

Los Angeles Times, April 9, 1993

This play on words in a 1993 metropolitan newspaper is no accident.[2] There is a growing awareness that something new is in the air of male sexuality. Today, lust seems to have an intensity about it—an aura— that is different from what was prevalent in the last century, even up to World War II.

John D'Emilio and Estelle Freedman, two historians of American sexuality, referring to the sexual revolution of the sixties and seventies, say:

> The reduction of women's bodies to erotic objects had debilitating effects. Women walking down the street were the targets of stares, catcalls, and whistles. Men would "use her body with their eyes," wrote Meredith Tax. . . . "They will evaluate her market price. . . . They will make her a participant in their fantasies. . . . No woman can have an autonomous self unaffected by such encounters."[3]
> [We would add that no *man* can be unaffected.]

Then look at this snippet from the *Los Angeles Times* of August 28, 1994:

> This season fashion is outrageous, sexy and glamorous, full of slick fabrics, tight miniskirts and dangerous stiletto heels. Spring's baby doll has become Fall's vixen, intent on showing off legs, hips and breasts. Hair is coiffed, lips are dark, nails are lacquered midnight red. Fashion hasn't been this blatant since the '70s. The message: Dress up. Provoke.

lustification \lus-ti-fi-ca-shun\ *n.*—the act or process of imbuing something or someone with lust. **lustify** *v.*—to imbue with qualities soliciting lust in the viewer. (From the author's *Pseudo-Dictionary of Fabricated Words*)

Today there is an intangible but crucial "something" in the air, but since most of us have grown up within this new atmosphere, it is difficult to see, much less evaluate. But something very potent is going on—the lustification of picture-women, and more recently of picture-men. So let's look at the historical development of that process. Without realizing it, our sexuality and very identity are being threatened and shaped by it.

Pictorial Magazines

Mass newspaper journalism in America got underway between 1830 and 1835. The press of London had already set the fashion for inexpensive, newsy papers for the masses. Literacy was being extended, and with it came the new appetite for news. Workers were being attracted to the New World, and a new class of people began to dominate population in the cities. The "penny press" was born in New York City in 1833 with Horace Greeley's *Morning Post*, the first penny newspaper. By 1884 in Britain, the illustrated magazine had become firmly established. A quick consensus developed among publishers that a magazine should give "wholesome and harmless entertainment to crowds of hard-working people craving for a little fun and amusement . . . light literature and *a large supply of illustration* to please the senses"[4] (emphasis added). How accurate their intuition of human nature. And what a revolution they unwittingly ignited.

By 1891 the *Strand* magazine, famous for carrying the Sherlock Holmes stories of Sir Arthur Conan Doyle, had the stated editorial policy to "put no limit on illustrations." There were 110 illustrations in one issue alone—woodcuts at that. The illustrated magazine was "a phenomenal success." Instantly, another appetite was born, and we humans have never been the same. The proliferation of picture magazines and pictures in other publications of every conceivable (and inconceivable) type is one of the phenomena of the modern era. For example, by 1987—at the beginning of our CAT-scan slice of the nineties—there were thirteen thousand periodicals and some eleven thousand newspapers published in the United States and Canada alone.

It may be difficult for us to realize that there was a time—a mere lifetime ago—when there were no lustified picture-women in the mass media. It is just as hard for us to realize that after the turn of the 19th century, within one generation, the American visual ecology underwent the most dramatic change in human history. The rate of change has been accelerating ever since, with pictures of women becoming the dominant icon.

A reality transformation has already taken place in the photograph itself. Actual reality "out there" is transformed into shades of ink on paper—millions of isolated microscopic dots. If you want to try an interesting experiment, take a printed photograph and put a 10-power loupe to it. Examine the photograph for what it really is—dots of ink on paper. Then ask yourself, How can this produce such a response within me?

When lusters *ingest* the image, reality distortion occurs inside us, energized by lust and shaped by the mediated lusts of others. (This will be developed at length later in the book.) We humans are a marvelous reality-transmogrification machine! This ability to distort—to actually change—reality tells us something very significant about human nature: that it is essentially spiritual, with forces more powerful and more complex than we are willing to admit. (Our use of the term "spiritual" or "spirit," refers to the core essence of the human psyche, as in Shakespeare's *Sonnet* 129.) However, the fact that the problem is in the luster should not blind us to what is being communicated in the picture itself.

Let's take a common example of how lust may interact with even "innocent" photos. I remember when the new athletic shoes became popular, the ones covering the ankles. The first time I saw them on a woman, I was struck with how unattractive and impractical they were. How clunky! Why on earth would anyone other than a basketball player ever want to be seen in them? But then female models began being photographed in them in poses designed to attract and sell. Now everyone wears athletic shoes as a matter of course. Such is the power of the media to manufacture desire. By association, the shoes became a symbol of power or glamour and "beauty"—all of which, for a luster, amounts to a potent lust-symbol. As we gaze at one still photo of this image, we see that the impact is by virtue of the pose, spiritual emanation of the model, and the intrinsic unreality of photographs. The photo itself is another distortion of reality. But this single, static two-dimensional "transform" of reality is a very powerful medium of spiritual communication and propaganda. Evidence? It *sells*! And much more than shoes.

Early Girlies

Production of an indigenous American pornography began after 1846, when William Haynes, an Irish surgeon who immigrated to New York, took the money he had made by publishing *Fanny Hill* in the United States and reinvested it into the production of cheap erotic novels. These became "barracks favorites" during the Civil War and encouraged increased production in the postwar years. "Obscene prints and photographs" were quite commonly kept and exhibited by soldiers and even officers. An example: "New Pictures for Bachelors," twelve-by-fifteen-inch pictures, most placing the man in the role of voyeur, looking at women posing (fully clothed) to be gazed at. Titillating pictures and literature continued to circulate during the late nineteenth century, seen in pool halls, bars, hotels, and in the popular crime and sports newspaper, *Police Gazette*.[5]

Imagine a Civil War soldier, getting hold of one of these "New Pictures for Bachelors" for the first time. Chances are he's never even seen a photograph before. He picks it up, mesmerized, quickly looking around to see if anyone's watching. He stares at the image again, spellbound, entranced. She's real! She's posed there for me! I can have her! A switch turns on inside his brain and soul. A spiritual connection is made. *Mis*-connection. That man may never be the same. And we're not even talking about the erection or what he then does with that picture. Is this something like how the new lust gets into the air? We can almost see the virus at work here, infecting its first "cell" and propagating itself. The virus vector—its means of replication and transmission—is the picture of a woman designed to elicit lust. And the virus host is an eager unsuspecting male.

Did modern lustification of the female image begin with the likes of "New Pictures for Bachelors" and those innocent woodcuts in nineteenth-century magazines? The key is intent; what is the intent or mind-set of the photographer or subject in creating that image? I'm a walking illustrated history of this progressive lustification of image-women from the mid-1930s on, when as a child I got infected and became a willing victim to the viral replication and transmission. Lustification of picture-women is a striking cultural phenomenon of our times, even from that date. Looking back on it all, the direction and rate of change is astonishing.

Life, *the Girlies, and the New Picture-Sex*

Lustification of picture-women probably got into full swing in the Roaring Twenties and Thirties. In a doctor's office I recently saw a photo from 1934 showing six "bathing beauties" in an automobile ad, which is toxic for me to dwell upon, even today.[6] Of course, this may say more about me than the picture, but I venture to say that there is in that shot a clear example of lustification in progress. The women are being coaxed into a come-on pose exuding that certain spirit intended to make males lust and buy. (Someone should write an exposé of the techniques that advertisers, photographers, and pornographers use—are most of them men?—to coax females into lust-enticing poses so they exude that certain "look." It would shock us.) How could the women—or ad men—have known that what they were really selling was something that would work against their own sexuality, promoting a false or pseudo-sexuality?

A great watershed in this lustification revolution is exemplified in *Life* magazine, launched in 1936, which rocketed to instant mass appeal in the 1940s and became the common coin and symbol of our new image-driven world. In its hey-day, *Life* could be found everywhere. No wonder that so many of us males could be found feverishly scoring our next lust and sex fix from that picture-fest.

Life was a training ground for the new photography and one of the mass media through which lustification could proceed smoothly and unrecognized for what it was. (But we picture-lusters recognized it!) *Life* was but one prominent example of pushing the mass art form past existing horizons: using the female image to sell everything—not only the female image but lust itself. These were the famous fashion, glamour, or bathing suit shots, which we knew could always be found inside and before which we could do our secret ritual obeisance. Not only a new appetite but a new iconography had been created.

Evidence of a rapidly escalating appetite for picture-women lust goes back to World War II. This was the era of pinups. They were so gorgeous, and it was so "masculine" to paint their salacious figures on the noses of our aircraft and sport them on our lockers and tattoos.

An interesting example of this glorious new "heterosexuality" in process is revealed in a rare incident recently brought to light. On February 21, 1947, a B-29 bomber named the Kee Bird departed from Fairbanks, Alaska, on a secret spy mission over the Arctic Circle and crash landed on a frozen lake in Greenland. When the plane was spotted by rescue aircraft, "crates full of supplies, including a nudie calendar from a Fairbanks bar, were dropped by parachute." As the Kee Bird crew members scrambled aboard, all supplies and nonessentials were left behind to keep down the weight of the C-54 rescue aircraft. "One of the few things the Kee Bird crew made sure to bring back was the pinup calendar."[7]

This was the new "freedom" and "sexuality" that helped glamorize the War. The new "heterosexuality." Who could discern that for millions of us it would also signify genital slavery and diminished sexuality and manhood? We lusters didn't have to encounter the criminal liability of our chemically addicted brothers and sisters in search for our next fix. *Life, Look,* and the popular media became Everyman's drug connection. And think about the title of *Look,* the other picture-magazine from that era; it's an imperative, commanding us into the new image-connection.

Once picture-lust is connected with the sex act, the lust-infected person has to find more and different and "better." Lust, as a narcotic, is always looking for—demanding—something more powerful. And that wide-open soul will now harbor the new mutant viral strain, which takes over more of him, generating the need for yet more, defiling his very essence.

This brings up an interesting point. Is the power in the picture or in the man? Lust can take the poorest intimation of feminine or masculine form, even cartoons and comics, and jazz it up into something that will pump up enough juice for orgasm.[8] This tells us there's some ingenious creativity at work within us. *There's a source of psychic energy within us that can not only distort reality but create and amplify unreality on demand. The perversion is inside us.*

I remember in 1949 the hottest pictures I could buy on the magazine rack—and only in certain select places, since publishers were testing limits—were in Peter Gowland's *Bathing Beauties*. Picture-perfect young women in bathing suits posed in what I thought at the time was a tremendous breakthrough for my lust (and, it turns out, a breakthrough for the genre). This magazine and a growing number of others of the same genre were called "girlies". *Webster's* Ninth dates the term from 1942, saying girlies featured "scantily clad young women." Such magazines are now passé—child's play compared to what is now on the open market and Internet—an indication of the progressive nature of our changing sexuality and the lustification driving it. Additionally, it indicates that not only individuals but masses of men, and also our culture itself, may be in a state of progressive addiction.

> *Tolerance*: more of the drug is tolerated with less of the desired effect. The tolerance principle is one of the three basic criteria indicating addiction. The other two are attempts at abstinence and withdrawal symptoms during abstinence.

The Nudies

In 1946 the Supreme Court decided against the U.S. Post Office and permitted mailing privileges for *Esquire*, a slick men's magazine with the famous and lusty Petty and Varga girl drawings. *Esquire* was a thick magazine with articles on a variety of topics. How many of us plowed through it in a frenzy, when we were lucky enough to run across one, to connect with those two fanciful darlings in every issue? As superbly drawn and salacious-appearing as they were, however, the drawings did not have the power photographs had for me, since I had cut my teeth on the "real" thing. Orgasm was more difficult to achieve with drawings than with photos. Those drawings did not emanate the spirit that could be captured in photographs. And capturing the spirit is what image-lust is all about—the enticement to be captured, and a deliberate provocation to "take."

This court decision paved the way for the future. Thereafter, the demand and accessibility of erotically explicit material increased steadily, and the revolution was off and running. The first issue of *Playboy*, December 1953, made old issues of *Esquire*, in its most uninhibited days, look like trade bulletins from the Women's Christian Temperance Union.[9] That's when the lusty girlies exploded into the lustier nudies. It's interesting that the terms "soft porn" and "pornography" are often used today for such magazines. "Pornography" used to be used only for the "hard stuff," material depicting the actual sex act. Is this an indicator of the acknowledged toxicity of this new *Playboy* genre?

A *Kinsey* Faux Pas?

The original Kinsey report stated that "use of literature and erotic pictures for stimulation during masturbation is not really common, and it is largely confined to better educated individuals."[10] This statement would be met with instant ridicule today. It is no longer true, and one wonders if it was really true in Kinsey's day. How many men being interviewed, though willing to admit to masturbating, would admit to using pictures? "You mean you have to use *pictures*?!" I doubt whether the Kinsey interviewers were able to break through this shame barrier. When asked in a 1993 interview whether they used pornography to masturbate the first time they ever had an orgasm, one of the young men at Duke University replied, "Oh, yeah, and *as touchy as it may be to say*, a lot of the men, in fact, almost all the men I've talked to have similar experiences."[11]

The Kinsey male research began in 1939 and lasted nine years, being published in 1948, five years before the *Playboy* revolution. Times have changed. Everyone knows what these magazines serve. Since *Playboy*, lustification has exploded (see following chart). These magazines became sexual staples, providing the absolute bare necessities, the drug of choice for millions of us. Today, Kinsey would have to devote a whole chapter to use of erotic images in masturbation.[12]

The fact that we all know what's going on in this business, but prefer to blink at it or act as if it's not there, is illustrated by an incident that happened to me a couple of years before I got my last "hit" from one of these lust "connections." A man I had business dealing with, who knew of a responsible and very sensitive position I had held with the government in the past, happened to see me coming out of a magazine store with one of the magazines in a brown paper bag. He looked at me in disgust and said, "Not you!"

This chart tracks paid circulation figures for *Playboy* and *Penthouse*, with *Time* magazine used as a rough index of growth for a magazine of general interest. The *Playboy* curve dominates the figure, since it was the first nudie to break the ban, peaking in 1973 at 6.8 million paid U.S. circulation per month. According to the Census Bureau, the U.S. male population figure for 1973 was 102,240,000. This roughs out to one *Playboy* for every fifteen males, regardless of age. No wonder; image-lust could well be the best-kept secret of the male sex.

Note that in 1973, *Time*, then the foremost U.S. news magazine, had reached only four and one-half million in its upward gradual slope, and it had been in the field since 1923. Also, note *Playboy* from

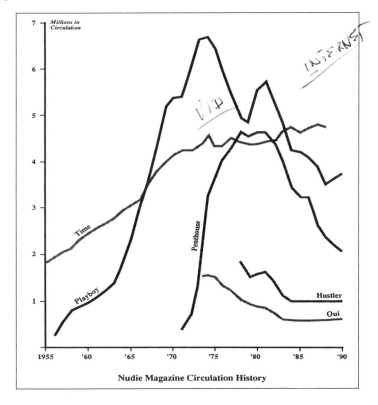

Nudie Magazine Circulation History

1955 to 1973. I doubt whether any other magazine has ever known such a steep rise in circulation figures. *Penthouse* followed and instantly became a close rival, pandering more salacious provocations of lust. Then *Hustler* and others carried us further, and in only one generation there was an unprecedented sea change in the landscape of male lust. (The leveling off of the *Hustler* and *Oui* curves on the chart is due to their failure to report circulation figures.)

It is impossible to chart here the advent of the thousands of "men's interest" magazines that flooded the market since the advent of *Playboy*, covering every conceivable niche of the erotic market. And we're only talking about the legal market; the illegal underground is so vast it defies the imagination. It took twenty years for *Playboy* circulation to reach 6.8 million, but by 1993, some forty years after that first issue, according to the *Janus Report*, there were 35 million copies of men's interest publications being circulated every month.[13] This figure includes only "girlie magazines like *Playboy, Penthouse*, and *Hustler*," omitting the entire homosexual pornography genre, which must be quite vast by now. Moreover, we know a large segment of this kind of publication never gets on the lists. But even 35 million was 14% percent of the entire 1993 U.S. population, some 28% of males of all ages!

Strangely, the Janus report did not delve into the significance of this, stating only that voyeurism has become institutionalized in our society. Is it too shameful for people, even sex researchers, to describe what boys and men were really doing with these magazines, resorting to image-sex? The real story is what's going on inside the psyche; and we've been missing that story (ref. Appendix 4 case studies).

Playboy corporate sources report that the reason for diminishing circulation in *Playboy* after 1975 was that magazine circulation generally was slumping due to increase in video entertainment and the explosion of specialty magazines.[14] Now, instead of *Sports Illustrated*, there is a magazine for every conceivable sport or aspect thereof. The same holds true for the men's interest magazines. Instead of *Playboy, Penthouse*, and the other leading lust dispensers, there is a specialized magazine—and now website—for every conceivable, and not so conceivable, aspect of male erotic interest.

Why the whole American women's movement has not rallied against this dismembering of women's parts into sexual menus served up in glossy, is one of the paradoxes of modern liberalism. This movement vented its outrage at the Anita Hill affair, but it seems impotent or uncaring about what most of their men are lusting after in the barber shop, not to mention what's hidden in the garage or car trunk. But then perpetual adolescence is still the least-acknowledged trait of the male sex. Or is it that women, even today, simply follow their men, even into allowing perversion of themselves as lust objects? Then again, how powerful must be the lure of being so idolized (worshipped), considering the tremendous payoff of being lusted after?

Think of it: If this many men were turned on to image-woman lust, masturbating to the magazine girlies and nudies, how many more did so without them or to ads in the daily newspaper? Using even the strict definition of masturbation (deliberate self-stimulation leading to orgasm), Kinsey reported back in 1948 that about 92% of the U.S. male population masturbated. This high incidence was verified and clarified somewhat in what was touted as "America's most comprehensive survey of sexual behavior"—the *Sex in America* survey of 1994.[15] However, that research also asserted that instead of masturbation being a substitute for interpersonal sex, it was just the opposite. The ones who were sexing out the most in other ways were the ones who were masturbating the most. Pseudo-sex simply doesn't satisfy.

It doesn't take another scientific study to determine how many males are having self-sex with images of women today. Or to images of men. The porn film industry in Southern California alone reportedly does a $9- to $14-billion business annually, creating over 10,000 new titles a year.[16] If one were to plot the Internet pornography curve alone, it would already prove to be exponential, approaching the vertical, such was the near-instantaneous explosion of porn Web sites appearing overnight. The number of porn Web sites in the Websense® URL database alone surged from approximately 88,000 in 2000 to 1.6 million sites in April of 2004. Nielsen/NetRatings estimated that 34 million people visited porn sites in August 2003.[17] In late 2004, Family Safe Media reported that porn is a $57 billion industry annually, with 4.2 million porn Web sites, containing 372 million pornographic pages, getting 68 million daily porn search engine requests, 116,000 of which daily are for child porn. And now with mobile phone porn. . . . (http://www.familysafemedia.com/pornography_statistics.html)

There's obviously a historically significant development here—not masturbation, but mass resorting to lustified picture-women and picture-men. Image-lust. Image-sex. Image-consumption. It is interesting that the *Sex in America* report also used the term "consumption" when referring to use of erotica in sex. (We will deliberately sidestep things like phone sex, that probably could only have been ignited after the image-sex revolution was in place.[18])

The Picture-Sex Incidence Curve

I suggest that if we were to plot a curve of the percentage of men masturbating to images against a time scale (strange that this has never been attempted, to my knowledge), we'd be in for a surprise. Somewhere in the mid-nineteenth century the line would probably start very low, begin rising with the advent of photography, rise slowly but steadily through the turn of the century, steepen as it goes through the 1920s and 1930s, make a significant jump around World War II, steepen sharply through the fifties and sixties, and by now be only hundredths of a percent shy of 100%.

Unlike the *Playboy/Penthouse* curves, which diminish due to the proliferating number of sources for the new lust, the image-masturbation curve keeps getting steeper and shooting higher. Image-lustified sex is new in the abruptness and magnitude of the *change in human sexuality.* This change is not easily recognizable, but will be revealed as we proceed.

If, as Shakespeare says, "the whole world knows," why does all this not ring an alarm? Let's look at the controversy over *Sports Illustrated* as an example. The magazine has an annual swimsuit issue featuring not only women but girls in "sexy swimsuits." It has long been their best-selling issue and by far its most popular one with advertisers. The magazine has also built a multimillion-dollar industry around that one issue, selling everything from calendars to videocassettes featuring the swimsuit models. *Sports Illustrated* claims the issue is "read" by one out of every four Americans.

The challenge to the swimsuit issue was being mounted for the reason that it "devalues women and children." This is very true, but it misses the real mark—what this tells us about the men "reading" the magazine, men getting a new supply of—why not face it?—their drug. What it means is another media-legitimized opportunity for self-sexing ourselves into the new pseudo-sexuality and passing that on to our sons and neighbors.

> "The decision [to publish the swimsuit issue] gets made in a male-bonding, Madison Avenue sort of way," said Cecilia Blewer, a steering committee director of . . . Women Against Pornography. "Advertisers should know that a lot of women intercept this issue when it comes into their homes and, in their one feminist statement for the year, they toss it out."[19]

Times may be beginning to change when wives toss out the stuff. A former model for the swimsuit issue, now disaffected, says of the advertisers in the issue, "They are promoting violence against women." This is closer to the mark but still misses the core issues: why the magazine is so appealing to men and the significance of the anti-sexual revolution ripping through our psyches and our culture. That Ms. Blewer makes the comment she does about male bonding is indicative of how women still do not perceive the real threat here. Male lusting over swimsuit picture-women is the very opposite of male bonding—*it is anti-male, anti-sexual, anti-woman, anti-love, anti-human.*

ISOLATING

The Addictive Wave

We've complicated our lives immensely. A new appetite has come on the scene overnight. Not pornography, lust, or masturbation; these have always been around. Every man and his father and brother, not to mention what the women might be up to, are scoring sexual connections with the spirit of lust communicated in *images*.

These photo-icons (if we can use the term icon, an image of worship) are pushed worldwide, and the new appetite they pander will be awakened in multitudes as yet unborn and uninfected by the ever-more-virulent strains of the virus. And the virus is being spewed into the air of the subconscious. If this sounds extreme, you have blissfully avoided the culture shock of Internet porn. *This* is the new terrorism.

Husbands may protest or bluff when their wives ask what the pictures are doing under the shelf paper in the bathroom cupboard or why they stay up so late "working" at their computers, but thousands in recovery from this sexual/lust addiction testify that these are their "connections" that turn solitary sex into such a super-powerful drug fix.

It was in 1978 when, apparently for the first time, a British journal article appeared, "to contribute to the widening of discussion about the nature of dependence," particularly sexual behavior.[20] That was apparently the first reference to what soon thereafter would be called sex addiction. There has been no end to such books and treatment programs since, especially since the publication of *The Sexual Addiction* in 1983 in the U.S.[21] And when a recent president's sex-capades were brought to the light, suddenly words like "sexaholic" were being bandied about in the media air.[22]

Also, the addictive wave is what's new. Each experience connecting with these lustified images builds upon the previous erotic level. At eight, ten, or twelve the boy begins by masturbating to images. But the newness and powerfully addictive "high" of that experience forces him to look for "more" and "better." So his addiction is progressively looking for more potent forms of the drug to produce the original lust high. And market forces capitalize on the commercial potential to create something a little more seductive in the next edition. The young man discovers this and simply must have the new stuff. On and on and on, such the fast-growing swell of this image-lust tsunami.

When I stopped resorting to porn in 1974, I was appalled at how young the nude models were getting. There's a cumulative effect building both within individuals and in the culture. That's why porn—and the types of sexual expression—must branch off into every conceivable form. And "orientation" has little if anything to do with it. This addictive wave is operating in the same-sex lifestyle (and with girls and women) just as it is in the so-called heterosexual world.[23] How could it be otherwise? It's a cultural force, as we shall see. And lustification continues—of the female image, the male image, the child image . . . .

> "It never seems to stand still, does it?" he said. "Once one crutch is introduced and you give in to that, it holds you up long enough for the next one to come along and carry you a step further. And that addictive wave keeps on advancing; it never stops. There's always that new enticing aspect of Desire out there—or is it in

here?—ready and waiting to suck you into it. And we keep riding the leading edge of that wave. The more there is, the more you want. The more you want, the more you have to have. Wanting more always leads to wanting more . . . . Like I have to keep riding the leading edge of my own desire! What is it that keeps us moving out, away from, farther and farther? And from what?"[24]

What *are* we moving away from? From our maleness, our masculinity, from Woman, from Man, from our humanness, from real sexuality.

Is there something new or different going on? Yes. What's new is mass-mediated image-lustified sex. The new lust has conquered reality.

Lustification in Process

In the 1980s Jim Palmer, the sports personality, showed up in an ad wearing only shrink-to-fit briefs, reportedly something of a breakthrough. Men's underwear, we are told, "awoke in the mid-1980s." The May 27, 1993, edition of the *Los Angeles Times* shows an ad for Jockey shorts for men. The main image is a 10 × 12 shot, showing a close-up, camera at crotch level, of the man's genitals bulging behind the stretch fabric. A knowing grin on the face of the model intensifies the erotic aura imbuing the shot. The very next issue of that newspaper featured an article on men's shorts with a brief history. We're told that "Clark Gable bared his chest and paved the way for the sensitive, semi-naked man in *It Happened One Night*." And a shot from 1946 shows slugger Babe Ruth in his Jockey "longs." We are told, "It is now acceptable for the male to think of himself as a sexual object." How did we jump from an ad for men's clothing to a pronouncement that it's desirable to be lusted after?

An extraordinary specimen of lustification in process of the male image appears in the February 11, 1994, edition of the *Los Angeles Times*. The front page of the View section (Style/Comics/Pop Culture) is filled with fifteen shots of men in shorts. Nothing unusual or startling here. But the piece is captioned "Leg Men," a slang term previously used only to describe men who got high on women's legs. And the masculine appendages are referred to as "gams," a colloquial or slang term that I remember being used exclusively for attractive women's legs (*Random House II* dictionary).[25] The nineties do seem to pinpoint a transition here.

Picture-Lust and the Desexualization of Women and Men

The new image-icons that have appeared in our culture are helping to promote pseudosexuality and result in the desexualization and defeminization of women. In allowing the exploitation of such images to attract and arouse men, women are unwittingly becoming *de*sexualized. Dependence on lust to be "attractive" actually winds up inhibiting natural sexuality. This may well be one of the factors in rendering men functionally impotent. For short-term advantage—attracting men or igniting lust—they get long-term male disability and paradoxically render themselves less sexual and less female. And hence ultimately less attractive.

And is the male lust-imperative the reason why women have to make so much of their "looks" and feel so inferior if they can't measure up? In letting their face and body parts be turned into icons, do women wind up actually denying their own reality? They must; pseudosexuality demands it! (See Appendixes 2 and 3.) These body parts have become unreal media images, semantic symbols, icons, imprinted not only in the male and female consciousness, but in the American culture-consciousness. And the image always appears more real than the real thing. That's the intrinsic character of photographs, as we shall see in Part III. We're in a lose-lose situation here—both men and women!

Due to the genius of media advertising and the human flaws it exploits, a new appetite has been created in both the American male and female. Picture-lust. This is propaganda in its most insidious aspect, appearing as an angel of light and beauty. But in allowing the reality of their own bodies to be perverted, women unwittingly validate, support, and perpetuate the loss of their womanhood *because* we validate, support, and perpetuate the loss of our manhood.

This must also apply to the male-to-male image-connection. How could it be otherwise? (Ref. Appendix 2, Pseudo-Woman and Fairy Queens.)

"Ah Women!"

A letter I wrote to the editor of a leading news magazine in 1972, just prior to my own recovery, is revealing.[26]

So *Playboy*'s new *Oui* wants to "turn on women" too! No wonder, considering the success they have had with so many of us members of the stronger sex. Just think. . . .

The naive adolescent, developing normally toward the opposite sex in the real world (difficult as that is), then given his first fix of "joy of living" and sucked into the *Playboy* delusion, unwittingly burns into the neurons of his formative sexual experience images out of the id of neurotic adults.

The boy, now naive, "liberated" husband, hooked on the spirit of the age and auto-adultery, finds marriage only complicates matters. Not only must he serve his continually renewed stable of media wantons, but he has a one-and-the-same, aging, childbearing, full-time, real woman on his hands! Finding self-indulgence only traps him into the cycle, and no longer free to have sex without fantasy, he resorts to the ever more explicit images and ideas so ingeniously pandered. And failing to see that rather than validating his manhood as promised, they only help reduce him to pubic slavery, he is easy prey to the forces possessing the models he so longs to possess; forever blind to what is on the other side of idolatry.

And the poor naive wife, unsuspectingly harboring in her own home her husband's meretricious favorites, has to settle for his dutiful, guilt-ridden, leftover amours. Far from ever knowing her, the real, he is merely scoring more connections with the anti-real. Confused and unfulfilled, she never guesses the best-kept secret of the male sex.

The ones really exploited, until now, that is, were not women at all—mere side effect losers—but men. Yet, this newly packaged fruit of the tree of the knowledge of good and evil claims that having "more units of eroticism" not only does not exploit, but makes for "better communication between the sexes." Really!

Ah women! Just think what is in store for you!

Lawrence Goldstein says, "As our 'society of spectacle' grows ever more powerful . . . the fantasy body, the body offered as sexual fetish, becomes more and more inescapable. . . ."[27] True, none of us can escape the lustified air in which we all live and move and have our being.

But we who use the picture-women or picture-men—our lust is the imperative driving the whole business.

Before we go on, let's briefly take a look at this "lustified air" of ours from another telling perspective—*memes*.

Memes and the Sociology of Lust

"Thoughts, like fleas, jump from man to man.
But they don't bite everybody."
Stanislaw Lec (1909–1996)[28]

The term "meme" (pronounced meem) was coined by a British biologist in 1976. Memes are to culture what genes are to biology. A meme is a unit of cultural information, such as a concept, belief, or practice, that is spread in a way similar to the transmission of genes. While genes control our biological makeup, memes control our socio-cultural and spiritual thinking and behavior.

"Examples of memes are tunes, ideas, catch-phrases, clothes fashions. . . . Just as genes propagate themselves in the gene pool by leaping from body to body via sperms or eggs, so memes propagate themselves in the meme pool by leaping from brain to brain via . . . imitation."[29] Certain genes in my body influence the color of my hair, while memes—cultural "genes"—influence my hairstyle, what I wear, how I relate to people, and how I think and act about sex, God, etc. While genes can only be transmitted from parents to offspring, memes can be transmitted among individuals through any cultural forces, such as the media, entertainment, education, religion, and so forth.

During the last ten thousand years, humans have remained virtually unchanged on the genetic level, whereas our culture (the total set of memes) has undergone radical developments. Looking at modern lust through the relatively new science of memetics helps correlate the psychology of lust with its sociology.

Memes can be transmitted in the space of hours. The number of individuals who can be taken over by a meme from a single idea, individual, or event is almost unlimited. For example, how long did it take for our new American-fear-of-terrorism meme to evolve after the Twin Towers attack of 9/11, and how many individuals did that meme take over? Millions of us were taken over within minutes, such was the awesome power of that imagery.

The backward baseball cap and the f-word are memes. Women's fear of snakes is a meme. Athletic shoe styles are memes. "The American Dream" is a complex of memes, as are the terms "straight" and "gay." Note how the male earring meme has evolved recently. And the plunging-cleavage meme, even more rapidly. All over the place now. Individual memes in the lustification of picture-women are obvious and legion. And if one were to start tracing the half-life of pornography memes (how long it takes for a new porn advance to become passé), one can easily see how the virus not only replicates but must continually evolve to maintain its viability and propagating power. Escalating numbers of memes are the viral vectors propagating the new lust.

Like a virus, a meme is a "contagious information pattern that replicates by parasitically infecting human minds and altering their behavior, causing them to propagate the pattern." A meme is said to be *auto-toxic* if it promotes destruction in its host, the smoking-is-cool meme, for example. The new lust meme is auto-toxic in that it promotes destruction of love and sex in the infected.

However, memes can also be negated. Resistance to the cigarette-smoking meme that was transmitted via generations of earlier movies and advertising, began to be conferred on the public through the anti-smoking campaign waged by Surgeon General C. Everett Koop. And thus evolved the smoking-means-cancer meme. Koop's tireless warnings about the health risks of smoking helped reduce the number of smokers among Americans from 33 percent of the population in 1981 to 26 percent only eight years later.[30] And today—where have all the smokers gone? Remarkable and unprecedented! Europe is said to be twenty years behind in this.

Immunity or avoidance is what some of us mistakenly sought in lust recovery. Avoidance was impossible, and there's nothing on the horizon for immunity from this virus. We've found that achieving resistance is from the inside out—spiritual—not from the outside in. However, if there ever were an anti-lust campaign like Koop's, there would doubtless be a comparable positive effect. Note however, that when cigarette smoking was considered a bad habit or even a sin, as it was around the Roaring Twenties and later, that only made it more attractive, since there were sexual overtones in the advertising and films. If, instead of anti-porn crusades, intelligent education and advertising focused on disclosing the true nature and effects of the new lust, as Koop did with tobacco, this would be dealing with the heart of the matter, offering hope for recovery from a deadly personal and social disease.

"If we accept that many of our actions are meme-based and therefore can be changed, we have the potential to improve our lives by evaluating the memes and overriding those that we believe have the potential to do us harm." This is exceedingly hopeful and realistic, but not always easy. Increasing numbers in lust recovery are slowly learning, from necessity, why and how to do this to live sober, joyous, and free.

. . .

It is important to understand what's going on in the lustification of our culture. Mass addiction to a new appetite is being created and fed here—an appetite of historic and global impact. In fact, we are now at the point where we embrace the new lust not only as a fundamental human characteristic, but as a fundamental human right and the very grounds of our personal identity. The impact of the new lust on human ecology tracks other recent reality shifts accompanying the advent of such things as photography, silent films, radio, the phonograph, modern movies, television, video, computers, and the explosive proliferation of cyberspace technologies. These innovations, benign in themselves, are used to create and feed new appetites, captivating our psyches, engendering and mediating our changing sexualities in ways previously impossible. A seemingly necessary part of everyday civilization, they are nevertheless carriers of the lust virus.

The steepness of the growth curves of each of these new tools as virus carriers increasingly overshoots the old *Playboy* curve. We are in the most abrupt and far-reaching psychic revolution that has ever taken over the human species. It's a global psychic tsunami. The new lust has immediate and total access not only to every area of the culture but to the most private secret recesses of the human psyche. It has captured the soul of America.

To appreciate the impact of all this within the male, let's continue by taking up where the young men at Duke left off and see how this developed in an actual case history.

THE QUEEN OF MAGIC—
GENESIS AND EVOLUTION
OF PERSONAL LUST

Privacy was used to protect the consumption of obscenity in the home, without any consideration of the effect of men consuming pornography on women and children in those homes.

Catharine A. MacKinnon[31]

What would happen if the boys at Duke could tell us what their sexual attitudes, behavior, and relations would be like far ahead into their futures? What would they tell us at age 45 about their sexuality having been shaped by image-women and the likes of *Penthouse Forum*? Where would those beginnings have led them? Fortunately, we don't have to wait to find out; the lives of recovering infected ones are beginning to cover that ground. The following is one of many typical stories, tracing the journey from innocence to disorder—if only they were to be revealed. This one happens to be mine, because after painful soul-searching, I feel that I should speak for myself. My story is typical of thousands in recovery, hundreds of which I have personally witnessed (see Appendix 4). Reading this may give others courage to examine their own histories.

In tracing the origins and stages of my own lust, I will be making a correlation between what's going on inside me and the various forces impinging on me from the outside. And that process will continue through the rest of the book. A considerable risk for the storyteller, perhaps, but well worth it to collect crucial data otherwise unavailable. "Scientific" descriptions of sex are meaningless without the subjective evidence of what is going on inside the person. Documenting the elements of this story began in 1974, when I entered recovery, and continues to the present time. Someone has called it "an autobiography of lust."

This chapter was written before I learned of the Duke University interviews. The two accounts are strikingly parallel, identifying the same principles at work.

It should gradually become evident that my so-called heterosexuality was really something else, *and this revelation was the catalyst enabling me to discover and make the case for pseudosexuality.*

The Queen of Magic

In 1935 at the age of eight, while reading the Sunday "Flash Gordon" comic strip, I had my first erection when I saw Azura the predatory Queen of Magic grab Flash and kiss him. That was my sexual awakening, and the beginning of what immediately turned into daily masturbation. I remember no sexual contact or education of any kind prior to my solitary discovery of sexual self-stimulation.

Imprinting

The year 1935 was the very time the Austrian ethologist Konrad Lorenz was discovering "imprinting" (ref. *Pragung*, the German word for impressing coins), referring to the newborn greylag goose's attachment to Lorenz. In the absence of the mother goose, the newborn reacted to Lorenz exactly as it would have to its real mother, following Lorenz around and copying his behavior. To the little gosling, Lorenz *was* its mother. Seeing the filmy-clad and aggressive image-woman Azura grab and kiss Flash definitely was my sexual imprinting, at least the first conscious experience, and one of the more important. Let me interrupt my story to develop this imprinting concept.

Drawn from the people and experiences of childhood, the map ["love map"] is a record of whatever we found enticing and exciting—or disturbing and disgusting. Small feet, curly hair. The way our mothers patted our head or how our fathers told a joke. A fireman's uniform, a doctor's stethoscope. All the information gathered while growing up is imprinted in the brain's circuitry by adolescence.[32]

Random House defines imprinting as a "rapid learning that occurs during a brief receptive period, typically soon after birth or hatching, and establishes a long-lasting behavioral response to a specific individual or object." A UCLA psychiatrist defines imprinting to be "postnatal, non-biological experiences that are crucial in the development of fixing gender identity."[33] Imprinting is well known in psychiatry with reference especially to infant-mother relationships.[34] In this book I take the liberty of broadening the concept of imprinting to include personal and cultural factors. This would extend sexual imprinting beyond infancy, not only through adolescence but into adulthood. The extreme suggestibility of our sexual response warrants this. The term describes my own experience and that of many others so very well. (Appendix 4)

Having Azura's image and actions coupled fortuitously with my sexual awakening, I would thenceforth be looking for more Azuras and Azura-Flash experiences to recapture the incredible high of that original dose of picture-woman unreality. I may have been abnormally susceptible, and I may have needed some sort of relief mechanism to cope with my own internal conflicts and familial environment. But it was my imprintings and early sexual experiences that were the catalysts for crystallizing my sexual attitudes and behavior out of the solution of predisposing factors.

Since to my knowledge I had been isolated from any prior sexual contact or exposure, I believe that my sexual response mechanism was programmed by the Azura experience, my sexual birth or "hatching," where "a long-lasting behavioral response" was impressed into my sexual system. The direction—why not just go ahead and call it orientation for now?—was strongly conditioned, if not set, by this initial and subsequent imprintings. But whatever that orientation was, it had *pseudo* written all over it. The rest of the case history will clarify that judgment.

What would have happened if, when my sexual system had reached that stage of ripening, I would have been exposed to mutual masturbation with other boys? To a baby sitter's molestation, or to someone exposing herself or himself? To watching animals have sex on a farm? What if it had happened while lying in bed next to a parent? While being disciplined? While playing doctor? Listening to hundreds of stories over the years confirms my own experience of the great formative power of sexual imprinting.

> [A] considerable amount of preliminary experimentation and practice is essential to biologically effective sexual intercourse in adult human beings. It appears that . . . particularly during the appearance and specialization of the higher primates, the mating behavior of the male . . . has come to be more and more dependent upon individual experience and learning. This implies, of course, a complementary decrease in the adequacy of the purely instinctive elements of the pattern.
>
> Erotic arousal is easily evoked in the naive male ape, but a great deal of experience and practice must take place before this generalized sexual excitement leads smoothly into a well-integrated and complete copulatory pattern." [We are told it is just the opposite with a naive female ape.][35]

Some male dogs masturbated by their owners forsake female dogs completely for the human.[36] Experiments with ducks indicate those of one species raised with a different species mate only with those of the adoptive species and reject sexual advances made by their own species.[37]

I want to show how the imprinting process over time helped shape my orientation to pseudo-sexuality. Today's media-driven categories seem too simplistic and unrealistic. What is often overlooked is the fact that generalized sexuality is shaped by learning and experience and is therefore highly susceptible to imprinting and cultural forces, as in lower primates and other species.

An interesting phenomenon occurs in meetings where people talk about a certain form of sex we have never experienced, and the next thing we know, we're entertaining that possibility. What would happen if—? It's as though any barrier we may have had may be weakened by merely *hearing* someone else relate their experience. An analogous phenomenon takes place in sessions focused on discovering one's childhood victimization. Before you know it, you find yourself reconstructing your own past and—lo and behold!—"discovering" how you too were molested or abused. We humans can be extremely susceptible to this kind of suggestion, especially to what's in the media air about us. Our sexual susceptibility is what gives imprinting such power.

The scarcity of reference to this broader concept of imprinting is incredible. We hear loads about sex, but little about imprinting. Even the *Janus* and *Sex in America* reports missed the golden opportunity to include an item that should have been added to their interview questionnaire: "Describe the events surrounding your first and early sexual experience(s) and what you were seeing, thinking, and feeling at the time." Have we been so caught up in a "Just-the-facts-ma'am" mind-set in gathering statistics and "scientific" data, that we leave the person out of the equation? Looking only at externals, we lose the true inner reality of the event. There is no such thing as scientific explanations of sex (which Kinsey and following have claimed) without the subjective evidence of what is going on inside the person! I doubt whether there is anything really scientific about the sexual behavior of the bonobo apes without knowing what's going through *their* minds.[38]

What may be the real reason for this unfortunate omission in the sex surveys is our philosophical and scientific mind-set today—a one-sided view of the human being. With all our knowledge about man, we do not know what or who man is.[39] I think the most fundamental flaw in the methodology of science has been its deficient view of man. Under the microscope, in the test tube, and on its many instruments, it cannot detect the essence of that other side of man—the spiritual side. Shakespeare did.

Why not see what an honest written inventory of your own imprintings reveals?

The Image Connection

Back to my sexual history, tracing more of the imprinting, and how my pseudosexuality developed. Having discovered solitary sex, I proceeded with it daily for a short time without it being picture-driven at all, even though my initial awakening was coupled with a pictorial image. I would lock myself in the bathroom and stimulate myself for as long as I could before ejaculation. Sexual self-stimulation induced a blank mind, a trance-like nirvana state in which I had no thoughts or fantasy whatsoever. Mindless pseudo-serenity. For me it was the pure drug experience, total escape from myself and the world about me. In my case, let's call this *Pseudosexuality* I. We'll try to identify these stages as the story evolves.

Why did I soon have to resort back to that original picture-connection? I assume the power of the initial image-imprinting with Azura had something to do with it. Plus, the principle of tolerance comes into play, where more is required to achieve the initial effects. Also, my father died when I was five, and my mother was non-touching. Perhaps this loss and lack of parental intimacy created a vacuum waiting to be filled, even with such a pseudo-person connection as Azura. However, any such contributing factors don't change the fact that I was simply hooked. Hooked on an image-connection with picture-women.

What had been pure escape became, with pictures, a totally new and different experience in an entirely different dimension. The only thing that remained the same was self-stimulation to ejaculation. Internalizing the image, "trancing out" on it—or rather, "trancing *into*" it—was everything. I had entered a whole new kind of experience affecting the very core of my being. And although these experiences were using the sexual function, they should not be called sexual. They were essentially anti- or pseudo-sexual. Call my self-sex affair using image-women *Pseudosexuality II.*

The French Connection

The next stage in the development of my pseudo-heterosexuality—my *mis*-orientation to women—came when I was surprised by lust one day, flipping through some newspapers for my next picture-fix. What jumped off the page into my soul was the *spirit* emanating from a photo of Danielle Darrieux, the French actress of World War II fame and intrigue, clad in the standard one-piece bathing suit of the times. What triggered this next imprinting was not the person—I had no idea then who she was—or even the amount of undress, but the pose and *spirit* emanating from the total body language and expression, the I-want-you-to-lust-after-me radiation. Now that's a very powerful meme! This woman wanted me. *She* wanted *me*! More than that, she wanted me to want her! That's what that image communicated to me. That's what it did to me.

Yes, my need undoubtedly influenced what I was perceiving, but the woman's "need" (to be wanted or lusted after?) was captured and transmitted in that photograph. That's spiritual. From the spirit of one to the spirit of another.

This experience brings to mind a line from Neil Jordan, director of the movie *The Crying Game*: "The only thing non-actors have to work with is themselves. What the movie camera sees is a person's spirit. You can't hide that."[40] Yes, the camera sees and captures a person's spirit. Maybe that's why primitive people fear that the camera will rob them of some part of their being. This was even true of the French novelist Balzac (1799–1850).[41]

When a person poses and thinks emanation, as Danielle did, that spirit is somehow captured and retained in the photo. It will be communicated to viewers whether they open their soul to it ("drink") or not. I was ready to want what she offered, conditioned by my prior imprinting, sexual thinking and behavior, and media exposure. My soul was open to a spirit-connection, a *mis*connection. Sexual imprinting today has to do with much more than merely the biological or physiological. More than the physical, sex is subjective. For me, at that early age, Lust was born. *Pseudosexuality III.*

A statement of Susan Sontag's is to the point here: "Our relation to photographs can inspire something akin to lust."[42] To the best of my recollection, my experience with Danielle's image is where image-*lust* was born in me. But lust for what? Not lust for real women, or even attraction to real women; those came much later at the age of about twenty. And not lust for sex as such; sex with myself was merely the mechanism for getting The Experience. Besides, I did not yet know what sex was or how it took place between people. And it surely was not lust for dots of ink on paper. Was it lust for the spirit of lust possessing the model? Lust for lust? This may be why we have such a difficult time tracing the genesis of sexual orientation. You cannot scientifically prove, much less analyze spirit. Shakespeare didn't try; he just told it like it was (*Sonnet* 129). From my total experience, the most significant component in sex is the disposition of the spirit, the inner core essence of the human being, the thoughts and intents of the heart—soul-set. And that is affected by what's "out there."

Pseudosexual Sex Organs

CROCK By Bill Rechin and Don Wilder   September 15, 1993

Another crucial element in my formative sexual experience was the image of Danielle's legs, prominently shown off in the photo's foreground. Having lusted after, masturbated to, and then forgotten hundreds of thousands of picture-legs since then, I can still visualize that image, burned into me in that powerful imprinting so many years ago. That memory still has a powerfully toxic aura associated with it. It's as though those limbs were in motion, signaling me, capturing me, assuming power over my very soul. Instrumentalities of lust. And I was only eleven or twelve, had never touched a woman, and knew nothing about sex.

> *Nothing beats a great pair of L'eggs*
> Advertisement for women's hosiery

Legs are still part of the feminine mystique. They're everywhere! Marlene Dietrich had hers insured for a million dollars. In a local square dance club one of the class prizes is for "Best Legs." *La Joie des Jambes* (The Joy of Legs) is a play that appeared locally in 2004. The imaging of women's legs and other body parts—bosom, lips, hands, eyes, figure—evolved into a cult in the twentieth century, giving us one of the most visible and powerful icons of this new religion (Appendix

3). This is a religion complete with creed, symbols, rituals, faith-as-risk, community, etc. For me, and apparently millions of other boys and men, the spirit inspiring these lust-symbols was another imprinting burned into the neurons of our formative sexuality, another term in the equation of our sexual orientation—our *mis*orientation—a potent element of our pseudosexuality.

Speaking of pseudosexual sex organs, my first erotic encounter with a girl—the first touch ever—was in high school. The girl (now deceased) came over to my house, ostensibly for help with her chemistry homework and sat in the living room chair next to the fireplace. She had given signals of attraction at school, so I sensed there might be more here than tutoring the balancing of chemical equations. We were in the room alone—a first for me. So as soon as she sits down, what I do? My generalized sexuality had been expressing itself in masturbation to a succession of Azuras and Danielles since age eight. So, what do I do? Following my imprinting, I go right up to her, trancing out on her legs, drop to my knees, and grab them. Surprising? I had been serving this icon of lust for at least six years.

Broadcasting

While we're on the subject of women deliberately provoking lust, let's talk about "broadcasting." This term goes back a ways. Taxi dancers are women who dance for hire in ballrooms set up for that purpose. You buy a ticket for so many minutes, you pick a girl, and dance until your time's up. In the taxi-dancing lingo that I heard, "broadcasting" was when a man's erection during the dance was obvious to the girl. The women didn't like it and coined that pejorative term. Well, why not call what Danielle was doing "broadcasting"? Experiencing that for me was a decisive event in the genesis of my perversion. The lusty-leg and plunging-neckline memes we have now are broadcasting. The whole lustified female image is broadcasting! Why the obsession to be lusted after? Don't they know that lust is never satisfied, that it always wants more? Don't they know they're being infected by the male lust virus meme, which is auto-toxic, promoting destruction of love and sex in the infected?

No wonder circulation figures for some of the girlies and nudies started going down. A daily newspaper—not to mention television and the Internet—can supply enough lustified picture-fetishes to keep half the population of lusters intoxicated all day. Once in a while today, as I glimpse these truncated appendages in a newspaper, the thought strikes me, How grotesque! The woman has been chopped off! (That may indicate progress in my recovery.) Whence this awesome power over millions of men? And women!?

Speaking of the "dismemberment" of women's bodies in advertising imagery, is that very far from chainsaw and snuff films? The idea behind all this is that a woman's body part becomes an object used to attract and sell. It's a commodity. An important question for researchers is, What is the connection between today's lust and violence? We'll see later that lust is always an act of violence within the luster.

Random House II defines fixation as "a partial arrest of emotional and instinctual development, at an early point in life, due to a severe traumatic experience or an overwhelming gratification." Mine was an incredibly overwhelming gratification. Why? Why did that leggy pose arouse me so? What did it give me? The same dictionary defines fetish as "an object or non-genital part of the body that causes a habitual erotic response or fixation." Something non-genital causing an erotic response. Due to the spirit in which they are pictured and used, the legs (and hence any other parts) become *virtual sex organs*. Note that legs are the largest "organs," having the most surface area and greatest form factor to engage the viewer. (Or is it dominate or threaten the viewer?)

We come away with an amazing thought: lust-driven sex has the power to create its own pseudo-sexual "organs." Hence the advertising boom in reconstructive surgeries of every inconceivable type, shamelessly exploited in the media. *This is pseudosexuality*, key to understanding what is happening to our sexualities. When we capitulate to lust, there's no end to it, because lust never satisfies, always wanting more and "better."

Do you see why I keep coming up with the concept of pseudosexuality to describe what's been happening with us, our culture, and our sexuality? Science is still stuck on the question, What is a homosexual? (For example, ". . . there is still no universally accepted definition of homosexuality among clinicians and behavioral scientists."[43]) But a more far more pertinent question would be, *What is a heterosexual and what is heterosexuality?* What if much of what we call heterosexuality today turned out to be pseudosexuality? The personal case history you are now reading is exhibit A.

"Peppy Stories"

Why is it that I can still remember the header on that torn and yellowed scrap of paper I happened across one day as a boy while walking barefoot across a field? The scrap contained about a third of a page torn out of some pulp magazine and had no pictures at all. This "Peppy Story" was about a woman being interviewed by a man at a modeling agency. I forget the prior dialogue but will never forget his asking her to disrobe as part of the interview and her ready acquiescence. The portion of the page was missing where it must have told what happened after she disrobed.

This was another first-of-a-kind experience for me, since most other erotic triggers had been and would continue to be pictures. Why did it have such power over me that I would subsequently masturbate to the memory of that story hundreds of times? (At that age I still did not know about sexual intercourse.) The point of this new experience is that with Danielle Darrieux, the invitation and seduction had only been intimated. Through this new-found medium of "peppy" print I was encountering a scene describing direct erotic interaction between a man and a woman—with lust in between the lines, obviously in the mind of the author. This dual conditioning with both pictures and words was to leave me a helpless victim to the new lust.

What is there to account for the print medium's extremely potent power to imprint? In the case of the story, the experience is communicated directly to the reader. I don't have to conjure up the force or imagination necessary to turn a pictorial image into the lust drug; the author has already done it for me, explicitly, with words. (This will also be the case, more potent yet, with the moving-image experience, as we shall see.) Many bear witness to this awesome imprinting power of pictures and words associated with their first sexual experiences. Witness the experiences of the Boys at Duke in chapter 1 (and other case studies in Appendix 4).

At any rate, the change this peppy-story experience wrought in me was apparently the thought of some kind of physical interaction with a fantasy-woman in contrast to being passively tranced-out on a picture-woman, as with Danielle.

This pseudo-interaction became a new term in the equation of my sexual learning, perhaps the initiation of the pornographic consciousness. Call this *Pseudosexuality IV.*

Aborted Adolescence

One would think that being sexually excited about interacting with even a fantasy woman would be considered normal. But in my case, sexualizing the fantasy again and again had the opposite effect. As part of my PS syndrome (PS for pseudosexuality), it helped *alienate* me from relations with real girls. That is one of the paradoxes of pseudosexuality. What was happening in my peppy story and every pictorial encounter was working against my relational ability and nurturing the anti-real. It kept me isolated within myself and progressively enhanced the isolation! Just like the boys at Duke—love cripples—only I wasn't having intercourse with real bodies.

My pseudosexual thinking and behavior kept me from advancing through normal adolescence. Physically, my body was advancing through the normal process—acne and all—but emotionally and inter-relationally, the development was aborted. I leave it to others to show how aborted adolescence appears in our culture in so many different manifestations. Cultural artifacts of PS. One reader of this book noted that whole parts of our culture seem trapped in perpetual adolescence: sports, gangs, popular music, TV, video games. . . .

A woman's remark overheard in a doctor's office:
Question: *"When do men leave puberty?"*
Answer: *"Six months after the funeral."*

In recovery, my arrested adolescence has taken up where it was lost in boyhood. Very awkward at times, at my age, but what an adventure! An awesome and scary awakening, but I feel good about it. I know I have to continue making the change, learning to relate to attractive women non-sexually, non-romantically, without mis-connection, yet honestly and sexually in the broad natural sense of the term. Actually, this aspect of my recovery is such a powerful experience, it's gender-bending. It's trying to turn me into something "different." Incredible change, but awesome! Why is it taking so long? Can this be anything like what gays feel if they think about "change"? Had I been badgered up front that I would have to change in this manner, I would have hid or run. I could not have understood or coped with it. And without recovery, it would have been hopeless.

In Transition

Skipping ahead to high school, I am rather embarrassed to relate that having a crush on one girl, all I could do was peek at her discreetly from a distance. I could never bring myself to speak with her directly. Was it any wonder, considering that my normal sexuality had already been thwarted in its development and my only "intimate" relation with girls was as picture-voyeur? I heard later that in high school various girls were attracted to me and even tried relating to me, but I didn't perceive that. I did not act on it. PS kept me in my mother's womb—the Womb of Picture-Woman. Women were not real. I had not broken through into the real world. In the U.S. Navy at age eighteen I walked a girl around the block once, even briefly holding hands for the first time with anyone—powerful!—but when she invited me to a movie, I canceled out, unable to cope. And this young woman was an attractive and talented musician who seemed to take to me.

Real Sex (?)

The young men at Duke were experimenting with sex in premarital situations. I did so after marriage. My first sex with a woman was with my first wife. I was twenty. It was marvelous! I had been "having sex" with myself for twelve years, jazzed up with picture-lust at that, but it couldn't hold a candle to this. That was pseudo-sex. This was real and good, even though I was incapable of mature emotional intimacy. It was sex without fantasy or resorting to images. It transcended any-thing and everything I had ever had with myself and picture-women. Totally different. Talk about a sea change—! The discovery was so overwhelmingly good, why didn't it cure me of the unreal? Within a matter of weeks, I found myself grubbing about, searching for picture-women again so I could score connections with the anti-real. Why, when I now had the real—and it was good? What kind of sexuality is this? What kind of "orientation"? Therein lies a tale of misery for the male of the species. And the female!

Marriage and wonderful, wonderful sex did not save me from my misorientation. And it would be twenty nine years later when I would finally admit and "come out" to full and exclusive pseudosexuality.

My pseudosexuality had been determined, my orientation and preference set, with those innocent imprintings, beginning with the Queen of Magic, and I failed to make the transition to true heterosexual reality. But lest we conclude I was *unable* to change, let me add that I freely *chose* to turn back to the anti-reality of picture-sex after those first weeks of real sex. It would only be years later when I would see that self-obsession, hidden under my religious "believism," was what blinded me to the truth about myself and powered the addiction. ("Believism" is formula-belief and religious observance instead of personal connection and life.)

We do our potential recovery a grave injustice if we fail to see the place personal decision making has in the making of our PS. "Attitude transcends the externals; attitude makes the person. We are what we think. Thus, regardless of other factors that may be involved, we help create our own predisposition to addiction. And, I might say, to orientation. We underestimate the power of the lust virus and pseudosexuality to our great loss. It is a super-powerful spiritual force—shall we call it a *Higher* Power?—promising a most-seductive high. There is a sense in which something in us chooses to believe the Lie, as it did with me. The unreal offers greater promise than the real (Plato).

The Resentment-Lust Connection

I say "innocent," referring to those early masturbations of mine, because they arose naturally and were not forced on me in typical back-alley encounters. However, I see now that *I* was not innocent. Through searching and fearless moral inventories of my early childhood I realized that I had created my own predispositions for the dependency and obsession. I discovered that I had carried suppressed resentments against two family members. And it was my continuing resorting to resentment—an addiction all its own—that kept me from seeing the truth about myself.

Resentment was for me just another form of lust, and hence another "drug." This is the *resentment-lust connection.* Just as lust distorts the reality of a woman, man, or child, resentment distorts the reality of the person against whom we unleash that negative spiritual force. We create a pseudo-person of the one resented, just as we create a pseudo-person of the one lusted after. And we shut the reality out. The resentment-lust connection may also be a key to the lust-violence connection, that we will look into later.

Real Women and the Misconnection

Once sex with a woman (my wife) was initiated, it was only a matter of time before I would run across the first "real" Azura, a physical incarnation of my picture-Woman, and then another, and another. . . . The fact is that I did not begin to see women as *sex* objects until I had had real sex with my wife. That was when I broke into the real world. I would see an attractive girl at college and would die inside because I was married. I wanted to connect with that person (or was it the image?) but couldn't have her! Eventually, lust for "the real thing" won out, and each affair or "relationship" began as a glorious, "liberating" experience.

Here was a whole new world of experience for me. This is where many women in sexual recovery identify a distinction between their stories and those of the typical male luster. Sex and physical lust are not the real issue; they only mask the real issue, which is what we might call the Velcro Syndrome. "*'Please connect with me and make me whole,' we cried with outstretched arms.*"[44] It's where I have my spiritual umbilical cord in my hand, with a plug dangling from its end, and I go around trying to plug into someone to get the juice, the life-force I need to exist. I'm the Connector and the woman is the Connectee. And the connection seems very real—super-real. But it's a *mis*connection. Just like the Boys at Duke. *Mis*-orientation. Let's call this stage *Pseudosexuality V.*

Here's how another misconnect puts it:

It is enmeshment with another person as a god. I used my partners as gods. It is my drive for God-hunger directed toward a
person. I will surrender anything for that person-connection. It's
twisted 180 degrees from where it should be, but it's got a kernel
of truth and therefore I keep on doing it. So if I have a relationship with this person which is like god-oriented, then everything
should be okay and everything should be right, and that should
be the perfect relationship.

I devour her. I surround her. I cut myself off from everything else, and I cut *her* off from everything else. Because I'm so
close and I want to be so connected. That's why it's so insidious,
because it seems like such a good thing. Only it's misdirected. It
seems like it should be the highest good. If you don't know about
the real connection, it is the highest good. And it's supported by
family, friends, and society. Right now this is the idolatry of our
whole society: focusing on "the relationship." That is The Good.[45]

An entry from this young man's journal, written at the beginning of his last "relationship," reveals the personal mis-connection as
Source-of-life:

Yes, you are the most dangerous drug to me. I used you to shield
myself from my mind and soul. I see your beautiful face and forget the abyss. No, I refuse to face the terror and instead melt with
your body. I am gutless and feeble and I rage against God-myself.
Clasp me tight and look into my eyes as I into yours. Let us transfer terror into joy. Let us dance with joy as we plunge headlong
into the void.

Here was a man who knew what was really happening, but was
powerless to stop.

Oddly, in my relationship history, even though availability of the
real thing increased, picture-woman masturbation kept increasing
too. For me, at least, this challenges Kinsey's (and Freud's) "sexual
outlet" focus, everywhere present in his 1948 report, where one of
his underlying (and unproven) presuppositions was that males must
have sexual "outlet." My new and unrestricted sexual outlets only

led to wanting more! I and many others are discovering tha
become totally optional.[46] However, when lust, the miscoi
or addictive demand is active, sex is not only not optional but seemingly mandatory—the neurology is triggered.

Pseudosexuality Continued

My pseudosexuality continued to progress in marked stages: affairs,
masturbating to triple-X rated films, arcades, this kind of sex, then
that. As strange as this may seem, each stage was a new imprinting that
stuck with me as though it were the one-and-only original, "establishing a long-lasting behavioral response." Instead of the newer activity replacing the former, however, all of the activities continued and
escalated, crossing new lines, including gender. As a footnote, I should
add that once I stumbled onto prostitutes, that became the obsession
of choice.

The Magic Piece—"Coming Out"

While nearing the end of my journey into PS one day, I met the actress-
dancer-prostitute who was the ultimate embodiment of all of the "best"
picture-woman fantasies and real bodies I had ever known. Beautiful,
intelligent, sensitive, exotic, she was the goddess of desire. Her willingness to continue seeing me—it would still be for money—and work
with me on my play was contingent on her staying in prostitution. For
me the decision would mean giving up my second marriage and new
family, job, career, all of life as I knew it—and God. Guess what won
out. Not who, *what*. Lust.

When closeted gays have their orientation made public, it's called
"coming out." This experience with the actress-dancer was my coming out into full and exclusive pseudosexuality. The conflict between
the dual natures was over. No more trying to be what I was not. I had
finally made a reluctant peace with what I was. There was sadness there,
but resignation. Capitulation. Lust was the higher power.

These various stages in the evolution of my PS might be summa-
rized as shown below. Each may be considered a formative imprinting
all its own.

Pseudosexuality I—Age 8. Solitary sex as simple self-stimulation without images or fantasy. The escape connection.

Pseudosexuality II—Age 8 or 9. Masturbation to image-women. The image-sex connection.

Pseudosexuality III—Age 12. Masturbation to lustified picture-women. The lust-connection.

Pseudosexuality IV—Age 13 or 14. Masturbation to a story-woman. The fantasy-sex connection.

Pseudosexuality V—Age 26. Affairs. The personal mis-connection.

Pseudosexuality VI—Age 30. Prostitutes. The *living*-image mis-connection.

Pseudosexuality VII—Age 49. Capitulating to full and exclusive PS.

Age 49—Recovery from PS begins . . . .

Crossing each new threshold, I would experience similar feelings: Wow! This is it—what I've always been looking for! And then I would pursue it with everything I had. What should have been the tip-off was that I always wound up wanting more. And "better" and "different." Compulsive masturbation to image-women never stopped. I just kept piling on more ways of feeding lust. I soon discovered I was not alone. The world about me was reflecting my own devolution into pseudosexuality. Everything was "out" with respect to the heterosexual "closet." "*Anything goes*," as the Cole Porter song had it. And I followed eagerly along. Who knows where this might have ended had I not stopped when I did?

I did not choose my orientations—my *mis*-orientations. They seemed to choose me. However, I chose the attitudes that would set me up for them and drive me deeper into pseudosexuality. This would be the key to recovery: *Captive I may be, but I can choose the attitude that will open the door to freedom.* Thank God!

Now I find that my "orientation" is changing. I'm going through delayed adolescence—real adolescence. WOMEN. They're real! Complex and difficult as all get-out, but real. Beauty doesn't have to be tinctured with my lust any more, even thought it's lustified "out there." And lust is no longer attractive to me! How marvelous! Don't give up, you boys at Duke; there's a way out of this mess. And you have hit upon the key— start talking about it honestly together, facing what's really going on inside you.

Do we begin to see why I'm so hard on us so-called heterosexuals? We're in denial. Worse, we won't face what's really going on inside. So let's take a deep look into the psychology and something of the sociology of lust.

THE PSYCHOLOGY OF LUST

*We would not have our guardians grow up amid images
of moral deformity, as in some noxious pasture, and
there browse and feed upon many a baneful herb and
flower day by day, little by little, until they silently
gather a festering mass of corruption in their own soul.*

Plato, *Republic*, III: 401

Now that we've seen something of the rise of image-driven lust-sex
from both cultural and personal points of view, let's take an in-depth
look at what's going on inside the very heart and soul of the luster.
This should reveal elements of a psychology of the new lust and help
illuminate what we are calling pseudosexuality. This chapter contains
the core material—the raw data—out of which the concept of pseudosexuality was first distilled.

Prior to coming out of denial, many of us thought anything we did
sexually was normal and natural. Others persisted even though they
felt it was wrong. Regardless of what the old laws or moralities were,
our sexual "liberation" freed us from those frames of reference, if for no
other reason than we had to do or simply wanted to do what we were
doing. And doing it made it not only legitimate for us but normal and
natural. I typically led two lives, in two conflicting realities; but *within*
each reality I was usually at peace with that morality and psychology.
That some of us went to pieces periodically was, to us, an accident or
anomaly, brought about by others or even an "unjust" God.

This explains how the lusting minister or priest, for example, can preach fervently against immorality in the morning and act out on porn or go cruising for sex on the other side of town that very afternoon. To some of us the contradiction between the two realities was profoundly disturbing, leading us to emotional illness and more addictive behavior to numb out the shame. Others of us would cover any doubts or inner conflict and flaunt it openly, seeking public validation and daring the world to disapprove. This indicates we suffered from a fundamental reality distortion. What is more difficult to realize is that we also suffered a distortion of our personal and sexual identities.

While in the obsession, there's no external reference with which to judge the anti- or pseudo-natural from the natural. However, if somehow we can observe it from the "outside," we should be able to see what's really going on inside. Since we're going to be talking about what is "natural" and "unnatural" in the area of male sexuality, what is real and what is unreal, let's look at two scenarios and see if we can detect any pseudo-sexual components in a typical lust event. First, the natural, without lust.

The Natural

A man goes for a walk and sees a neighbor woman getting into her car. They have spoken briefly before about local matters of mutual interest to the community. He finds her attractive, and there have been indications she puts out some energy his way too. As he walks past, he looks her full in the face, smiles broadly and waves; he enjoys going outward in this connection with Woman. She smiles back, waves happily, and drives off. He walks on with a buoyant step. Both feel a positive energy. The exchange is both a going outward of one to the other and a taking in of each other. It is complete in itself, enjoyed, and not demanding repetition.

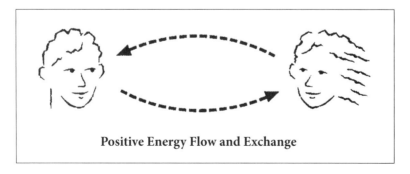

Positive Energy Flow and Exchange

Watching this exchange, we would say there was a good deal of healthy sexual energy in the air between the man and the woman. Normal sexuality was expressing itself without sex or lust. (Sexuality is not sex.) We witness the clean joy of two sexual humans responding to each other and enjoying the free exchange and impulse of life mediated thereby.[47] The diagram shows this face-to-face encounter and the positive energy vector between them.

The Anti-natural

Bear in mind that whatever else this book attempts, it is an exposé of what we are calling the new lust. Lust can hardly be called unnatural today; it is practically omnipresent, a way of life. I use the term *anti-natural* because, as we shall see, no matter how prevalent lust is in our culture, whatever damages human sexuality and interpersonal relations works *against* the natural and hence must be regarded as unnatural.

The event described below is some blank verse I wrote several years into recovery from sex and lust addiction. It would have been impossible to discern that had I still been captive to lust. This revealing piece captures the inner sequence of mental and spiritual states by dissecting the various components in the anatomy of a single lust event. It is, in effect, a CAT-scan of the man's psyche as the event proceeds within him.

As you read, it will become readily apparent that apart from any allusions to gender, what's going on is not gender-specific at all. It can apply equally to what may transpire between a man and a woman, a man and a man, a woman and a man, a woman and a woman, or an adult and a child. Non-lusters may not identify and may not even understand. However, whenever I've read this before audiences of self-admitted lusters, the piece has evoked instant identification bordering on an awakening.

Imagine this is the same scenario as in the natural one, above—a man going for a walk, seeing a potential lust object. Only the man in question is a habitual luster. The formative experiences of the boys at Duke had created this very kind of person. The visual encounter with another person that is described is exactly the same inner scenario as someone taking a lust "drink" or "hit" from a still or moving picture or from a memory or fantasy. I use a man-to-woman example here to depict the deviancy in a so-called heterosexual incident. This points up the underlying pathology that drives pseudosexuality.

In the following analysis I was able, in an extraordinary way, to go deeply inward within myself in a subjective freeze-frame process and do a replay in slow motion. I had developed this technique in previous scientific research.[48] (It may be that only those who have been in the throes of lust recovery can understand or identify.)

> Warning: As we enter the very soul of the luster caught in the act, be careful that you do not open your soul to this evil. And if you, the reader, happen to be one who was ever victimized, you may not want to read it at all, since what we have here, though not sexually explicit, is the very essence of violent, diabolical corruption.

Notice how the intoxication and transformation build and deepen within the luster as normal visualization moves into spiritual perversion.

Anatomy of a Look

There it is—
Over there.
That image in the corner of my eye.
Light rays impinging on the retina of my peripheral vision.
Rays coming in. Neutral. Passive.
Innocent.
Brain processing the data as a computer.
Man the benign machine.

Then, the image moves closer and more data is processed.
The computer sets a flag: "Trigger material."
Recognition.
Now I, the practicing luster, face a moral predicament:
Decision!
To drink or not to drink?
Suddenly I'm a spiritual creature with a higher will *using*
      the computer.
Man the autonomous being!

I choose to drink.
Not just look. *Drink.*
Only the luster knows the difference.

What is the drink?
Instead of light rays coming in passively
    and registering a neutral image,
Something is now going *out* of me.
Taking. Plundering.
Against the knowledge and will of the other person.
And lightning-fast.
Doesn't have to be the hard "drool."
Can even be oh, so quick and "gentle."

Lust is always an act of violence.

Rebellion. Demand. I want. I must have.
I must have or I'll die!
So I take. And get. . . .
It's free! And secret. No one knows!
Or will ever know.
I don't even acknowledge it to myself.
The perfect steal.

But it's an act *against.*
Against the man or woman, yes.
But what about a mere picture or fantasy?
There's something in *me* I have to transgress.
Something in *me* I must turn against.
The light inside.
An act of defiant will.
Against the Light I take.

Isolation. Separation.
Escaping inward, getting lost—inside myself.
Losing my self.
But *seeming* to gain a shot of life.

And instead of the image serving oneness with that person,
I choose to use it against the natural.
Perversion.

The one glance is enough.
I now process the image any way I choose.
It's no longer a person or picture out there;
It's something *in here*.
Greedily I ingest and possess,
And am possessed.

I invest the image with a super-natural Power and Presence.
Larger-than-life.
Infused with spirit to fill the emptiness within.
Spiritual intercourse.
With myself!
(Or with . . . with *what?*)

This creative power I get—
Is it from being in the image of God?
Is that what I use to imbue this thing with its super-force?
I pervert the very image of God?
But this is what I want. Must have!

It's taking me out of myself!
Mood-altering. Mind-altering.
Self-transcending! Spiritual! Ecstasy!
What power! I'm in total control!
I!
Create!
And possess!
I'm GOD!!!

The saliva of the false god juices a voracious appetite.
I gulp and devour this inner entity.
And am devoured!
Lust is self-consuming; I'm doing all this to *myself*!
No wonder it unleashes the negative force:
Rage,
And the litany of all my sins.

And what was once neutral, innocent reality,
 a person, a mere picture in the brain,
Has become a perversion—
Twisted distortions of reality out of the inner darkness.

I, the Destroyer at work.
I, now the god of my own life,
Creating my own goddess of Desire,
In my own lust-image!
Idols out of the Id,
False worship!

And I have what I truly want: my own god—*Me!*
The giver of "life" to me.

To what end?
Death!
Shutting out the light and love of God and man—
And woman—
Blinding me to the truth about myself.
For to see *that* truth would be to fall down and cry
Oh God—!!
What's *wrong* with me?!

Hard to Believe?

To the reader who is not a recovering luster, the above description may elicit strange reactions or outright rejection: "What in the world are you talking about?" Thus, to give this "Anatomy" of a lust look some corroborating credibility, let's look at what a psychologist has discovered relating to captivity or bondage of another sort.

 "In August of 1971, social psychologist Philip Zimbardo performed an infamous experiment at Stanford University, one whose results still send a shudder down the spine because of what they reveal about the dark side of human nature."[49] The horrors of the Abu Ghraib prison scandal in the Iraq war of 2004 were a real enactment of what his experiment showed had happened to nice middle-class college students in the Stanford Prison Experiment of 1971.

Dr. Zimbardo relates: "I designed the experiment that randomly assigned normal, healthy, intelligent college students to enact the roles of either guards or prisoners in a realistically simulated prison setting where they were to live and work for several weeks. My student research associates and I wanted to understand the dynamics operating in the psychology of imprisonment. How do ordinary people adapt to such an institutional setting?" As it turns out, they had to terminate the experiment prematurely "due to its character-imploding power." The experiment's startling revelation was the "transformation of character"—good people suddenly becoming perpetrators of evil.

We're told that the key factor in this character transformation is a situation that *promotes anonymity and therefore reduces personal accountability.* "When people feel anonymous . . . as if no one is aware of their true identity . . . they can more easily be induced to behave in antisocial ways." In such an anonymous situation, we're told that one's "mental functioning changes: they live in an expanded-present moment that makes past and future distant and irrelevant. Feelings dominate reason, and action dominates reflection. The usual cognitive and motivational processes that steer behavior in socially desirable paths no longer guide people."

There we have it; that's exactly what's happening inside our luster. He enjoys perfect anonymity in that eye-blink and the dark spiritual drama going on inside him. The luster is imprisoned in that expanded-present moment. There's no past or future. Time stands still. Reason and one's best motives are shut out as the action of lusting takes over and dominates. And I, for one, can identify with prisoners becoming "pathologically passive in response to . . . forces acting on them"—a prisoner, captive to the power of lust.

We are forced to conclude, with Dr. Zimbardo, that *"[T]he line between good and evil is in the center of every human heart."*

Analysis of the Lust Episode

Let's take this test-tube sample of a lust event and examine it stage by stage.

- Visual contact is made with the object.

- The object is instantly recognized as potential for lust. The sub-conscious lust "radar" is always on and scanning. Identification! Lock-on occurs automatically; the luster has no choice.
- In the snapshot of an eye-blink, a "drink" is taken—the visual snatch. But what is the drink? In this case, what the man is seeing—the image appearing on his retina—is a female, but what he is perceiving really isn't there; it's a product of his own desire, coming from deep within. The retinal image is cool and neutral; the processed image is hot and engaging. This is the first indication that some kind of distortion is going on. Thus, *a negative spiritual force is at work within the luster.*
- Fantasy, energized by lust, builds on the perceived image. It may focus and obsess on only one bodily part or attribute of the person. This can be almost anything, depending on prior imprint-ing and experience. Forget the genitalia or obvious leg or breast fetishes; a woman's lips, hand, fingers, fingernails, or glove will do. Or merely the sexual aura a person emanates. In same-sex lust, a man's shoe and sock in an ad or window display triggers one man. Another was overheard saying hair on a man's chest drove him crazy. The variety of triggers for the luster testifies to just how prominent learning and experience are in the forces driving human sexuality. Lust imbues the image with an aura and intensity not in the original. *The reality of the sex object is distorted and made unreal.*
- The force imbuing this snatched image is most powerful because it must and does *overpower* the person's own natu-ral reality and sensations. The obsessive luster is doing this against his will or conscience, regardless of how submerged it is under years of this activity. And yet, he is doing it *with* his will; hence inner conflict is engendered. At the same time, he is taken over—"possessed," experiencing a rush of "energy" and power. The distortion is within him; hence it is his own identity that is being distorted. He wants that distortion; thus, isn't the man unwittingly lusting after distortion of his own identity? *Perversion of sexual identity.*
- One of the reasons this "drug" is so increasingly craved is that the luster becomes abnormally energized and empowered, as

though some force is actually charging him up. Although his personal reality is actually overpowered, he has the feeling that he is empowered. The person feels *super*-human (another tie-in with violence?). This is an incredibly insidious entity, clever and deceitful, and testifies to the huge ego force driving lust. *Self-deception; the Lie builds.*

- The lust hit produces a powerful shot of what feels like "life." That time and time again this later proves to be *anti*-life, producing the letdown of "huge blackness," doesn't deter the man from perpetrating again. This feeling of "life" is the great payoff of lust; it delivers the sensation of more transcendental ecstasy than mere sex or love can ever give! Lust packs the Great Wallop, a high-voltage discharge of awesome power. Lust is the sex-enhancer, the ecstasy amplifier, the Cocaine of the luster's soul. Lust is *power*. What the person is experiencing feels not only real, but *super*-real. In such moments as these, the person will feel more "alive" than at any other time in his life. *Delusional pseudo-reality.*

- Since this is all happening within the luster, and since lust has to "feed" on something, it must be feeding on himself, even though he thinks he is consuming the image. This is one of the diabolical delusions of the lust event. Feeling sustained and enlivened by this devouring snatch, he is actually being devoured. *Lust kills.*

- A kind of alcoholic "*blackout*" accompanies the experience. Other sensory data are shunted out, and sensory and emotional "tunnel vision" occurs, so overpowering is the intense inner involvement with the lust event. I have personally witnessed cases where the man was so overtaken by the visual drink and so locked on to it, that he lost all social consciousness and became functionally mute and deaf in the conversation he was having with me as he was tranced-out on the woman walking by. (It takes one to know one.)

I have come to detect other physiological changes while in such a state, such as dryness of throat, change in pulse, blood pressure, respiration, anal moistening, and galvanic skin response. I believe many of the symptoms are similar to those experienced in the fear response. Note that whatever else these and the host of other changes being discovered are, they are *chemical changes*, and chemistry affects neurology. How can this type of thinking and behavior *not* affect sexuality?

- The person creates a mental scenario enabling him to "connect" with the entity now possessing his inner being. This non-physical Connection is intercourse—spiritual intercourse. But intercourse with *what*? He's still just standing there staring, not moving a muscle. He feels like he's really possessing the woman out there, but he's really lusting after something within himself. Intercourse with self. (This is a very crucial concept, if difficult to comprehend.) What is happening inside this man is not only perversion of female reality, but *perversion of his own reality*.

    In losing contact with reality—a deliberate distortion of the reality of the other person and intercourse with the false "reality" within himself—the man has deceived and violated himself. This immediately becomes a *new way of being*. No wonder that the greatest barrier in recovery is seeing the reality of our own defects and wrongs. And if anyone dare drop a hint of what they see in us— Watch out! We lash out in murderous rage or a hundred other ways. In deliberately losing ourselves, we become blinded to ourselves. Called "pride blindness," this is the blindness of ego-lust, the most insidiously damning sin of all, because we sin against our own being. *Perverted self-obsession.*

- As the lust event builds, the experience becomes mind-altering and mood-altering—the essence of the drug experience. Personal reality is being altered by the negative force. The man's natural relation with the woman—intrinsic to his maleness— has been subverted. Continued subversion *changes the person.* "How?" you might ask, "it's only mental!"

    Consider: If the luster were to perpetrate only ten visual snatches per day, as our man above is doing, he will have repeated this event 36,500 times in a ten-year period. Recovering lusters testify to something more like a hundred such lust events just flipping through an issue of *Time* magazine, and an untold number of visual and fantasy hits throughout the rest of the day. This would get him millions or billions of lust events over that ten-year span. Science may soon be able to detect the chemical and neurological changes produced in such hits. Why not? Everything else we experience seems to have a chemical/neurological counterpart. We now know that the brain is actually changed by such behavior.[50] "As a man thinketh in his heart, so is he." Besides, there certainly is *character change*.

As though this inner spiritual scenario were not enough, occurring within the space of a few eye blinks with the man caught staring time-suspended into his own inner darkness, imagine what happens when this awesome lust event is coupled into the sex act. Natural sex involves all of the many systems comprising the human organism—muscular, circulatory, sensory, endocrine, nervous, emotional, spiritual. . . . These all converge and peak together in a neurologically massive input experience, chemically affecting not only the whole brain but the whole person. Just one *natural* sex experience, and the system will seek its repetition. Add mind- and spirit-altering lust to the sex act, and the system is instantly hooked, crying out soon for another fix. And another. . . . Talk about human sexuality being shaped by learning and experience—! Lust shapes sexuality. Lust distorts sexuality. *Lust destroys sexuality.* Has anyone plotted the accelerating male impotence curve lately?

Have you ever witnessed a boy's first reaction to porn? I have. He came from the neighbor boy's house, where he had just been shown the father's *Playboy* stash. (His reaction was similar to the time a year or so before when he had been introduced to acid rock music.) He was visibly deranged, acting as though he had just mainlined speed. When I gently asked him what was wrong, he told me. I had to carefully help him come down, and then fumbled around trying to give him some sex education.

• Our analysis shows that lust has all the characteristics of an addictive "substance" and then some. Even though there are no chemicals to shoot up from the outside, the new image-driven lust has proven to be one of the most potent "gotta-haves" known to addicts. This lust event in our friend, above, must be repeated again and again and again; and not only is there no real satisfaction and joy, as in the natural scenario, ultimately there is inner darkness, alienation, and dissatisfaction. The man is cut off from his own life. Can we begin to understand what the British doctor was writing about in his *Onania* pamphlet of 1712, when he was talking about effects of the new masturbation (see Introduction)? Also, the tolerance principle comes into play—increasing doses are necessary to achieve the original effects. Our typical luster, ostensibly "faithful" to his wife, will be compelled to go online or pull a magazine from his stash and gorge and sex out over the "real thing."

- Sadly, the more lust-sex progresses within this man, the less truly sexual he will become. By "enhancing" sex, lust is destroying his sexuality. For this man, the term heterosexual becomes a malapropism or oxymoron. *He's really a pseudosexual.*

Summary of the Lust Event

To the non-lustaholic reader, this may all sound strange. But such readers would be surprised to learn of the nearly universal identification recovering lust junkies admit to when they read or hear "The Anatomy of a Look" or these analyses. "I've been waiting for this book all my life," said a Chicago investment analyst.

The lust event begins with a conscious decision to snatch, pervert, and consume, leading to an overpowering reality distortion and mood-altering high, energizing a false spiritual empowerment and distortion of personal identity. This results in a distortion of sexuality, the perversion of sexual identity, and character change.

Note what has taken place. As the diagram below shows, what could have been a normal, natural visual encounter with another sexual human being becomes something totally different, going in the opposite direction, coming back upon the luster. From the very first instant, there is no thought of interacting with the *person*. The thought is, "Is there anything there I can have?" and "I am going to take". This is akin to the impulse-buying programming of the consumerized society. It is diametrically opposed to the natural, and hence is *anti-natural*; diametrically opposed to real sexuality, and hence *pseudosexual*.

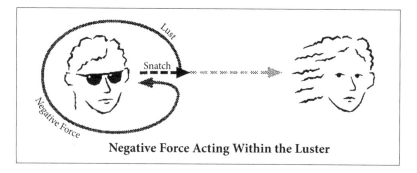

Negative Force Acting Within the Luster

Watching our luster, we are amazed. This attractive, healthy-looking specimen of manhood standing there before us is a cauldron of conflicting energies, sucking everything into the vortex of—what—? Into the vortex of the ravenous black hole within him. He is at once a ruthless victimizer and pitiful victim of forces of which he is unaware, losing his very masculinity and manhood with each drink. Infecting the spiritual air with his psychic pollution, he stands there with his invisible addiction validated, supported, reinforced, encouraged, and driven by the incredibly powerful forces we have unleashed in our culture.

That's my story; I was that man.

Observations and Implications

The effects of this lust-viral infection on the person and his relations deepen and broaden our understanding of the concept of pseudosexuality and its impact on our world. Again, the following is a description of my own experience, corroborated by that of many others.

- This so-called heterosexual man's concept of woman is distorted. The man does not know a woman for what she is naturally. Thus, opposite-sex reality—and hence sexuality—is progressively diminished; the man's capacity for true union with woman is damaged. The man becomes a *love cripple*. Many things can masquerade as love, but love becomes alien to him. Incapable of true intimacy, yet needing and seeking love, he unwittingly pushes love away. Not only is love for woman short circuited, *the very capacity and ability for love diminish*. (Recovery from this has been most painful and slow for me, but most rewarding. To finally discover and begin to experience real love—How can there be anything deeper or greater than that?)

- To the perpetrator, the object of lust is really asexual. It is difficult to grasp this elusive but very important concept. When our poor friend was lusting after that woman, *she* did not really matter; for him, she was not there at all. The force of lust did not emanate from her, regardless of how attractive she was, how she was dressed, or how she was acting. Lust emanated from within *him*. Thus, *the lust force is asexual.*

- **Note:** Paradoxically, if it is gender-connected at all, *lust must be same-gender connected, even when fixated upon the opposite sex.* Because lust is generated within and acting upon the gender doing the lusting. This is important to consider. I wonder if this is what Karl Stern, professor of psychiatry at the University of Ottawa and psychiatrist-in-chief at St. Mary's Hospital in Montreal, was getting at when he wrote, ". . . the seducer [read *luster*], the man who approaches woman [read *lusts after woman*] for conquest's sake only, without the possibility of lasting inner involvement, is always homosexually tied."[51] There's something here we should carefully consider, and it could prove to be another burr under the saddle of Marlboro Man.

  This raises an important question never asked: Does my "heterosexual" lusting help engender personal and cultural predisposition toward same-sex lust or tendency? Is there any connection between this century's explosive rise in opposite-sex lust and the corresponding rise in same-sex lust? (I believe the pseudosexual revolution has driven the evolution of both so-called orientations simultaneously, as we'll see in Part II.)

- Lust seems to produce a field effect. An ancient wisdom says, "None of us liveth to himself." Is there really a "collective unconscious" floating about (Carl Jung)? A cultural ESP? Multiply the above lust episode of our solitary male by the millions upon millions of lust events going on each day in the minds and actions of men around us. Women who happen to catch the luster in the act certainly feel that negative power in the air, but that's the visible tip of the iceberg; most of it is submerged and invisible. It is still the best-kept secret of the male sex. Then let this foul spiritual smog hover over the city and within the home and persist over time and over generations, and what do we have? Spiritual pollution. A polluted culture. We are the product of our times. "The sins of the fathers . . . ." Have we not created our own plague, an HIV of the human spirit, wreaking havoc upon human sexuality? And how can female sexuality remain unaffected when it lives and breathes the same polluted air and has to connect with *this*?

- The man reaches a point where he cannot have sex without activating the lust force and having some lust scenario working in his mind. Sex is energized and enabled by lust, instead of flowing naturally out of human intimacy, love, and passion. Many of the lust-oriented like myself never had sex without lust, so they don't know there is anything different than lust-sex as they know it. This is simply another way of describing *functional sexual impotence*. If I must have an unnatural force released within me in order to perform sexually, then I am functionally impotent. 'Cures' like Viagra frequently depend upon concealing the dysfunctional and anxiety-causing role played by pornography in promoting impotence.[52]

  Sadly, many sex therapists use lust to treat impotence and criminal sex offenders! Functional impotence is common enough in lusters still acting out sexually; it is very common in recovery, when men start having sex again and their programming screams out that they can't maintain an erection or have orgasm without bringing the images or memories back. The modern dilemma of man-woman relations has created enough performance problems for men as it is! Lust thoroughly complicates matters and adds an intolerable burden.

  This man, apparently sexually attracted to the opposite sex, becomes less sexual, we might even say less male. Human sexuality is a function not only of bodily factors, but the psycho-social and spiritual. Freud called it *psycho-sexuality*.[53] Sex is subjective.

- Passive lust—wanting to be lusted after—works the same way, whether the subject is man or woman and the object is man, woman, or child. When I want to arouse lust in another, I am lusting after lust, and the same spiritual forces are active in me as they are in our poor friend, above.

Of course, women are caught in the same complex of pseudosexual forces affecting men. It must be wonderful to be released from clothing sanctions and be free to celebrate the joy of one's own bare parts flopping around, if that's all there was to it. But unfortunately, today that cannot be divorced from the insidious LQ factor—the Lust Quotient. That glorious freedom has been infected by the lust virus and has lost that primal innocence we so long to recover. One cannot enjoy breathing clean air while one's own lungs remain fouled.

- Distortion of reality in this deep core of the human psyche means that the man's relation to reality in general is disturbed. This is perhaps most apparent in interpersonal relationships, even though making the connection between the malady and his relations is so often missed. But how can a man's relational "mechanism" with one human population—women—be perverted and his relations with others remain unaffected? It's one and the same relational mechanism. Thus, every intimate relationship gets botched.

Man to wife: "What do you mean, 'Do you know how you came across just then?' I was *not* rejecting and hateful; I was merely questioning whether we had made a firm commitment to go out tonight. I didn't think we had." No, the man does *not* know how he comes across to the woman; she's too much a part of his pseudosexual system. He's so in touch with his pseudo-Self, he's out of touch with the reality of his wife.

Often, even today, I find the first thing I see when I look at my wife are the results of aging. I don't see the person behind the body. I suffer not only from my self-induced programming to unreality but from the cultural force of the beauty-lust revolution. Whenever I notice such crippled perversion in myself and surrender it, I can usually look at her again—taking "the second look"—and see through to the person. What a marvelous gift.

The lust-oriented suffer from a profound sickness. We are spiritually diseased, and our immune system is disabled. How can women hope for a life of normalcy with us without our recovery? Much of the time they unknowingly *support* (not cause) our illness!

- The love cripple becomes an interpersonal cripple. We wind up with low RQs—low relatability quotients. We may do well on the job and in situations where no intimacy is required, but when it is required, we don't have the tools with which to cope in a normal manner. Interpersonal life is not easy for the lust-oriented. That's why the luster is such a tragic failure at being male, man, husband, father, and friend.

- What is virtually impossible for the religious luster to see is the fact that this relational perversion holds just as true, if not more so, with his relation to God. (The man can never see this without first surrendering his addiction.)* This may help explain some of the religious addiction and perversion of our time. If we can see it.

- Subconsciously, the person knows he is damaging himself, even though he may remain in denial. This pops up in other areas and in other manifestations of the negative force—resentment, rage, self-hatred, etc.—which in turn call for more of the drug to push away those negative feelings. At the same time, his self-obsession produces feelings of greatness and rightness out of all proportion to reality.

- This addictive process produces isolation. The man has never joined the human race; he's unable to do so. This luster is not only a love-cripple, but deep inside a very lonely person. Increasing amounts of time are spent fantasizing and masturbating in restrooms, cars, before TV and computer screens, etc. The man lives alone with his thoughts, even when in the company of others. He who would *possess* woman or man can't let anyone *in*!

- Once this addictive pattern is set, the man is susceptible to other addictions, whether chemical, behavioral, or spiritual (resentment and negative feelings about others, for example).

- Reality perversion creates a lie within the man's very identity. The Lie, however denied or repressed, produces guilt and shame, which require continued repression or expression via other negative attitudes.

The person must either go into denial about what is happening within himself, see it and descend into destructive self-

* "Surrender" in the 12-step recovery program refers to giving it up to God.

loathing, seek help, or seek to justify his lifestyle as "natural." Or all of the above. We often try to convince others to validate ourselves. But it never satisfies. We have to seek more and more validation for what we're doing, from higher and higher levels of authority—the media, religion, and state, for example—but deep inside we remain unconvinced. This propagandizing in the so-called heterosexual area has been so pervasive over such a long period of time, we don't recognize it as propaganda anymore. How can it be any different in the same-sex area? It's part of the PS propaganda across the board. The reality distortion is now part of the subliminal cultural mind-set. *Pseudosexuality seeks—insists on—validation from without because there is no real validation from within.*

In my acting-out days, I recall articles and editorials in the nudies attempting to offer an apologetic for lust—*Oui*'s entrée issue, for example. Maybe they are still doing that.[54] This "defense" of lust is a tip-off that they know what's going on. They know what they are pandering to. Lust sells! But we are the ones who create the market for the stuff and go to any length to get it. Lusters make porn and all its effects a necessity in our world. *Any cure must begin in the hearts and minds of lusters.*

- The negative force behind our rage and wrath seeks expression and validation by finding others doing the same, by pushing itself onto others and pulling others down with us, by promoting itself, and by trying to convert others—even the world, if it can—to the Lie. This is precisely what we males have done and continue to do. When one of the new nudies came out, the accompanying press release touted it as "joy of living;" that "more units of eroticism" (read *more intensely lustified pictures*) made for "better communication between the sexes."[55] And notice how aggressive, propagandizing, or even shrill we get when our way of life on either side of the orientation divide is threatened. The *Playboy* delusion was one of the most powerful forces shaping today's sexualities. During the 15th World AIDS Conference in Bangkok in July of 2004, a display in the lobby honoring prostitutes declared: "It is not necessarily degrading to have intimacy with strangers. In fact, it is one of the most liberating things you can experience."[56] That's pretty good propaganda.

Lust as a Function of the Primordial Warrior Response

We've tried to describe some of the elusive psychological or psycho-spiritual characteristics of this new lust. But does even this account for the super "adrenaline rush"? There may be another factor involved—what I will call the primordial Warrior Response (or, the Response). This Response derives from the threat of the predator population—lions, for example—endangering a hominid or human tribe. We were the minority creature on that vast prehistoric landscape—the prey. Imagine the scene from our village surrounded by the savannah. When we see the beast threatening on the perimeter, we are struck by the power of this predator, the Leopard Lord. With power over life and death, she is Queen of beasts, powerful, cunning, and beautiful, inspiring both fear and awe. Encounter with her is both terrifying and fascinating. We either galvanize to engage her or flee. To survive back then, the fittest did not flee; they had to conquer the beast. That instinctual patterning is still within us; witness war games, gangsta rap, etc.[57]

Today our global village is surrounded by another "savannah." The "predator" out there all around us is the lustified female image. This image "preys" directly on the male. Indirectly it preys on the female by forcing her to assume that image, react, or adapt to it in some other way; but that's another story. This lustified image has its turn-of-the-century origins in the clothing and advertising industries' aping of the prostitute garb, pose, and demeanor.[58] This lustified image has increasingly penetrated our world since the confluence of photography, advertising, consumerism, the media, the existential vacuum of our culture, and other forces.

Look at a typical lustified female image as Predator in any magazine or on any high-fashion runway, for example: elevated (high heels); hips thrust forward; costumes and color accentuating the ritual awe; tantalizing exposures of shape, skin, and limbs; the exaggerated ritual makeup mask and pose, accentuating the emanation of power over the male. This Predator is poised and "dressed to kill." She is "cunning, baffling, and powerful,"[59] inspiring fascination, awe, and fear. Her presence occupies the village and now dominates our virtual reality. Today's male is being relentlessly "stalked" and preyed upon at every turn. By his own choice! (Or is it?)

In the warrior response, the heart and respiratory rates increase, blood is withdrawn from the surface of the body and the viscera in favor of the voluntary muscles to prepare for the sudden exertion of fighting or fleeing, pupils dilate, the bronchi distend, glucose is released by the liver for use by the muscles, and blood clotting is sped up, in case of injury.[60] This response aroused within the warrior produces a "high," an altered state of consciousness supporting his ability to survive. I suggest that for the male, *fixating on the lustified Predator image activates that very Response.*

However, the lustified female image is designed to elicit even more than that primordial Response. The image is not only threatening and aggressively overmastering, but is designed to *attract* the male, offering to be taken. Models in the media are *attract*-ive. The meta-message of the image come-on is saying, "I'm here for *you*. I'm offering myself to *you*; I want you to *take* me." The image says, *Drink, take, and have!* And the primordial Response says *Kill!* Or be overcome! So, the luster "kills"—scores, snatches, consumes.

Interestingly, the other possible response is *Flee!* Is there any subconscious connection here with why so many of us today find "the easier softer way" to be with the same sex? Fearful of engaging Predator-Woman, do we find it easier to "flee" and gravitate to men? Is She simply too awesome to deal with? There may be a finer line than we think separating the so-called orientations. Regarding recovery, if my lust or sexualizing is even partially fear-driven, how important it is that I overcome fear of Woman in order to love and be loved! That's what I'm trying to do today. Not easy for me, but it is working. And for that I am joyously grateful.

Whatever else is involved in today's "male gaze," the mere act of visually "drinking" (compared with normal looking) may well be triggering the primordial Response. The luster is not free *not* to experience it. Fixating on the lustified Predator image not only is a quick-and-dirty way of experiencing the warrior Response, it creates a *"super* hit," by adding the sexual come-on.

Conversely, I've noticed that activating the Warrior Response—playing chess or "taking sides" in scenes of violence in movies, for example—lowers the threshold of my Lust Response.

When we connect this powerful primordial Response with the Lust Response, then tie both in with the highly complex all-systems-involving transcendental ecstasy of the sex act, we have something incredibly powerful and new in the sexual ecology of the human race. Through virtual reality, we're doing Nature one better. We might say that by activating the primordial Warrior Response, the Lust Response achieves "critical mass," resulting in sexual nuclear fission. A Big Bang, yes, but also disintegration. And sex becomes something not only more powerful, but *different*.

Masters and Johnson—on Lust?

One final thought on the psychology of lust. Masters and Johnson, the famous sex researchers, have described in detail the place sexual fantasies play in both heterosexuals and homosexuals. In their book *Homosexuality in Perspective*, they describe and provide statistics for both free-floating and short-term fantasies in a select subject population. Free-floating fantasies are "spontaneously evolved by men and women in response to sexual feelings or needs without restraints of time or place." Short-term fantasies are "stimulative mechanisms, frequently in response to imminent sexual opportunity . . . 'old friends' used to initiate or enhance a sexual experience or as a supportive mechanism when concern for sexual performance develops."[61] Recovering lusters like myself know exactly what they're referring to with such jargon. Stimulative mechanisms used to initiate or enhance sexual performance is a euphemism for lust, the easy remedy for functional impotence.

One concludes from their research that sexual fantasy is alive and doing very well indeed in both heterosexual and homosexual populations. But more than this, it is highly probable that Masters and Johnson, in their scientific analysis of sexual fantasy covering the years 1957 through 1977, have unwittingly been documenting evidence for the new lust.

. . .

These glimpses into the luster's conscious, subconscious, and social self reveal what men and boys are turning into, though they—and their parents, girlfriends, boyfriends, or wives—can rarely see this at the time. Incubation of the lust virus goes undetected and remains so, even after it has metastasized into the cancer of full-blown pseudosexuality.

There's a pseudosexual revolution going on. Is it any wonder we're burning out so soon?

THE LUST-VIOLENCE
CONNECTION

"For me lust is spiritual. A spiritual drug. This drug for me is absolutely tied to violence. Lust is an act of violence for me. This drug of lust is rooted in my violence, for myself and others, especially women. This drug of lust seems to be the way I calm myself from my fear of violence; the medication I use to come down from my fearful, anxious and angry/violent states. A big lust trigger for me is to be threatened in some way!"

From a male sexaholic trying to recover

Lust and sexual violence and abuse are imbued with the same dark spiritual energy. Note the string of adjectives having connotations of violence that Shakespeare connects with lust (see his Sonnet 129 in the Introduction): "murderous," "bloody," "savage," "extreme," "rude," "cruel." Lust is a destructive force—within, even if it never finds its way out.

"Take me!"

Some years ago, I had occasion to pick up one of the adult video industry news magazines. Until a newspaper covered the story, I had no idea that the world center for that $14 billion industry was in my own back yard. I wasn't prepared for what I saw. The trade "news" was more pic-tures than text. And what pictures! I hadn't held any such magazine in my hand for twenty five years. What a shock! No nudes, mind you, just pages crammed with head shots of the models posed for video covers, like they're trying to out-lust one another, their facial spiritual aura cry-ing out, Hire *me*! Buy *me*! Snatch *me*! It was like suddenly walking into a cage of hungry tigers. I had the strange but unmistakable sense that the overall feeling around that coterie was *violence*. The women seemed like they were posing to elicit a violent snatch from the buyer—"*Take me!*" I actually felt attacked by the images. This was a whole order of magnitude darker than what I had seen in the girlies and nudies twenty five years before. These predators were not being beautiful and sexy, as they were back then, they seemed to be soliciting and expecting a fero-cious response. I felt the spirit of lust-violence hovering in that image air. These are Women?! Predators! Get me outta here!

I got this feeling, not by looking at any single image, but by flipping through, trying to find the publication masthead so I could write a letter, and being accosted on every page. I can't tell you how grateful I am to have stopped resorting! How can anybody survive, connecting with that spirit today? And what I hear tell about what's happening on the Internet—! To think that our children— What *is* lust today? Where is it going?

Epithumia

Let's go back to the "Anatomy of a Look" in chapter 4 to see the lust-violence connection:

> Instead of light rays coming in passively and registering a
>   neutral image,
> Something is now going out of me.
> Taking. Plundering.
> Against the knowledge and will of the other person. . . .
> Lust is always an act of violence.
>
> Rebellion. Demand. I want. I must have. . . .
> So I take. And get. . . .
> The perfect steal . . . an act against. . . .
> I the Destroyer at work. . . .

The Greek word for lust is *epithumia*, a compound word made from *epi*, meaning "intense," and *thumos*, meaning "passion," "anger," "wrath," or "rage". Did the Greeks know something we don't? In some strange kinky way violence is like lust, and lust is like violence. On more than one occasion, when I've watched gratuitous violence on the screen, I've become more vulnerable to lust. That's another reason why I can't watch it today.

The Violence Is in the Taking

In the forties, one of the street terms for having sex with a woman was "snatch." Another was "tear off a piece." Was this latter terminology related in any way to the common practice of tearing a picture out of a magazine, then masturbating to it and throwing it away, or was there even then the idea of taking by force what was suggestively offered in the photo images? Why the violence in these and other sexual expressions? When woman is just a disposable paper image and not a real human being; when, since childhood, you've been letting yourself be overcome by the lust mediated through those images—then gorging on her, tearing her up and throwing her away—you've conditioned yourself to a brutally self-centered kind of inner violence. What we fail to see is that pseudosexuality not only does violence to our ethical sensibilities but to our very sexuality itself.

Earlier in my personal story (chapter 3) I related how I grabbed a fellow student's legs when she came over and sat down in my living room. This is revelatory and may provide insight into the microgenesis of a person's predisposition to violence-prone thinking or violence-prone fantasy. I have no doubt that the toxic imprinting in me of masturbating to that photograph of Danielle Darrieux's legs at age twelve not only set me up for the "take me" trigger but gave me "permission" to grab this girl's legs. Note today's plunging necklines, a very infectious meme, propagating so rapidly it's hilarious to me now.

But there's more here. Implied in the "taking" of those legs was the idea that I had such a right. Can you see the disposition or frame of mind that's implied here, the hint of the *spirit* of violence asserting itself ever so subtly? When we say that every act of lust is an act of violence, we aren't saying there's physical violence involved. What we are saying is that the idea of "taking" a person without permission is on the same order as the spiritual essence of violence. That's why more than one religious teacher has said that lusting after a woman is the same as taking her and resentment is the same as murder.

The lust-violence connection is in the heart.

The Violence Is Against the Luster Himself

It is the inner psychic and moral violence that corrodes the tissue of the man's being, even if he never breaks out into physical violence. This conflict within him adds to his distress and self-hatred, which are inevitably inflicted on others in some way or another.

Paradoxically, the man in our story of The Anatomy of a Look must continue his pursuit of woman; she is his drug connection. She actually becomes an *it*, since lust erases gender and person. This conflict adds to his distress and inability to form lasting union. It drives him to more of his drug in order to sedate the conflict, stress, and self-negation which invariably increase.

Self-hatred must progress either inwardly or outwardly, or both. Anger turned inward can turn into depression, a host of other emotional illnesses, and more self-destructive attitudes and behavior. Outwardly it can manifest itself in hostile attitudes and physical violence. This negative force can break through into overt acts against women, from passive rejection to physical and sexual violence.

Using the analogy of Newton's Third Law of Motion—"For every action, there is an equal and opposite reaction"—I suggest that for every lust event there is an opposite (negative) force acting within and back upon the luster himself. "What goes around, comes around." (See the illustration on page 70.) Lust is always an act of inner violence. But the luster is unaware of this, blinded by the overpowering payoff of the experience. Since the lust event is a willful perversion of the object-person being lusted after, that perversion must be a *perversion of himself*, because it's all happening within himself.

A psychosis is "a major mental disorder in which contact with reality is usually impaired" (*Webster's*). This habitual impairment of reality is certainly pathological, damaging and changing the person, and feeding the growing disorder within. At least subconsciously, I was doing something I knew was against my well-being, so anger-resentment came into play, feeding a pool of self-hatred and resentments inside me. Unless the man is drinking, drugging, gambling, entertaining, or eating these negative feelings away, with a life given over to lust he's bound to have negative ("violent") feelings about what he's doing to himself. In recovery I eventually came to view this as terminal self-hatred. Psychiatry and therapy had failed to discern the lust-resentment connection; they blamed it on childhood environment, that I was suffering from low self-esteem, or just wasn't getting enough sex at home. Inability to cope with the tyranny of lust against oneself has led some men to self-castration.

Of course, my "low self-esteem" would jump out and hit the shrinks in the first five minutes of the initial session. But how facile, such diagnoses, and how trite the typical admonitions, "Start thinking better of yourself! Look at yourself in the mirror every day and say, 'I love you.'" Telling this to a self-worshipping narcissist is like telling an alcoholic to take a little wine for his upset stomach. Today's psychological paradigms often miss the all-important personal-responsibility component in mental illness that the Twelve-step program is capable of uncovering.

There could thus be a connection between the new lust and the new violence. Yes, there's a new violence in the air today. And a lust connection. The Amish School massacre of October 2006 says it all, too horrible to recount here. The new lust may not create physical violence directly, but there's an inner spiritual attitude of violence unleashed within the luster himself, based on that self-centered snatch mentality. This fits perfectly the perpetrator at the Amish school. Also, there's an expectation of wrath from the man's own guilt and self-judgment. In some, this may stay inward as escalating self-hatred or depression. In others, this negative force may be coupled with the sex act itself—even in sexual violence. In many, as was true in my case, this inner self-violence pollutes the spiritual atmosphere of the home in emotional abuse toward wife and children.

CALVIN AND HOBBES By Bill Watterson   February 15, 1995

The Violence Is Against the Symbol of His Tyranny

In our luster, caught in the "Anatomy of a Look," we see that subconscious negative feelings can develop against women, since the lust object—that image—may be subconsciously perceived as the "cause" of his sexual tyranny and self-hatred. This can create a chronic love/hate relation with women, lovers, and wives. Without her even knowing it, the man's sexual partner is "in the way"—in the way of lust—cramping his style. Lust always wants more of the pseudo-real, but the woman out there is real.

By 2004, California was experiencing over 100,000 reported cases of sexual violence per year. And ". . . more than 75% of female assault victims age 18 or older were raped and/or physically attacked by someone they knew, and nearly six out of 10 rape/sexual assault incidents were reported to have occurred in a familiar place."[62]

One of the former models for the annual swimsuit issue of *Sports Illustrated*, awakened to what is really going on, said of the advertisers, "They are promoting violence against women." Of course; she felt it, she knew it. But under the influence of being lusted after, there's often a voluntary suspension of disbelief. Lara Roxx, implicated in the HIV outbreak among porn actors in the San Fernando Valley, relates how she felt one night while dancing on stage in a strip club in Montreal: "[W]hen she looked down at the 'perv row' [actor's slang for row of 'perverts'], the man staring back up at her was sizing her up like 'a piece of meat without a brain in my head. I started to cry,' she says. 'And I ran off the stage.'" (*L.A. Times* May 5, 2004) Forget "perv row"; what's the look on a man's face when he's consuming a porn image in private? And what's the line being crossed *inside* a person when he is openly that rapacious? Porn actresses and the like know the truth; there is not only "perversion" here, but something powerfully *pseudo-* and *anti-*.

Serial killer Gary Ridgway, the Green River Killer, known to have had sex with and then murdered at least forty eight prostitutes, said, with intense feeling, when asked why he killed the girls, "I can't stand it to have woman in control over me!" (televised documentary) How were these girls controlling him? They weren't; he controlled them. But it was the power of the prostitute *image* that controlled him, the image of porn woman he had probably burned into his psyche at an earlier age. When and how did his exposure and consumption of those images begin? And, if he's typical of picture-lust junkies, had he ever had serious misgivings (religious? parental?) about being under the power of those images and wanted to stop but couldn't, thus leading him to transfer his self-hatred onto others or eliminate the source of his tyranny by killing them? Only the powerless can know or understand the extent of shame, self-hatred, or rage when trapped in the slavery of virtual Woman. Or virtual Man.

Donna Ferrato, a New York photographer, will never forget how her quest to document love [read lust] broke her heart and changed her focus from romance to domestic violence.[63]

The Violence Is Against Society

Many of us seem to succeed in keeping the negative force directed inwardly, against ourselves, though unaware we're doing so. For a long time I've sensed a huge negative force building up in our society, requiring all the cultural "medications" at our disposal to keep it at bay. It is mostly under the surface, but is breaking out more and more. Note the recent phenomenon of freeway shootings, where irate motorists blast away with something stronger than their car horns, and the new "road rage." Note the church burnings, unthinkable in the past.[64] And note the wrath expressed in the recent school shootings. Note the fierce hateful wrath expressed about current sexual and political issues. Increasingly, the wrath is breaking out.

At the beginning of this chapter we said that "lust and sexual violence and abuse partake of the same dark spiritual energy." Astrophysicists tell us there is increasing evidence for "dark energy," a mysterious, repulsive force throughout the cosmos that appears to be speeding up the expansion and hence disintegration of the universe. This begs for an analogy with what we're discovering about the new lust—an invisible dark force permeating our spiritual cosmos and speeding the disintegration of our sexuality and humanity

We talk about violence in the media. But the lust snatch and its progressive buildup of self-hatred point up what may be a missing question in the pornography debate: Is there any connection between addiction to *pornography* and violence? A single act of lust in my heart is an act of violence against another, even though the object of that lust may not know or feel a thing. Isn't it interesting, though, how violated a woman can feel when she does happen to catch a man gaping in raw lust. And the man, when caught doing this, reacts as though he were caught actually violating that person. If you've ever encountered or been involved in a raw act of lusting after another, you probably know what I mean. Addiction to lust creates a *rapacious attitude.*

There is much ado about genes and violence. Some researchers feel people with low levels of the brain chemical serotonin may be predisposed to violence, and research is looking for "vulnerability genes," which create the serotonin deficit (*Los Angeles Times*, December 30, 31, 1993). Is it possible for there to be a relation between lust and low serotonin levels? Could this be one of the results of lust's inner violence upon the self?[65]

Lust is violence, and our culture is promoting lust in virtually every aspect of our lives today, not just the sexual. A fertile field of investigation would be to plot the rise of sexual violence against the rise of the new lust and pseudosexuality, looking for possible correlations by careful analyses of the subjects' related thoughts and attitudes. And because of our intimate intercourse with the media, our connection with lust is more immediate and pervasive than at any other time in human history. A great overlooked solution to the drug and violence problems is to mitigate lust-pollution. And the only way to mitigate lust-pollution in today's America is to start eliminating it in our own lives, one life at a time, one day at a time. May this book help serve that end.

We had fed the heart on fantasies.
The heart's grown brutal from the fare.
William Butler Yeats

The F-word, etc.

World War II was the time when the great f-word burst into the male vocabulary. It has spewed increasingly into the cultural psyche ever since. In the military there were countless examples of abusive dehumanization associated with the term used in describing sex with women. They were so utterly crude, vile, and obscene I can't repeat them. But they give graphic insight into the real nature of this new "heterosexuality," lest anyone think I'm making more of a case for pseudosexuality than is warranted. Why was that word primarily a man's word, at least then? Because it was sex-plus-violence all balled up into one negative vocalization, often accompanied by the giving of the finger. Yet that is the force behind every lust snatch. *That single image epitomizes pseudosexuality more than anything we've said in this book.* There's an unholy spirit of lust-violence unleashed in our midst. This was the glory of 1940s American manhood? What's it like today?[66]

In the Navy I remember being simultaneously repelled and attracted by all this—secretly (even to myself) yielding to its power, but only because the progression of my lust over the previous nine years of my life had been setting myself up for it. And we should remember that this was war time—world war. If lust predisposes us to violence, there's plenty of evidence that the spirit of violence in the atmosphere of war breeds lust. Why can't we face the lust-violence connection head on? Quite possibly because "lust" doesn't fit current psychological paradigms. Again, because of science's one-sided view of man.

When and why do hatred and violence become coupled with sex? When our sexuality has become distorted, and when we as humans are becoming perverted. It happens when we hate ourselves for missing the mark of being human—misusing ourselves and others—and we transfer that hate onto others. This one word has become an evil force in our racial subconscious, an unclean spirit fouling our spiritual and sexual ecology, a prime artifact of pseudosexuality.

The f-word is the symbol of the new terrorism insinuating itself into the spirit of America through the new lust.

Finally, let's take the preceding Calvin & Hobbes cartoon that probed the connection between media violence and violence in the culture and do a lust paraphrase of it:

"Graphic lust in the media. Does it glamorize perversion? Sure. Does it desensitize us to perversion? Of course. Does it help us tolerate perversion? You bet. Does it stunt our empathy for our fellow beings? Heck yes. Does it *cause* perversion? Well . . . That's hard to prove. The trick is to ask the right question."

. . .

Now let's turn from studying the new lust and its malignant brood to tracing its fascinating historical role in driving the pseudosexual revolution.

PART II
THE PSEUDOSEXUAL REVOLUTION

In Part I we saw how symptoms of the lust virus infection were already manifesting themselves in the young male students at Duke. We then saw the infection developing over time as reflected in the lustified female image, traced its progress in the author's life, dissected the anatomy of a lust look, and from all of this developed beginnings of a psychology of lust and its effects within men and their relationships. This led to discerning threads of the lust-violence connection and other social ramifications. And we began to give it all a name—*pseudosexuality*.

"The Sexual Revolution" is a well-worn phrase referring to that transitional period in the American fifties, sixties, and seventies—roughly from Kinsey and *Playboy* through Viet Nam—where "Make love, not war" became the mantra of sexual "liberation." In reality, that revolution was part of a larger, broader change in human culture brought about since the Industrial Revolution.

But there's another revolution that's been going on within the Industrial and Sexual, one so covert it's impossible to see without stepping outside the stream. And unless we step outside, we cannot appreciate its profound effects on human identity and sexuality—*The Pseudosexual Revolution*.

Understanding that all of us without exception are a part of and live within this revolution helps us appreciate the enormity of the effects of the lust virus contagion. Thus, in Part II we will try to step outside to trace the cultural evolution of our sexuality along two parallel tracks— the so-called heterosexual and the so-called homosexual—and discover what is driving both. This will force us to see our changing sexualities in both a broader and clearer light. We haven't always been what we are, and it didn't happen overnight. The new lust and American sexuality gradually evolved into what they are today. This fascinating history will also help us see that recovery-wise we're in for more than we could have possibly imagined, both in the work we'll have to do to recover and the incredible prospect of the benefits that accrue.

THE RISE AND SPREAD OF
THE NEW SEXUALITIES

The big changes in history, the ones that fundamentally alter how we think and act, have a way of creeping up on us until one day everything we know is suddenly passé and we realize we are in a whole new world. It wasn't until the late 19th century, for example, that the British historian Arnold Toynbee coined the term "the Industrial Age," nearly 100 years after it first arrived on the world scene.[67]

Jeremy Rifkin

Obvious to any student of history, "big changes" are happening faster and faster, and on a scale and magnitude inconceivable even a century ago. Not the least of these are dramatic changes in our very sexuality and personal identity. But to see them, we must stand apart from the flux of currents swirling about us, driving us along, and see the whole course of the river itself.

Stepping Outside

If we can see that today's sexuality in its various expressions arose within and in response to the same complex of cultural forces, we shall have come a long way toward understanding the many shapes of today's pseudosexuality. This will be an eye-opener and will call for nothing less than absolute honesty, understanding, identification, and communication, at the deepest levels of human experience and intercourse. This kind of truth does not come easily.

One of the great cultural blind spots I hope this book is revealing is the true condition of today's heterosexuals, so-called. Illusion is too weak a word; delusion is more like it. But how can we see our own blind spots? We can't. That's why we must "step outside" our situation, so to speak. But how can we do that?

Let me suggest a novel approach—looking at the prevailing sexual scene through gay eyes and gay history.

As it turns out, the history of homosexuality in America helps reveal what I call the new "heterosexuality," the mutation of our sexuality engendered by the new lust. The two movements are really in sync with each other and share common origins. If we will see it! John D'Emilio, writing as associate professor of history at the University of North Carolina, is a historian of the gay movement in the United States. His book, *Sexual Politics, Sexual Communities: The Making of a Homosexual Minority in the United States 1940–1970*, is a well-researched and very readable history of the roots, origins, and development of the gay movement.

The broader context of D'Emilio's treatment is the history of sexuality in America, which he and Estelle Freedman have presented in a subsequent work, *Intimate Matters—A History of Sexuality in America*. These historians have shown how the meaning and place of sexuality in American life have changed over the last three and a half centuries, being continually reshaped by various forces. In tracing evolution of the same-sex lifestyle, they unwittingly expose the blind spot in the opposite-sex lifestyle. This will become increasingly apparent as we examine this history from such a unique perspective.

These historians show "the ways that historical forces continually reshape our sexuality, and the ways that individuals and groups have acted to alter the contours of sexual history."[68] I propose to show how the same forces that gave rise to the gay movement also brought the new heterosexuality into being.

I suggest that what was really happening in this history of American sexuality was the genesis not only of a gay movement and a gay per-

*sonal identity, but also the genesis of a new heterosexual "movement"
and a new "heterosexual" identity, and that both movements arose
from the same cultural forces and are part of the larger pseudosexual
revolution.*

The new heterosexuality did not appear to be as much of a media
phenomenon as was the gay movement, but in reality it was, as we
shall see.

The following sampling of historical highlights (used with permission) draws selections from the D'Emilio and D'Emilio-Freedman histories. Readers are referred to these two volumes for the full scope and
wealth of detail. Page numbers are listed for reference. The two titles
are abbreviated *SPSC* and *IM*. Block excerpts not in quotation marks
are condensations or paraphrases.

The Historical Angle

We begin with D'Emilio's informative survey of recent changes in historical thinking:

Excerpt:

> ". . . [S]ome historians have discarded the view that sexuality is
> primarily a biological category, an innate, unchanging 'drive' or
> 'instinct' immune from the shifts that characterize other aspects
> of social organization. Instead, as a number of writers have
> argued, eroticism is also subject to the forces of culture. Human
> beings learn how to express themselves sexually. . . .
>
> "[S]ome historians have begun to entertain the idea that
> human sexuality is a socially constructed, changing category. In
> recent books several writers have argued that 'the homosexual'
> or 'the lesbian'—that is, the person defined by society and by
> self through a primary erotic interest in the same sex—is a
> nineteenth-century invention. . . ."[69] (*SPSC* 3–4)

Comments: This trend is very instructive: Historians and sociologists
are beginning to explore the *formative* aspects of the larger historical-
cultural context of our sexuality. Eroticism is subject to the forces of culture. Humans *learn* how to express themselves sexually, and the content

of that learning is socially conditioned. Human sexuality is *socially constructed*. And changing![70]

If our homosexuality as we know it today is "socially constructed" and subject to the forces of culture, what about our heterosexuality? How can it remain unaffected? This "social conditioning" of the new heterosexual is precisely what I have been describing in this book—the lustification of picture-women, for example, an obvious symptom of the conditioning. The new heterosexuality is socially constructed. Look at what was going on in the *Playboy* revolution, to name only one element in the genesis of today's "heterosexuality." The technique of having pictures of nude women posed to arouse and feed lust associated with articles by famous writers—all of it blessed by the Supreme Court and quickly assimilated by the media—created a social environment that not only legitimized the image-lust connection, but forced it into the public consciousness, influencing our sexuality. If these gay and lesbian historians call homosexuality a nineteenth-century invention, we'll see that what now passes for heterosexuality is also a nineteenth-century invention. (In this context, they refer to "homosexuality" and "heterosexuality" as recent social designations, distinct categories or "orientations," not kinds of sexual activity.) The emergence of these concepts into the modern vocabulary should become clearer as we proceed with the history itself.

Colonial Sexuality

Excerpt:

> "For the North American settlers who migrated from England in the seventeenth and eighteenth centuries, the imperative to procreate dominated the social attitude toward and organization of sexuality. The production of children by each conjugal pair was as much a necessity as the planting of crops in the spring, since the cooperative labor of parents and their offspring generated the material goods that sustained life. . . . *'Heterosexuality' remained undefined, since it was literally the only way of life"* [emphasis added].
>
> "Same-sex erotic behavior remained sporadic and exceptional. Even the [court] trials of persistent offenders document

daily lives that revolved around a heterosexual family role." Homosexual acts were not conceived as different in essence from other sexual transgressions—such as adultery, fornication, or bestiality—that occurred outside the sanctioned bonding of husband and wife. (*SPSC* 10)

Comments: Heterosexuality being undefined back then because it was the only way of life gets your attention. It's hard for us to imagine a time when the word did not exist. But the word heterosexual doesn't even appear in the 1928 edition of the *Oxford English Dictionary*. In the 1933 *Supplement* the first known usage is in 1901 from *Dorland's Medical Dictionary*: "abnormal or perverted sexual appetite toward the opposite sex." Yes, you read that correctly; the first known literary reference to heterosexuality in English is "abnormal or perverted sexual appetite toward the opposite sex!" Pseudosexuality rests its case (smile)! The next (common) usage is from a 1920 translation of Freud's collected works.

Had I been practicing my lust-driven heterosexuality in the colonial culture, I would have stood out as a transgressor, just as my brother who transgressed with the same sex. My "heterosexual" transgressions would have been deemed the same in essence as his. I remember cruising that special boulevard for prostitutes, and over the years, watching the scene gradually shift to gay hustlers evenly spaced on every block. *On the street* we were all in the very same pseudosexual world. We were all part of the sex-market, the sex supply-and-demand system, which was really the lust supply-and-demand system—advertised, promoted, and legitimized in the mass media.

We all had the grounds of our being in the same moral and spiritual environment. My secret pseudosexual self was "out" in that environment; I felt comfortable, real, and at home there. ("Out" is used in the same sense as when gays "come out" by openly declaring their preference for the same sex or are "outed" by others.) I was in my real element. What a liberating feeling to "be myself!" To "find" myself. That cruising ritual connected me with the pseudosexual "movement," where heterosex was "out" on the streets, in massage parlors and "model" joints, in bars, in the X-rated theaters, peep shows, arcades, and book stores—available, friendly, welcoming—and often dangerous or illegal. I was at home with my "real" self out there! That was my "heterosexual" lifestyle, which was really a delusion, because without my knowing it, that was working against my real sexuality—real because of what I have discovered in recovery.

It is no wonder that I had to have more and more of that "reality" until finally, one day, I capitulated completely, becoming willing to give up wife, family, and career so I could finally "come out" and have an unending supply of "what I really wanted, what I really was." Less easy to see is that the same thing was happening to the millions of men—the majority of the new heterosexuals—who did not go out onto the streets for sex, like I did. Their meretricious (prostitute-like) favorites were in the media and served them in solitary sex or in their fantasies while having sex with their wives.

We shall see that the same American history has spawned both "movements," both lifestyles, the "homo" and the "hetero." Whatever forces there are in our time acting in and upon the opposite-sex experience are acting in and upon the same-sex experience. How could it be otherwise? There are few culture warps in the aftermath of the reality revolution where discrete areas of life are left unaffected. (We begin dealing with the reality revolution in Part III.)

Post-Industrial Revolution—
19th and Early 20th Centuries

Excerpt:

> "During the second half of the nineteenth century, the momentous shift to industrial capitalism provided the conditions for a homosexual and lesbian identity to emerge. As a free-labor system, capitalism pulled men and women out of a household economy and into the marketplace, where they exchanged their individual labor power for wages. . . .
>
> "The family, deprived of the functions that once held it together as an economic unit, became instead an affective entity that nurtured children and promoted the happiness of its members. [Note the importance of this term *affective*—based on emo-

tion and feeling.] Birth rates declined steadily, and procreation figured less prominently in sexual life."

In place of the closely knit villages of the pre-industrial era, huge impersonal cities arose to attract an ever larger proportion of Americans. "The interlocking processes of urbanization and industrialization created a social context in which an autonomous personal life could develop. Affection, intimate relationships, and sexuality moved increasingly into the realm of individual choice, seemingly disconnected from how one organized the production of goods necessary for survival. In this setting, men and women who felt a strong erotic attraction to their own sex could begin to fashion from their feeling a personal identity and a way of life." (*SPSC* 11)

Comments: Look at the parallel effect on the opposite-sex lifestyle: Men and women pulled out of a household economy into the marketplace. Pulled out of being part of the family-village. Now, instead of being one-as-part-of the extended family, the bonding and unity of the whole, I become a single isolated market entity. I'm an asexual work machine as part of the larger asexual factory machine or office machine.

My gender no longer matters. Note the tremendous impact *efficiency* begins to play in the new work environment (the Charlie Chaplin movie *Modern Times*, for example). Man's identity now begins moving in the direction of the machine.[71] The more impersonal I become, the more efficient and useful I become. And man has shifted from being useful as a male—son, father, grandfather—to being used as market commodity. *How could our sexuality not be drawn in the same direction—to use and be used?*

Family now focuses on itself and individual happiness. Procreation becomes less necessary, and even in the way. The shift is from the focus on the larger good to individual "happiness." This must have marked the deadly beginning of me-ism, which has been progressing ever since. The ME generation. This process of individuation in itself is an isolating force creating a "hole in the soul" that needs to be filled, where "anything goes," and my sexuality can keep straying.

"[H]uge impersonal cities arose." CITY is born. An impersonal entity. City as System, replacing Life. If I, someone formerly in love with City, discern the development of city life correctly, what is impersonal becomes anti-personal, another aspect of pseudosexuality. A new "social context" based on "autonomous personal life" emerges.

I leave the farm-village and am thrust into CITY. *And City becomes the new pseudosexual "family," replacing the colonial inner-bonded family.*[72] Uprootedness. Pulled into the marketplace means I am part of the market. My being exchanged for wages is depersonalization. And if I am being depersonalized, so is my sexuality! And sex, divorced from the familial and community survival function of colonial times, *must now seek its own ends.* Now it becomes a force pushing me to mis-connect with the young woman or man working next to me in the factory to make up for that loss. The very System that predisposes us to the "hole in the soul" now offers the promise of filling that hole and dispenses the antidote for that isolation and alienation. And sex, pressed to fill the spiritual deficit, takes on this unnatural or *pseudo* role.

Of course, our brothers and sisters in City who had same-sex feelings would find identity and a way of life, just like our opposite-sex brothers and sisters would find their new identity and way of life. Which raises the tough question: Could such cultural changes these authors describe so well also be predisposing forces that help engender these new opposite-sex tendencies within individuals, just as they help engender the new same-sex tendencies? Why not? How can anyone be immune to such powerful forces? The pity is that apparently, these historians are more honest about such effects on their sexuality than the heteros are to those effects on theirs. But there are blind spots on both sides of the orientation divide.

The New Heterosexuals

Excerpt:

> "In American cities from the 1870s through the 1930s, there emerged a class of people who recognized their erotic interest in members of their own sex, interpreted this interest as a significant characteristic that distinguished them from the majority, and

sought others like themselves." "Some were or had been married; others were single. . . ." (*SPSC* 11–12)

Comments: In American cities from the 1870s through the 1930s there also emerged a class of people who recognized their erotic interest in members of the opposite sex in new ways and from new inner needs. These were the *new heterosexuals*. These men and women interpreted their erotic interest as a significant characteristic that distinguished *them* from the majority. After all, it was a new heterosexual minority that was enjoying the ambience of "ragtime and the blues, of barroom and bordello 'perfessers' in spats and hats, of Tin Pan Alley song pluggers and sidewalk player pianos, whose invisible hands held passersby enthralled with their fascinatin' rhythms."[73] It was this new "heterosexual" minority, with souls wide open to the new lust, that pioneered the new sexuality reflected in the silent films and popular music of the era and led the way into pseudosexuality.[74]

Excerpt:

"Gradually finding methods of meeting one another, these men and women staked out urban spaces and patronized institutions that fostered a group life. During the first two decades of the twentieth century, male . . . transvestites and their ordinary-looking comrades made their liaisons in saloons and clubs scattered through the least respectable parts of town. . . . By World War I . . . . men regularly cruised certain thoroughfares and parks. . . ." (*SPSC* 12)

"Gradually a subculture of gay men and lesbians was evolving in American cities that would help to create a collective consciousness among its participants and strengthen their sense of identification with a group." (*SPSC* 13)

Comments: What were the neo-*heterosexuals* doing at this time? They were also "gradually finding methods of meeting" sex partners in saloons and cruising parks. In 1910 in the average poor neighborhood in New York City there were twenty dance halls, twenty nickelodeons, and one hundred saloons (see chapter 10). Twenty dance halls in one neighborhood? This is the new heterosexual subculture emerging in the cities. The magnitude of this new heterosexuality far outweighed the simultaneously emerging neo-homosexuality. That's why I suggest that *the new heterosexuality was a prime factor in "constructing" the new pseudosexuality across the board.* The new "heterosexuality" was the wellspring of the new lust and its propelling power.

"Freud, flappers, petting parties, Hollywood scandals, even the crusade of Margaret Sanger for easy access to birth control, all pointed to the same conclusion: the sexual mores of the times seemed infinitely freer than those of bygone eras. . . . the liberated moderns of the post-World War I decades, the young men and women who danced the Charleston, discarded the heavy corsets and starched collars of their parents' generation, enjoyed double entendres, and appreciated the pleasures of intimate, erotic companionship." (*IM* xi)

Look at the title of George Gershwin's first published song (1916): *When You Want 'Em, You Can't Get 'Em, When You've Got 'Em, You Don't Want 'Em.* How we lusters can identify with that! It says worlds about the neo-heterosexual subculture evolving in the cities, overwhelmingly more prevalent than the homosexual. And it tells us something about pseudosexuality. It would be interesting to trace how the history of our popular music reflects our evolving pseudosexuality. That's a book waiting to be written. Certain artists singing certain songs can easily put me into a pseudosexual state of mind even today. They are entrancing, captivating. I can be possessed by the overpowering spirit, which is so beguiling it wants to reconfigure my inner being to its meta-message.

Had I been a young man then, I too would have been trying to pick up women in the new dance halls, movie palaces, beaches, parks, eateries, and bars. But don't just look at my external behavior; look at what was going on inside me, as I have tried to depict earlier in this book. What was going on in my sexual thinking? Was it real or pseudo? And what was it? It was lust, now in the newer forms being legitimized in the emerging culture. We can only discern this by looking back from a vantage point in recovery. The flow of imperceptible increments in the progressive evolution of the new lust permeating the culture blinds us to the changes taking place, as it blinds us to the changes taking place within the mind and heart of the individual.

Apparently, when we were living within the extended family, as in colonial times, with no such physical separation between the sexes, our sexual identities were more stable and secure than when the sexes became isolated in city life. Apparently, "exacerbating the gap between male and female" helped give rise to the new lust and helped create the new heterosexuality, the new bisexuality, the new homosexuality, etc. They were all in process of change together.

World War II

As this process of changing sexuality continued, this is what we see on the eve of World War II:

Excerpt:

> The mobilization of American society during WWII seriously upset patterns of daily life. Following in the wake of a depression that saw both marriage and birth rates drop precipitously, the war further disrupted family stability and social relations between the sexes. It uprooted tens of millions of American men and women, many of them young, and deposited them in a variety of non-familial, often sex-segregated environments. (*SPSC* 23)
>
> "Young adults who in peacetime might have moved directly from their parents' home into one with their spouse experienced instead years of living away from kin and away from settings where easygoing intimacy with the opposite sex led to perma-nent ties. Families endured prolonged separations, divorce and desertion occurred more frequently, and the trend toward greater sexual permissiveness accelerated." (*SPSC* 23)

Comments: World War II pulled me out of high school four hours a day to buck rivets on B-17s with 80,000 others around the clock in the bomber factory. That was my "back-alley" speed-reading course in lust-sex. War fever equaled sexual fever in the bomber factory. Everyone was talking sex, thinking sex, acting sex. The man I bucked rivets for and my fellow high-schooler both introduced me to the "real world." The same with the girls drilling holes in the very same square foot of fuselage I was working on. The cacophony of noise, the stress, the closeness, the sheer number of bodies of young men and young women thrown together . . . *Rapid mass changes in sexual ecology.* Pseudosexuality in process. And it's nobody's "fault."

Hello, John Wayne, *Easy Rider*, and Marlboro man!

Excerpt:

> "In releasing large numbers of Americans from their homes and neighborhoods, World War II created a substantially new 'erotic situation' conducive both to the articulation of a homosexual identity and to the more rapid evolution of a gay subculture. . . . The unusual conditions of a mobilized society allowed homosexual desire to be expressed more easily in action. For many gay Americans, World War II created something of a nationwide coming out experience." (*SPSC* 24)

Comments: A "substantially new 'erotic situation'" was also creating a new *heterosexual* identity and formation of a new heterosexual subculture. But because of the mass media and other forces, this new heterosexual subculture became the new *culture*. That's why it's harder to see it as something new or starkly different when compared with how the homosexual is perceived. That's the heterosexual blindness, denial, or delusion. *Heterosexual* desire could now be "expressed more easily in action." And World War II was the grand "coming out" of the new heterosexual. I was there!

A "substantially new erotic situation" for me personally was what was in the air at Lockheed-Vega, Burbank, California, with those 80,000 others. Grease-pencil graffiti carried it on the very fuselages we were sending out to war. With camouflage netting above us, bomb shelters outside, and the brain-battering noise around us, the atmosphere of sex was ubiquitous. (Sex and violence—sex and war, for example, or sex and violent noise or violent music—do seem to go together.) It was all out in the open. I'll never forget the "Pay as you enter" sign below the reclining female figure heralding the new "sexuality" and the tales of "hot sex" and conquest from my high school cohorts and adult superiors. This was where I began *wanting* what they were talking about. My orientation—my mis-orientation—was being culturally conditioned and driven. But with my eager consent, mind you! "Heterosexual" lust was "out." (We've already noted the rise and impact of the f-word earlier in the text.)

Another symptom of deepening pseudosexuality during World War II is pictured in the great disparity in the way male heterosexual expression and male homosexual expression were treated by the military. The whole idea of sex education in the male military was disease prevention. The way this was communicated not only gave free license to hetero-sexual promiscuity but actually encouraged it. "Go ahead and get what you can; just don't get careless. We don't want your tail dragging after lib-erty. Short arm inspection [a euphemism for checking for VD] at 0700 hours." In the Navy, we got *Destroyer 96*, the indoctrination film on why and how to use condoms. Homosexuals, on the other hand, often got dishonorable discharges.[75] Do you see the hetero blindness—blindness to our pseudosexuality?

What was happening was the legitimizing of the pinup-girl revolu-tion. *Private Snafu, Censored,* a Warner Bros. cartoon for the military, circa 1942–45, shows Pvt. Snafu writing his girlfriend back home from an army barracks with walls cluttered with female pinups. The cartoon creators were juxtaposing thoughts of the girl back home with the new lust. This is the essence of pseudosexuality. How seemingly innocuous. And how blind we were to what was really happening to our sexuality!

I was infected with the same entitlement mentality when I wrote to a girl back home, a girl I had never dated and hardly knew (remember the living room incident?). Exposure to the military sexual ambience encour-aged me to turn her into one of those pinups in my mind. She was dis-torted to fit what the pinups communicated: "I'm here for you; take me!"

What does this tell us about what was going on *inside* us heterosexu-als? It's what's going on inside that matters most.[76] All this is indicative of the changes in man's concept of and relation to woman, male sexuality, and the very concept and meaning of sex. This represents the entirely new American sexual culture where *"heterosexual"* desire would be "expressed more easily in action." This is pseudosexuality. No wonder that women, increasingly affected by all this, would eventually have to revolt!

Science Intervenes

Excerpt:

> The intervention of science initiated a profound reconceptualiza-tion of the phenomenon of homosexuality. Under the scrutiny of medical professionals "homosexuality shifted from being an aberration . . . to a condition that inhered in a person and defined

one's very nature. By transforming same-sex eroticism into a clinical entity, doctors hastened the evolution of a new form of identity that was based upon sexual expression." (*SPSC* 18, 19)

Comments: A new form of *identity* based on sexual expression? My identity as a human being based on how I have sex?! That tears at the fabric of what it means to be human. But that was also going on in the hetero world. But it didn't stand out as the gay phenomenon did because it was the quiet, invisible revolution taking place within us so-called "normal" heterosexuals. And it never hit the courts as explicitly as homosexuality did. Man-woman, woman-man, so it was "natural" and okay. But the seeds of pseudosexuality had taken root and the new sexuality was "out" in *both* camps.

Why was there no analogous changing medical opinion about heterosexuality? Was it not changing just as dramatically as homo-sexuality? The answer may lie in the fact that the new heterosexuality *appeared* orthodox, if a little frayed around the edges. Plus, we never realized how the new lust was developing and what it was doing to us! *This was the illusion of heterosexual orthodoxy.* In the same vein, the *appearance* of religious piety in the church masked the loss of the very reality it was preaching. This was the illusion of religious orthodoxy. I call it "believism."

Excerpt:

> There was a continuing torrent of media attention given the famous Kinsey reports on sexual behavior in the human male and female, published in 1948 and 1953. These reports legitimatized sex-uality as a topic of discussion in the popular mass-circulation press, confirmed what many gay people in the 1940s were experiencing as the sense of belonging to a group, and encouraged those in isola-tion to accept their homosexual inclinations and search for sexual contact. Kinsey's work gave an added push at a crucial time to the emergence of an urban gay subculture and provided ideological ammunition for lesbians and homosexuals. (*SPSC* 37)

Comments: Did the legitimizing of sexuality as a topic of discussion in the media resulting from the Kinney reports encourage heterosexuals to accept *their* new inclinations and search for sexual contact? It certainly did for me! I remember giving a girlfriend sexual partner a copy of Kinsey's *Sexual Behavior in the Human Female*—for Christmas. How glorious it seemed, being a free-ranging pseudo-sexual, under the delusion that I was realizing more fully my true heterosexual identity!

Pseudosexuality Comes Into Its Own— The Sexual Revolution

Excerpt:

> "Heterosexual mores had been in flux at least since the first decades of the twentieth century, as birth control advocates, sex radicals of the post-World War I generation, adherents of Freudianism, modern writers, and others mounted challenges to Victorian orthodoxy. In the 1960s several decades of gradual change came together in a new synthesis that legitimated non-procreative heterosexuality and affirmed erotic expression as a part of the good life." (*SPSC* 245)
>
> ". . . . Supreme Court decisions removed legal barriers to the presentation of homoeroticism in print and in visual media, and a bewildering variety of images and viewpoints about homosexuality appeared. This barrage of information made it easier for people to come to a self-definition as homosexual or lesbian, strengthened the institution of the subculture, and gave activists more opportunities for action." (*SPSC* 5)

Comments: Can you see the parallelism in these two excerpts? The sexual revolution helped spawn and accelerate both the new heterosexuality and the new homosexuality. The presentation of *hetero*-eroticism in the visual media in "a bewildering variety of images"—what was *its* impact on strengthening the institution of the pseudosexual infra-culture across the board? The "barrage of information" made it easier for people to come to a self-definition as *the new heterosexuals*. It "strengthened the institution" of pseudo-heterosexuality.

Excerpt:

> "At one extreme, pornographic books, magazines, and films
> proliferated, with their sexual content growing 'progressively
> stronger.' . . . Of greater import, perhaps, was the effect of these
> decisions on mainstream media. Popular novels, mass-circulation
> magazines, metropolitan newspapers, Hollywood films, and even
> television, the family's entertainer, rushed to take advantage of
> the new liberal climate sanctioned by the courts. . . . The slow
> movement, evident since World War I, toward the inclusion of
> the erotic in the public sphere, suddenly rushed ahead, as sex
> became a daily staple of American popular culture. . . . Sex was
> now on display, for all to see." (*IM* 287–288)

Comments: Sexual content of the pornographic media growing "progressively stronger" is what was happening ever since the "barracks
favorites" of the Civil War. *Why* did the mainstream media follow this
new liberalization—for the most part uncritically? Maybe the key word
is "follow." And of course when pseudosexuality is in process, pseudo-
sex sells. At any rate, this progression of sexual content in the media
is an index of pseudosexuality. What was happening in the media was
what was happening in my lustaholism. This is the tolerance principle
at work, characteristic of addiction: more of the drug is required to
achieve the initial effect. This tolerance principle is still going on—at
the mass-market cultural level.

What *Life* and *Look* did for the gay subculture (featuring photo
essays and articles) was nothing compared to what they did to propagate the gospel of the new heterosexuality. It was thus in the late 1950s
when I remember discovering the "meat markets" around town—
"dance joints" that were places to pick up girls. It was so exciting! All
those bodies, the loud music and dance, sex fever in the air. I felt like
a kid in a candy store. And I was one of the more reticent ones, a slow
learner. I remember too, dating the women I'd meet there and discovering how mixed up they were, all the while being blind to myself, of
course. Looking back on it all, I see the situation had pseudo-sex written all over it. The toll it took on all of us in that subculture was tragic,
but I could not see it then. It takes some recovery to even begin to come
out of denial and see. I can't imagine what it's like out there now.

"Coming Out"—The Erotic as Personal Identity

Excerpt:

> "Coming out" was both a unique product of its time and an important road mark in the history of sexuality. At a time when the hippie counterculture was urging the young to "do your own thing" and feminists were redefining the personal as political, coming out seemed perfectly to embody both. Coming out represented the adoption of an identity in which the erotic played a central role. No longer merely something you did in bed, sex served to define a mode of living. (*IM* 322–323)

Comments: The erotic becoming central to one's very identity—that's powerful! That's new in American culture.[77] But that's exactly what happened to me, finally coming to realize my free and glorious "heterosexual" erotic identity. However, this expression of identity can work two ways, as witnessed by the following two men. The first describes the liberating feeling of finally "coming to terms with being gay." (No one should ever underestimate the profound nature of this dilemma![78]) The second man went through the same tortuous process of finally being able to "own his homosexuality," but then went beyond that.

> **Rayford:** "Accepting my sexual orientation at the age of 27 was a great awakening, like being born—finally accepting my feelings, my self, turning a light on inside and no longer running away from what I saw there. It took many more years for me to overcome the self-hatred and self-doubt I had learned and to develop a healthy sense of who I was and what I wanted to do with my life."[79]

> **Michael:** "There was a certain integrity and freedom in finally being able to own my homosexual identity. But then I got frozen in that affirmation. After one and one-half years of sexual sobriety [total abstinence in his case], I concluded that I did not know what I was saying yes to when I was asserting 'I'm gay' to my circle of friends and confidants. So my speech shifted to speaking of my homosexual history and homosexual lust (my targets). I simply did not want to label myself any more, and that label, that name or identity, gradually receded from my consciousness. I had

to let go of a resolution that I had experienced as integrity and freedom. I was beginning to feel secure enough to find out who I was, and the picture of my identity is much richer now. I see that every male in recovery goes through this, regardless of orientation. Every male addicted to lust or sex has to let go of his 'sexual identity' in recovery."[80]

The whole point of the sexual history we've been exploring is that these self-proclaimed "identities" of ours are relative; it all depends at which point in our lives we intersect them and from which cultural angle. In this connection, note the following honest insights from a feminist lesbian historian:

"Perhaps the most serious limitation of gay and lesbian liberation is that sexual identity, which has so far proven to be a sufficient basis for sustaining a mass movement, may over time be insufficient. For many, sexual identity is as central to self-definition as race, ethnicity, or sex. But it may lose this character. . . . Will decreased opposition to homosexuality lessen its significance? . . . If lesbians and gay men become much more assimilated into mainstream society than they are now, they may no longer be self-consciously gay. In that case, since a heightened awareness of being different is fundamental to motivating people to identify with gay liberation, the movement might not be able to survive."[81]

The commonality between the evolution of the new homosexual and the new heterosexual movements is evident in the following passage from the D'Emilio-Freedman history:

Excerpt:

Though few [gay] activists seemed aware of it, the gay movement was moving "in the same direction as mainstream sexual culture. By emphasizing the centrality of sexual expression for their own well-being, they were echoing themes that the ideologues of sexual liberalism had applied to heterosexuals in marriage. And, the commercialism that came to characterize the gay male subculture of the 1970s was not different in kind from the consumerist values that had already made [heterosexual] sex a marketable commodity." (*IM* 323)

Comments: This is precisely what we see in tracing the evolution of pseudosexuality: Mainstream "heterosexual" culture and the gay movement have been moving "in the same direction"—pseudosexuality. Both movements reflect similar reactions to the same cultural phenomena. It is a tribute to the authors' competence and honesty that they record that few gay activists seemed aware of this. Well, few, if any, *heterosexual* thinkers were, or are, aware of this. The ideological energy in the air was—and still is—*the centrality of sexual expression for one's well-being.* This is our common delusion, the credo of our new mass religion.

Whole segments of those wanting sexual recovery bear witness to the fact that sexualizing is *not* central to one's identity or well-being. We're discovering just the opposite: when sexual expression is central, one's well-being is jeopardized and gender identity weakened!

Even though D'Emilio may not have had this point in mind, a passage from the conclusion of his book sums up this interesting phenomenon of the cultural congruity between recent homosexual and heterosexual history and experience:

"As the life cycle of heterosexuals exhibits greater variety and less predictability, they have come to face many of the choices and experiences that gay men and women confront. If heterosexual life is coming to resemble in some ways its gay counterpart, the experience of homosexual men and women likewise shows signs of converging with the heterosexual norm." (*SPSC* 248)

It should be obvious by now that there's an intrinsic commonality to the gay and "heterosexual" movements; a common denominator. They're growing out of and being driven by the same cultural forces. This has tremendous implications for all of us, if we have the clarity and honesty to be able to see it. In remarkable ways, both are caught up in and mirror elements of pseudosexuality we've been trying to identify. We're all in this PS revolution together, whether some of us like it or not.

Summing up the 1960s

Excerpt:

> In less than a decade [1960s], American society had witnessed "an explosion of things gay." "In just a few short years, the system of sexual liberalism had come apart. The premium that it placed upon fulfillment and pleasure compromised its ability to point sexual desire toward the institution of marriage. *The logic of consumer capitalism pushed the erotic beyond the boundaries of the monogamous couple* as entrepreneurs played with erotic impulses and affluent youth pursued their pleasures outside the marital bond [emphases added]. Women's liberation attacked modern marriage as an oppressive institution, while gay liberation challenged the supremacy of heterosexual expression." These movements succeeded in removing some constraints on sexual expression and refashioning how many Americans looked upon sex. (*IM* 324-325)

Comments: Sexual liberalism, with its demand that sex serve "fulfillment and pleasure," helped drive *pseudosexuality*. So did consumer capitalism, which is still pushing the erotic toward obviating marriage. "Refashioning" how we look at sex sets us up for how we act it out. Culture helps shape orientation.

The Pendulum Swings Back

"HELP!" In the late 1970s a very unusual phenomenon—an underground movement of sorts—was quietly getting underway in the U.S. Several different anonymous organizations were getting started, all unknown to each other. Of the most consequential of these were one in Boston, one in Minneapolis, and two in Southern California.[82] These groups were started by those wanting release from their "relationship addiction," "sex addiction," "sexual compulsion," and "lust and sex addiction." They looked in varying degrees to the recovery program of Alcoholics Anonymous for their inspiration.

Gabrielle Brown's *The New Celibacy*, begun in 1978, documents a post-sexual-revolution impulse toward sexual recovery among singles and marrieds alike in the U.S., unrelated to the sexual addiction recovery movement getting underway then. About the same time, *The New York Times* reported "the wave of asexuality" that was beginning to "sweep the nation."[83] And in 1988, *Joy of No Sex* came out, reflecting the popular trend begun in the sixties toward Eastern religion and sexual abstinence. This growing interest in abstinence was another reaction indicator that something was amiss in the Revolution.

Also in the late seventies, a whole raft of religious organizations (they number over a hundred) got started for "recovery from homosexuality."[84]

This is also when the NO SEX people of Los Angeles must have gotten started. I remember meeting members of this small group in the center of downtown L.A. at 7th and Broadway; it was before AIDS had hit the scene. These were African-American young men and women who appeared to be in their late thirties who had been "all the way there and back" in the matter of sex. They were now preaching a gospel of no sex, such was the devastation it had produced in their own lives. Once sober from that destructive way of living, they concluded that they were better off with no sex whatever, even in marriage. They seemed most content with this discovery and were beautiful people. All in all a very touching and sobering encounter.

How strange it seems today, for so many to be discovering that sex is optional. And indeed it is optional. Unless, that is, lust or demand is active, when it becomes seemingly mandatory.

The recovery phenomenon is much broader than I have pictured. The therapeutic community has jumped on the bandwagon as it did with alcoholism earlier, after AA, and diagnosis of addictive sexual disorders is now part of the *Diagnostic and Statistical Manual of Mental Disorders* (DSM-IV).[85] And many religious organizations are trying to deal with what is hitting them all in the face. There are recent signs of a more generalized turn toward sexual sobriety, manifest in the "abstinence-only" movement and a movement back toward monogamy, for example.[86] New symptoms of a reappraisal of our sexual attitudes and behavior continue to surface.

What's happening? Why are hundreds of thousands seeking help in the sexual area? Is there something we're missing? What invisible force has altered the orbit of human sexuality? Something defying scientific analysis. A visitor from another planet, viewing our history from a distance, might well discern plague-like symptoms and look for a virus. Why can't we see it? The greatest flaw in scientific methodology is its reductionist view of man, reducing man to his mere biology.

> *molecules and cells,*
> *matter, motion and spells*
> *and all that there*
> *for all I care*

Pseudosexuality Full-blown— The 1970s to the Present

Excerpt:

> With the advent of AIDS, there was a drastic shift in attitudes. As with the explosion of herpes and the host of other sexually transmitted diseases a few years earlier in the heterosexual community, a dread disease brought an undercurrent of guilt to the surface, transforming a medical condition into a moral commentary. (*IM* 354 and 356)
>
> Between 1984 and 1987 the proportion of gays who were celibate rose from two to twelve percent, while those in a monogamous partnership jumped from twelve to twenty-eight percent. "As the case load mounted, the potential ramifications of AIDS for reshaping American sexuality spread." (*IM* 356–357)

Comments: An undercurrent of guilt? Reshaping American sexuality? That's a telling admission. Guilt for what? You mean there's some kind of moral consciousness inside us that we easily push out of sight? I was "doing my thing" out there when I picked up a rusty nail. But even disease and guilt were never enough to stop me. This searching reappraisal that went on in the gay community after aids was disclosed—Isn't that the same kind of thing that happens to us so-called heterosexuals when we get infected with a sexually transmitted disease? Picking up a "rusty nail," getting caught by the wife, or getting arrested didn't stop me. The moment of clarity may not last very long, but our reaction is qualitatively the same. We are forced to look at the reality of what we're doing and who we are.

Yes, American sexuality is being reshaped as the result of historical forces. And if changes in attitudes have propelled the new lust, then changes in attitude will prove to be the key to recovery. But who wants to give up eating lotus unless they're really hurting?

"The Sexualized Society"

The essence of this sexualization of America is captured in the following article by cultural historian Neal Gabler, author of *Life the Movie—How Entertainment Conquered Reality*:

> As a young boy, I remember racing through our morning paper, on my way to the sports section, when my eye was caught by a small item. It involved a controversy over the movie, "Anatomy of a Murder." The film used the word "rape," thus offending delicate sensibilities and sending local censors into session to determine whether they would allow the film to be shown. I had no idea what "rape" meant, but I recall the item these many years later because whatever the word meant, I knew it was illicit—a term not permitted in general discourse.
>
> My children, now roughly the same age I was then, will have no such memories. Today, there are no forbidden words because there are no longer any taboos. . . . For the first time, words like "masturbation," "anal intercourse," "orgasm," "vagina" and "penis" were appearing regularly in the mainstream press and on prime-time entertainment. . . . For decades, we have been subjected to ever more graphic depictions of sex on the movie screen, in literature, in music and in art. For nearly as many years, we have exhibited greater frankness in our public discussions about sexual matters. As nearly everything else in America has become . . . . soaked with sex.[87]

Comments: This sexualization of our society is the greatest indicator and index of our lost sexuality, our *pseudo*-sexuality. It reveals how desperately we're trying to find it, not even knowing what we've lost. C. S. Lewis's analogy in the 1940s is even more cogent today: If we were to observe a society where burlesque houses featured tantalizing pieces of meat—"steak-tease," for example—we would know something was drastically amiss with their relation to meat.

Well, something is drastically amiss with our sexual thinking and behavior. The increasing number of media ads for male impotence may be one small indicator of our problem. Why the epidemic of functional impotence among so many sexually liberated American males and the Viagra revolution? I wonder how many otherwise healthy males are being treated annually for impotence. How many others do not seek treatment? When did this trend take off? The National Institute for Health (NIH) statistics for 2002 show that "20 percent to 46 percent of [U.S.] men aged 40–69 years in community surveys self-reported moderate or complete erectile dysfunction." Lurking behind such statistics may be another index of pseudosexuality. Lust kills more than love. Lust kills sex. The wave keeps advancing.[88]

D'Emilio and Freedman's comment is to the point regarding this sexualization of America: "The reshaping of sexuality in the 1960s and 1970s was of major proportions. . . . And all of this took place *in a social environment in which erotic imagery was ubiquitous*" [emphasis added] (*IM* 343). We are reminded again of the awesome power of the modern image connection (which we will treat in Part III). We live in an image-driven world that is altering human sexuality. It is not an altogether idle boast that *Playboy* is called "the magazine that changed America."[89] Let's look at the situation:

- Any man who has to resort to images or fantasies while having sex with himself or his partner is engaging in a pseudosexual act.
- Billions of images across the whole media spectrum are offered up daily to serve this practice.
- If one man can't have sex without resorting to images or fantasy, his sexuality is false; he is a pseudo-sexual.
- If untold millions of men across the whole "orientation" spectrum are doing this, we're in the midst of a *Pseudosexual Revolution*.

Summing Up

The Seizure and Manipulation of Our Sexuality. It can be terrifying to realize not only the psyche-bending power of today's image-driven lust, but also, as our authors point out, that the entire weight of capitalist institutions supports the visible public presence for the erotic, that everything that makes America America is suffused with the erotic and the new lust, and that it supports and perpetuates a delusion. But though we have inherited this cultural predisposition to pseudosexuality and have been victimized by it, it is at the same time of our own making and choosing. Powerless over the culture, I am responsible for my choices and attitudes *toward* that very culture. I choose the attitude I take toward my victimization.

The proof of this is that in recovery we have been able to make choices that go counter to the cultural forces and other predispositions—choices that go counter to what we perceive to be our very identity. Life-changing forces!

Finally, as we leave the historical scene, consider D'Emilio and Freedman's realistic conclusion:

> "Birth control is so embedded in social life that a purely repro-
> ductive matrix for sex is no longer even remotely possible.
> Women's role in the family and the public realm has [been]
> altered so profoundly that a gender-based system resting on
> female purity is not likely to be resurrected. The capitalist seizure
> of sexuality has destroyed the division between public reticence
> and private actions that the nineteenth-century middle class
> sought to maintain. Perhaps what the study of America's history
> allows us to say with assurance is that sexuality has become cen-
> tral to our economy, our psyches, and our politics. For this rea-
> son, it is likely to stay vulnerable to manipulation. . . ." (*IM* 360)

Yes, there's been a seizure of our sexuality. And not merely a capitalist seizure. Our sexuality has been seized by a power so formidable, so omnipresent, that it is now within us, possessing us. Possessing the very heart and soul of America. Lust.

This seizure has snatched something from us. Our humanity. Our very manhood. And, in consequence, our womanhood. Lust is the great Sexist Sin, not only against women and the feminine, but first against men and the masculine.

Cast adrift on a sea of relativism, we must rediscover the place and meaning of sex. What is sex for? Here and now. Today. For twenty-first century American men. What is *Man* for? What is Woman for? Our two historians talk of female purity as something now passé. But what of male purity? When will we men take responsibility for our own sexuality and sexual purity? It only appears that sexuality has become "central to our economy, our psyches, and our politics." The truth is that *lust* now plays that central role.

Yes, our sexuality "is likely to stay vulnerable to manipulation." That means our orientations—our *mis*-orientations—have been manipulated. They are being manipulated today. As never before. Our culture has manipulated our sexuality. Lust has manipulated our sexuality. We have lost our spiritual immune systems. There's no defense against the lust virus. Our sexuality has become distorted, and we are diminished. For increasing numbers of us vulnerable ones, self-damaged to the point of sexual insanity and sexual suicide, there is no option but to stop and find remedy. Today, in the devastating aftermath of the pseudosexual revolution, there *must* be another option.

THE "SHAKESPEARE" SCALE— PSEUDOSEXUALITY AND ORIENTATION

"When I moved to L.A. 2½ years ago, I was definitely heterosexual," said a British expatriate. "Now I think I should be bisexual, or trisexual or having sex with plants or something."

Los Angeles Times, August 3, 1993

How does all of this impact the general question of orientation—"the orientation quandary," as it's been called? What we have reviewed so far is telling us that in the human male the sexual response is highly generalized, is subject to imprinting, and gets directed and shaped through learning and experience under the power of a vast array of cultural forces. As we have already indicated and shall continue to see in Parts III and IV, these forces have tremendous power affecting the whole range of our sexual thinking and behavior.

Let's clarify something here. I am not saying that all males are infected with the lust virus and are pseudosexuals. I am saying that all of this makes a very strong case for the fact that we're in a pseudosexual revolution—that millions of men across the orientational spectrum are infected with the lust virus and exhibit pseudosexuality to some degree or other. My plea is first to so-called heteros: Let's look at ourselves honestly, even deeper than the honesty evident in the histories we've been considering. There's something wrong, and we're in denial! And we're the losers if we don't face up to it together.

Pigeonholing

I want to challenge the dangerous tendency of pigeonholing, which reduces infinitely complex human beings with their infinitely complex sexuality into ridiculously simplistic absurdities. We are more, and we deserve more than being forced willy-nilly into pseudo-scientific straitjackets! In an article looking forward to commemorating his ninetieth birthday, it is said of the late famous conductor-composer Leonard Bernstein that "He was bisexual and probably bipolar."[90] Note the casual certitude in the diagnosis, as though that facile label actually *explains* the man's sexuality, sexual identity, or orientation. But slipping him into that pigeonhole, far from explaining the artist's sexual thinking and behavior, actually helps *obscure* the man. It keeps us from asking the deeper questions and from seeing the man from within the tortured doubts and complexities of his mind, soul, and life—factors which lay behind whatever forms his acting out took. One trite label, from a journalist, and the manifold complexity of the person is reduced to an absurdity. Worse yet, listen to this: "Most gay men and women still marry a person of the opposite sex. Most of them never come out, even to themselves."[91] (Actually, that supposition supports our concept of pseudo-sexuality!)

Strangely, in the last several decades, the media message, exacerbated by the politicizing of sexuality, has fostered too limited an impression of human sexuality—namely, that it is either heterosexual or homosexual, with an occasional tip of the hat to bisexuality.[92] This oversimplification is the muddle of sexual orientation, which, with our new understanding of pseudosexuality, might better be labeled a myth. Anne Fausto-Sterling, developmental geneticist at Brown University, says, "There are many gradations in sexual orientation. What do you call men who have sex with their wives while fantasizing about men? Or guys who are mostly straight who pick up male prostitutes, or transsexuals, or serial bisexuals who may switch between exclusively gay and exclusively straight relationships? How do you count sexual behavior that changes over time in different circumstances?"[93] "Homosexual activity among men who consider themselves to be heterosexual is so prevalent in minority communities [as of October 2004] that public health officials have developed a new category—called 'men who have sex with men'—to identify them"[94]

George Chauncey, historian of the gay New York culture, shows how "it is almost impossible today to think about sexuality without imagining that it is organized along an axis of homosexuality and heterosexuality. . . ." He says "the hetero-homosexual binarism, the sexual regime now [prevailing] . . . in American culture, is a stunningly recent creation."[95] Why does this simple historical reality escape so many? Probably because most of us, including the media, are either not trained historians or have not researched this history of American sexuality. It's easier to go along with the media flow and be just another passive patsy in the American Republic of Entertainment.[96] Notwithstanding its failures in other areas, the Kinsey report puts it succinctly:

> Males do not represent two discrete populations, heterosexual and homosexual. The world is not to be divided into sheep and goats. Not all things are black nor all things white. . . . Only the human mind invents categories and tries to force facts into separated pigeon-holes. The living world is a continuum in each and every one of its aspects. The sooner we learn this concerning human sexual behavior the sooner we shall reach a sound understanding of the realities of sex.[97]

The Kinsey Scale. Pointing up the seamless continuity of the gradations between exclusively heterosexual and exclusively homosexual histories, Kinsey goes on to explain the famous "Kinsey scale," from 0 to 6. I think these were convenient, even arbitrary, pigeonholes he created, into which he could sort his statistics. Men are rated a Kinsey 0 "if they make no physical contacts that result in erotic arousal or orgasm, and make no psychic responses to individuals of their own sex. Their socio-sexual contacts and responses are exclusively with individuals of the opposite sex." At the other end of the scale, "Individuals are rated as 6's if they are exclusively homosexual, both in regard to their overt experience and in regard to their psychic reactions." Ratings of 1, 2, 3, 4, and 5 were supposed to cover everything in between.[98]

How About a Shakespeare Scale for Lust?

Why do the self-proclaimed arbiters of our sexuality (science, academia, religion, and the media) seem to restrict the labeling to acting out? Externals. Again, I fear it is because of that basic flaw in the thinking of modern science—Man as Materiel. How sad, how tragic, to limit man to the externals, to the behavioral, when it is the internals that make us what we are. But how fortunate, we lusters in recovery, that we cannot deny or escape lust, both within ourselves and the culture. That we must come to know it for what it really is. That we've been swept through the spirit-warp, past the event horizon, and sucked into the annihilating black hole of the Dark Force itself. We've been there, and out the other side! And we have something to say about it. As insiders! Just as it is now admitted that hopeless alcoholics in the 1930s in Akron, Ohio, had something to say about alcoholism, which they could not have understood until after *they* were in recovery together.

So, with tongue in cheek, why not devise a Kinsey-type scale for lusters—for acting *in*—and call it the Shakespeare Scale? (The reference here is to Shakespeare's *Sonnet* 129 on lust; see the Introduction.) Rate the man a 0 who never lusts after female or male images, fantasies, or people in the flesh. Rate the man a 6 who cannot fantasize or look at either images or flesh without lusting. Between these two extremes would be those along the whole continuum of 0 to 6. This is about lust, without respect to orientation. Let's classify ourselves from the inside; we may find that's where the real problem is. Hetero and homo—where are we with lust, and how has that influenced our sexual thinking and behavior? Maybe the real question isn't where we are on the Kinsey scale, but where we are on the Shakespeare scale of lust.

I am incredibly grateful and joyful that my orientation on the Shakespeare scale has been progressively changing in the last thirty years of recovery. I've moved from being a 5 or 6 to hovering somewhere between 0 and 1, with long periods at full 0. Thank God for the impossible!

The Orientation Quandary

Let's be critical here; can prevailing categorizations square with the full range of reality we see along the whole continuum of our current sexualities, which must include those in recovery? Again, let me offer my own case history, which becomes typical for many of those of us recovering from the infection. As Anne Fausto-Sterling has observed (above), my "orientation" was not static; it was a process characterized by internal changes manifesting themselves in external action: solitary masturbation without any lust (no images or thoughts of women or men or anything else), addictive masturbation, masturbation to picture-women, infected with lust, then masturbation to picture-women with lust, sex with a woman without lust (when I got married; this lust-free sex lasted only for a few weeks), resuming masturbation with increasingly lustified picture-women, discovering women wanted me, lusting after women in the flesh, trying to realize picture-woman-lust in sex with women, addictive lusting to women in the flesh, crossing the gender line, then progressive victory over lust in recovery, sex without any lust or lust scenario in marriage, increasing ability to see and relate to women and men normally, and total sexual abstinence with freedom not to lust.

See how misleading these classifications can be? At which point in our life experience, considering both the subjective and objective, do we take the orientation snapshot? Had Kinsey scaled me at age eight, I would have fallen outside the scale completely, because neither gender was involved, subjectively or objectively, even though I was sexing up a storm. If anything, he would have had to rate me at least a 3, since I was having sex with a male—myself. When I was twelve and later, he might have categorized me as a Kinsey 0 because I was using pictures of women and lusting after image women. But sex was still with myself, a male, so—? In the first weeks of marriage I'd be a 0 for sure. Perfect sex with a woman. After my encounter with male sex, I'd have graduated to a Kinsey 3 or higher.

Today, Kinsey would be very confused about me; he'd probably throw down his pad and pencil and stomp off. I'd have fallen outside the scale again! Sex is totally and joyously optional for me now, and I've gone through periods of total celibacy for over a year at a time in my current marriage. I've had erectile sensations when anticipating eating certain savory dishes my wife has cooked up for me, or when the bluebird on our patio alights on my hand for a piece of walnut. That doesn't mean I'm a 3 on the Zoo Scale. And feeling an erectile sensation in some affectionate male or female touches or embraces doesn't make me bisexual. I've heard recovering alkies say "My drinker is broke," meaning there's something out of kilter with their drinking, since they can't take a drink without getting drunk. Well, my *lover* is broke, my *sexer* is broke. Something's out of kilter with my love-sex connection. And it's okay, because I'm recovering. I'm me—complex, sure—but it has nothing to do with my "orientation."

The broader imprinting concept (chapter 3) should be added to the biological and psychosocial influences as a major player in the much-debated predisposition question of sexual orientation.[99] And there is a growing body of evidence that attitudes and behavior affect blood chemistry and the brain.[100] This offers real hope to many of us. In my case, though still having some of the effects of my imprintings, I have been able to change my attitude toward them and move from the pseudo toward the real. What victorious relief! According to the authorities cited in the above two endnotes, my changed attitudes and behavior are being reflected in altered chemistry. But this does not come automatically. It takes time and hard work (ref. chapter 16). Diseased attitudes and actions took me in; changed attitudes and actions are taking me out.

> **Questioner:** "Then what do you call yourself, heterosexual?" *No.* "Homosexual?" *No.* "Bi-sexual?" *No.* "Asexual?" *No.* "Then what *are* you?" *I'm me.* But since you insist on pigeonholing identity in sexual terms, I'll say that I am a recovering pseudosexual. Because all of my sexual thinking and behavior prior to recovery worked against real sexuality, which I am now discovering.

Exposure to the Virus, experience, and personal choices led me deeper and deeper into full and exclusive pseudosexuality, and recovery is progressively bringing me out, *into a sexuality and manhood I never knew.*

Let's dispose of the myth! This should give us pause and a little humility and help us "different" male pseudosexuals identify with one another, instead of allowing media or politics or culture or *lust* to pander to the lie of our uniqueness.

The PC Factor

The pigeonholing itself is what clouds the whole issue, preventing us from seeing the truth about ourselves. Since "orientations" are now part of our culturally mediated identity tags, they force people into trying to make a "fit" into one or the other—either go or no-go. In New York City I saw it being painfully forced on a man, a married man who was simply confused and caught in the pseudosexual trap. This pigeonholing preempts any considerations that might provide other perspectives for our feelings and experiences. And now that the media consciousness is crystallized into the orientation mind-set, it becomes a matter of political correctness to follow the line. No longer merely politically correct or an unwritten journalistic guideline, it is considered an inviolable rule that must be followed. And it's increasingly journalistic and academic suicide to question it.

America's lover is broke. Something's out of kilter with our sexuality. We need honestly to rethink the whole ball of wax. Too much has been omitted for too long from the complex equation of American male sexuality. We are the losers when we refuse to see the subjective elements and dynamism in our sexualities. Let's be more scientific about this thing!

Masters and Johnson on Cross-Preference Fantasy

The following excerpt is from *Homosexuality in Perspective*, by Masters and Johnson, pages 186–187. This may further clarify what we've been saying:

> By far the most intriguing return from investigation of the fantasy patterning reported by homosexual and heterosexual men and women and most relevant to this particular investigation was the high incidence of cross-preference fantasies. In cross-preference fantasy, homosexual men and women imagined overt heterosexual interaction and, conversely, heterosexual men and women fantasized homosexual interchange.
>
> Frequently, the content of the cross-preference fantasies returned from the in-depth interviews differed markedly from material reported by the same study subjects during intake

interviews and from opinions expressed during their periods of laboratory participation. In handling sexual fantasy material, particularly that which runs counter to cultural mores, there must be a constant awareness of the great difference between what men and women publicly profess as acceptable sexual conduct, what they report as fantasy content during most interviews, and what they fantasize privately and reveal only in unusual [more relaxed and unguarded] circumstances. (Interpolation added.)

Cross-preference sexual interaction had been described as "unthinkable," "revolting," "inconceivable," during discussions with small groups of fully committed heterosexual or homosexual men and women. Yet the very men and women whose public condemnation of variant sexual activity was most vitriolic evidenced a significant curiosity, a sense of sexual anticipation, or even fears for effectiveness of sexual performance when musing in private interviews on the subject of cross-preference sexual interaction. . . .

[T]he recorded fantasy patterns of the Kinsey 5 and 6 male and female subjects were just as frequently directed toward cross-preference imagery as those reported by the remaining members of the homosexual group with sexual preference ratings from 1 through 4.

This is very revealing. Note that these subjects of the Masters and Johnson studies were all sexually active and willing and able to have sex on demand in a laboratory setting. This brings up the interesting question of whether these subjects may have been sex/lust addicts. Did pseudosexuality skew the "scientific" analyses? Probably, if their laboratory sexual behavior was being considered representative for humans generally.

One cannot help but wonder whether Masters and Johnson, in their study of sexual fantasy, were unwittingly provided telling evidence for the new lust and pseudosexuality.

Those in recovery know exactly what Masters and Johnson are talking about here. This complex fantasy life is our story. We're the ones who fantasized, What would it be like if—? That's how we set ourselves up for crossing the next line, and the next. Lust, even in its "kinder and gentler" forms, pushes all boundaries and is amenable to every suggestion, from within and from without. But in true recovery, even though we are apparently never "cured" in an absolute sense, we find that we can be released from the obsessive-compulsive power of all such sexual fantasies, regardless of the orientation of the fantasy. It is possible to be no longer controlled by such fantasies and temptations, and for their number and intensity to gradually diminish. And this is amazing.

What recovering lusters must guard against, however, is either fear-driven sobriety or self-driven sobriety—trying to modify behavior without attitude and character change. It is change from within, *from the inside out*—spiritual change—that makes true recovery, seemingly so impossible, nevertheless very very real and so rewarding.

Especially noteworthy is the fact that temptations will still be in the framework of one's so-called orientation. Recovery does not imply immunity from fantasy or temptation. Our biological memories don't have to be erased. Recovery is being released from their power in the temptation, one event at a time. *This contradicts a common misconception (especially among the religious?) that recovery means* temptations *must stop, change, or shift to the other gender.* Of course we're going to be tempted, and of course temptations are going to be with the gender or mode involved in our past misconnections. This is very, very important and sadly misunderstood. Temptation is part of life—and recovery! Many may be stuck with the shame and guilt that the temptations are still with the gender or activity involved in their lust or acting out. But that's the very place, the only place, where the Remedy can work!

Orientation to Self

Finally, if we look at this whole pseudosexuality and orientation business through a wide-angle lens, another observation may help clarify the muddle. The real problem with lust—and our modern sexuality—is that it has become so *self*-oriented. As is our entire culture. Since the Renaissance, the teleology of Western culture has moved toward individualism, the doctrine that self-interest is the proper goal of all human actions. And individualism's response to today's in-your-face consumer capitalism has pushed this to the limit in *selfism* reigning supreme. In such a context, how could our sexuality *not* have moved as it has into self-sex and its consequences? We fail to appreciate the significance of the growing incidence of masturbation in the last few centuries. And how could our sexuality *not* have moved into every possible expression? Self-centeredness in the individual and selfism in the culture conspire together, creating predisposition to pseudosexuality. Why all the hullabaloo, animosity, and political and religious warfare about "orientation"? (Ref. Appendix 5, The Spiritual Basis of Pseudo-reality.)

Labels notwithstanding, most of us are really in the same PS boat. There's room for some humility here. And honesty. Identification. Yes, even understanding, accord, and recovery! Let's give it the light touch—this whole orientation business is really hilarious, when you think about it.[101]

. . .

The real issue is personal, spiritual: can I see what I really am in the light of this history of our common pseudosexuality, and am I willing to identify with the American sexual pathology across the board? Or, will I hang on to the notion of my orientational exclusivity—heterosexual, homosexual, or whatever? Against the mass of this historical, cultural, and inner-personal evidence, will I still cling to the notion that my orientation is absolute, unique, integral, whole? That it is isolated from the forces shaping the rest of American sexuality? In today's global village there is no such thing as cultural—or sexual—isolation. We're all in this together. We suffer from the common American illness—pseudosexuality. We need recovery. Our whole culture needs recovery.

For me to assert my so-called heterosexual—or homosexual—preference as the core of my human identity is nonsense and sheer folly. I am a human male. Broken, erring, addicted, obsessive, yes. Most of my fantasies and acting out happened to be with the opposite sex. That's irrelevant, because lust is asexual, and I'm infected with the lust virus. So are millions of others. We're in the same boat, even though most of us haven't come out of denial—yet.

To make my particular expression of the common pathology the basis of a claim for orientational uniqueness is crazy and keeps me in denial. In this my "coming out" into pseudosexuality, I thus refuse to legitimatize the cultural illness. Why should any of us tolerate this seizure of our sexuality any longer? Let's come out! All of us! Out of denial! Denial that we live and move and have our being in the Matrix of the Lust Lie. Out into the Light. And come *in*. Into the truth of ourselves.

PART III
IMAGE-CONNECTION AND THE NEW LUST

I had stopped all forms of sex with self and others for a year-and-a- half to save a new marriage. When I came home from work one day, I got the mail, and flipping through a magazine, saw the small photo of Argentine stripper Fanny Fox, a famous Congressman's nemesis, in a bathing suit. I glanced at the shot and turned the page, realizing it was a trigger. My hand turned the page back for a second look. As it automatically flipped back for the third look, I "drank." And the compulsion was reignited, initiating a three-month lust/sex binge where I crossed new lines I had never thought of.

The author

What makes image-connected lust so potent? How and why have we connected the human sexual experience with pictorial images? How can such photographs hold such power over millions of us and keep us in thrall so we cannot live without them? What lies behind the power of this mass addiction to ingesting picture-women and picture-men?

In Parts I and II we have delved into the genesis, nature, and historical evolution of pseudosexuality, making the case for PS. In Parts III and IV we will look at some of the cultural forces empowering this revolution.

In Part III we will assess the role pictorial images play in creating cultural and personal predisposition to pseudosexuality. Chapter 8 provides a broad historical background describing the reality revolution in which all this is taking place. Chapters 9, 10, 11, and 12 approach this problem from four different but related perspectives: the impact of still photos, the impact of moving pictures, the new image religion, and a personal experiment.

Our use of the term "image-connection" will require a special note. The emphasis is on *connection,* thus the hyphen. Being immersed in a world of pictorial images is the lot of almost everyone today. It's unavoidable; we can't seem to live without it. Not seeing or looking at pictures, per se, is not what we're talking about. It's the image-connection—how the total experience has affected our personal reality and the way we see and relate to others. If you think of it as the way drug addicts speak of their "connection," you get the idea. Our spiritual *connection* with Image is the new element in our sexual and relational ecology. It is thus spiritual *mis*-connection that's the issue. This is not an easy concept to define; it requires some introspection. It should become clarified by the time we're through Part III. And its power in and over our lives is astonishing.

8

THE REALITY REVOLUTION

Having introduced the concept of pseudosexuality, let's look at one of the most powerful forces driving it: mankind's new image connection. We shall see that our relation to photographic images—irrespective of subject matter—has introduced a new term in the human ecology complex, one with profound implications regarding lust and sexuality. First, some general observations and a look at the broader cultural context.

"Stop the World; I Want to Get Off!" This expression, the title of an American drama from 1962, captures the essence of our modern predicament. The general feeling is that things are coming at us too fast and heavy. For example, the psychic avalanche of radio, television, print news, Internet, and entertainment today is so assaultingly overwhelming, few, if any, can avoid the impact. Contributing to this feeling of being overwhelmed is the fact that not only is the human organism in an environment today that is totally different from all that has gone before, but also that this environment is in rapid flux, changing at a rate that the human race has never before experienced and for which we are totally unprepared. Increasingly, the masses are affected, yet choose to stay buried in the avalanche. Since we have grown up within this environment and it has grown up around us, it is very difficult to comprehend the suddenness of the shift, what it is, and the extent of its effect upon us. We're like fish in water; we don't realize what we're in because we're in it. Again, we'll have to "step outside" to see it.

Look at some of the most obvious factors in today's world, such as population explosion, industrialization, globalization, technology, the advent of leisure time for the masses, the entertainment revolution, and especially the new media: camera, telephone, phonograph, radio, movies, television, the computer, video, popular music, MTV, interactive TV, video games, the Internet, cyberspace. Each of these alone is a powerful force affecting human relations and sexuality. Consider, for example, the life-changing religious force that popular music and its stars have on the entire youth culture. Combined with an increasing rate of acceleration, all these forces have converged upon us with powerful impact.

Within the last hundred years—only one long lifetime—civilization has experienced the most dramatic, sudden, and cataclysmic changes in human ecology in the entire history of the human race. As incredible as it may seem, one has to wonder whether this surpasses the combined effect of all previous changes, from Neolithic times at the dawn of history to now.

We and our sexuality and relations are directly affected by all of this. The only event of comparable suddenness I can think of is the extinction of the dinosaurs, which apparently took place when a large meteor or comet struck the earth polluting the atmosphere. Something with as much impact as a meteor from outer space has covered our world—the Lust Virus cloud. Our atmosphere is poisoned, and we're gasping—dying for a breath of Love.

Let's look at some of the key elements of this *reality revolution* as it relates to human ecology, and then see how all this helps drive the pseudosexual revolution. Every advance in civilization and technology has enabled humankind in obvious positive, even necessary ways. At the same time, however, each advance carries with it a negative potential, considering what we are. And each of the new tools—technological, social forces, or ideas—forever alters human ecology and thus affects us and our sexuality. This is nothing less than a new direction in human evolution, propelling us into a new dimension. In the next chapter we shall deal with the psycho-spiritual impact of photographic images, but first the broader context involving the advent of writing and reading.

Writing

As far as we can tell, writing appeared on the scene between four thousand and thirty-five hundred years B.C., say five or six thousand years ago. Anthropologically speaking, that is very, very recent, and it was the beginning of a revolution whose impact it is difficult if not impossible for us to measure. Writing had a decisive impact on mankind as did the shift from nomadic hunting/gathering to agriculture and settlement in villages, which began some six thousand years before that, and as did learning to use stone tools long before that. With writing, for the first time we could communicate with others remotely. We could record and thus leave a permanent record of our experiences. Without printing, however, such written communication—usually via clay and later papyrus and vellum—was not only very slow, but very limited in scope, used mostly by the priestly castes and in trade.

Reading

It took some 4,900 years for us to get from writing to printing, which appeared in the fifteenth century. As late as the thirteenth century A.D., in Italy, France, and Germany combined, there were only about one hundred different works published during that century, all written by hand. The first movable-type printing presses appeared in Europe in the 1440s and 1450s, the Gutenberg revolution. And what a revolution it was! The total output of titles from those first presses from 1440 to 1500—a mere sixty years—is estimated at 40,000. Incredible, when you think about it. However, the total number of *copies* of books printed in the European market alone in that same period is estimated at 20,000,000—and from those crude, slow presses!

This is amazing. It's as though almost instantaneously, *a whole new human appetite was created*. Not reading—that is merely the tool. The new appetite was a mass reality shift to pseudo-life. What was new psychologically was a fundamental reality shift, one of the many ways we can get out of ourselves or alter our reality. Competition among fifteenth century printers was so great that they printed everything the public would buy, which was anything.[102] (This should not only tell us something about human nature, but about sexuality.) In our era, in only one year, 1987, some 800,000 or more titles were published worldwide, with the sale of 1,804,000,000 books in the U.S. alone.[103] In 1992, the American public bought $8.8 billion worth of books, 822 million books for adults alone.[104] In 2003, more than 100,000 books were published in the U.S. alone, with 2.222 billion books being sold here.[105]

Mass Communication of Soul-Set

Writing and printing enabled humankind to conquer time and space. We could reach remote peoples and influence later generations with our own experiences, knowledge, religion, dreams—and *soul-set*. I use this term to try to convey, in the spiritual realm, something akin to what we refer to as mind-set, only deeper. An example of mind-set induced through advertising might be, "I like this car better than the other; it looks classier." An example of soul-set mediated through the cultural air might be, "Having a beautiful car or body is a necessary end in itself and is intrinsic to my personal identity." Do you see the difference between mind-set and soul-set? Soul-set plays an important part in our pseudosexual revolution.

With printing, each subsequent generation—and individual—was thus enabled to experience the soul-set of prior generations and individuals. One might even say that we were more prone to experience the soul-set thus mediated and more susceptible to it *because* of writing and reading. Thus, a kind of accumulation and transmission of soul-set came about to an extent undreamed of. This seems to characterize the development of mass media generally. Awesome, if you stop to think about how we are shaped by culture.

Perhaps reading is also where our trend toward isolation began to accelerate. Women and men were no longer dependent on actual social intercourse between persons to learn and survive; we could stay by ourselves and read it all in books. Reading quickly introduced *a substitute reality*, which, in Susan Sontag's words, resulted in the "first fall into alienation . . . [engendering] that surplus of Faustian energy and psychic damage needed to build modern, inorganic societies" (interpolation added).[106] That is an extremely powerful concept! The first fall into alienation? Alienation from what? From others and even myself?

One poignant illustration may suffice: George MacDonald was thirty four when he wrote *Phantastes, a Faerie Romance*, in England in 1858. Typically for his time, indoor diversion and entertainment included reading books and writing and receiving letters. In it he tells the story of Cosmo, the university student, with whom MacDonald admittedly identified.

When he looked from his window on the street below, not a maiden passed but she moved as in a story, and drew his thoughts after her till she disappeared in the vista. When he walked in the streets, he always felt as if reading a tale, into which he sought to weave every face of interest that went by

Today we have not only a society without father, we have the substitute in books and other media—a pseudo-father of any and every conceivable nature. In effect, we choose our own "father" by exposing ourselves to the images and soul-set communicated in the media. Note how the boys at Duke learned what they did about relating and sexualizing with females not from fathers, family, or friends, but from *Penthouse Forum*. More than we realize, we are shaped by what we see and read.

With reading, we could now interact creatively with the written word out of our own psyches, and we could experience more internally than before. What I mean by this is that in reading, not only can I escape reality, I can also alter reality by projecting myself into the physical scene, mind-set, and soul-set communicated by the author. This is amazing and impactful enough. But I can also build on and amplify that through my own creative imagination (fantasy or lust, for example) to experience something totally new, without even leaving my chair, something even the author may not have had in mind. I creatively interact with that communication out of my own psyche. In other words, I can have or create an experience that doesn't exist, an unreal experience—in isolation! Reading becomes a catalyst for unreality—whatever I want to make it. Of course, this has tremendous potential, positive and otherwise.

In ancient days, communication from others at least had personal encounter associated with it—oral story telling between poet or actors and audience, for example, where there was still some level of social intercourse of persons. However, reality, which we previously had to experience physically, is now something different. Instead of "out there" in the real world, reality is "in here," in our minds. And we are now open to forces from without and within that affect us to an extent previously impossible and even unimaginable.

Reading allows us to glimpse and touch and be touched by the loftiest in man's experience and even beyond, to extend our soul's reach beyond its grasp, partake of the noblest and the best. It can inspire, uplift, and save. However, I'm saying we should also recognize the changes this has produced in human ecology, society, psychology, spirituality, and sexuality and see how we have been affected.

The advent of books and reading was an incredibly powerful change in the human environment. Instead of going inward only occasionally, before the printed word, we can now *live* on the inside of ourselves through this new medium. For many of us, here's an addiction waiting to happen—escape from reality, mediated by the marvel of the innocent and necessary technology of the printed word. Totally benign—in itself—yet it offers another technique we can use against ourselves. Have you ever wondered why sex scenes have become required for novels and PG-rated movies? It's more than "sex sells." There's not only an advancing wave of accumulating lust in the air, but the advancing wave of pseudosexuality, which calls forth more simulations of the intimacy we have lost.

Reading thus represents the first mass reality shift in human ecology. Call it the beginning of the Reality Revolution. You will doubtless sense the connection even this basic concept has with your own sexual thinking and behavior. But this was just the beginning. Mankind would never be the same. And the rate of change would keep accelerating.

Photography

Mallarmé, the nineteenth-century French poet, said everything in the world exists in order to end in a book. Today everything exists to end in a photograph.

Susan Sontag

The ability to capture images on film came in the 1830s with the cameras of Daguerre and Talbot in France and England, but it wasn't until the turn of the century that film on conveniently replaceable rolls was invented, and Box Brownies sold for a dollar apiece. Almost instantly, most families in the western world owned a camera, and a new human appetite was created. Not photos—they are merely the tool, the instrumentality. What was created was another fundamental reality shift, *a whole new way of looking at the world and ourselves.* And we would never be the same. Just as it was with reading. As we shall see, this jump was farther and deeper than anyone could have imagined. We're still jumping.

Anthropologically speaking, humans are visually oriented, versus being oriented by the sense of smell or hearing, such as in dogs or bats. Processing visual images in the human brain is all-involving. The occipital lobes, which handle initial processing of visual data, occupy no less than fifteen percent of the human brain. Neurons devoted to visual processing take up about thirty percent of the brain, as compared with eight percent for touch and only three percent for hearing.[107] By the time visual data are organized into recognizable forms, fully one-third of the brain is involved. And further processing of those images continues throughout other portions of the brain, depending on what we want to do with the information. It is difficult to exaggerate how pervasive the influence of visual images is in the human brain—even neutral images without associated feelings or emotions. When we get to *moving* pictures, as we shall see later, this influence becomes incredibly impactful. And when we add scenes that stir the feelings and emotions to the highest degree—sex, romance, and violence—there's simply no defense against total brain, system, and psychic involvement.

For now, let's consider the impact of the still photograph. It will boggle the mind.

IMAGE JUNKIES

"Industrial societies turn their citizens into image-junkies;
it is the most irresistible form of mental pollution."

Susan Sontag, *On Photography*, p. 24

What gives the photograph such power? One cannot begin to appreciate the impact of picture-sex on sexuality until the impact of the photograph itself is understood.

I will rely heavily on the insights of Susan Sontag, and later, Hugo Munsterberg, for film. These two probe respective ends of the image revolution spectrum. At first glance, one might ask, Why delve so extensively into images and the analyses of these two authors? The answer is that we are mining hard ground here. It is not easy to comprehend, much less communicate how we live in an unreal world today. A shift in reality. These two image psychologists, as I call them, have discovered the mother lode, but we must do the digging to come up with any nuggets of practical value. Theirs is the genius; it is left to others to apply these original insights to our specific problems and needs.

It's never easy to question the very basis of one's own life, to examine how we are so programmed that we live and move and have our being in an unreal world. If we are willing to look inside ourselves and our image environment as fearlessly as Sontag and Munsterberg, we will be amazed at what we'll find. This isn't for everybody. However, we the afflicted must help pioneer our own way back into reality.

On Photography

What makes image-lust so potent? How can it possibly be an addiction? What's it doing to our sexuality? The following excerpts from Susan Sontag's book *On Photography* reveal incredible insights as we wrestle with these questions.

I doubt whether anyone has more insightfully probed the impact of photography on humans than Sontag.[108] The statements below should cause us to think about a subject we take too much for granted and do not understand. To better appreciate the force of some of these expressions, imagine yourself leafing through a magazine in your dentist's waiting room. Note how the pictures control your perusal of the magazine. I believe that what we experience there represents one of the most profound changes ever to occur in human psychology. It's what I call the *Image-Connection*. The human connection with images. And for the lust-oriented reading Sontag's statements, the stark realization may begin to dawn as to why the lust pathology is so widespread, has become so much the very fabric of our lives, and is so "impossible" to overcome. As you read, remember that Sontag is just talking about still photography, usually without reference to any particular subject matter.

The following excerpts take on vastly more meaning when read in the light of what we have already considered in the "Anatomy of a Look" and the rest of Part I. Excerpts as revelatory as those that follow appear on almost every page of Sontag's work. Limiting the selection was difficult. Someone should write a book applying the fallout of her slim volume of essays to our subject.

Excerpts not in quotation marks are my paraphrases. Some statements are condensed for brevity. My editorial comments are in brackets. Page references are to the 1989 paperback edition (Noonday Press, Farrar, Straus and Giroux). Excerpts are used with the kind permission of the late author and her publisher.

Image Junkies

Sontag: "Needing to have reality confirmed and experience enhanced by photographs is an aesthetic consumerism to which everyone is now addicted. Industrial societies turn their citizens into image-junkies; it is the most irresistible form of mental pollution." (page 24)

Implications: Tough stuff, but this says it all. Talk about predisposition—*If those of us in industrial societies are image junkies, then we've all been set up—predisposed—to become lust junkies.* It is a revolution!

The term *image-junkies* reveals that a more powerful appetite than the merely physical is at work in our relation to photos. This aspect of man's being is more significant than the physical because it is out of attitudes and soul-set that behavior is determined and driven.

Needing to have photographs *confirm* and *enhance* reality implies that we have some kind of reality deficit. And pictures help fill that deficit. Filling the Deficit will be a key to recovery from PS. Not easy, and it will take work.

What is *most irresistible* is the image-*ingestion* aspect of our relation to photos. Eye candy. They taste so good! They feed an appetite. They feed the appetite they create. But both appetite and food are pseudo!

Have we become more prone to ingest image reality than experience real reality (whatever that is)? I suspect that my need to ingest image reality has been programmed not only by the larger image-driven culture, but abetted by my addictive spiritual relation to images in masturbation.

Sontag says *everyone* is now addicted to image consumption. Who today looks through that issue of *People* or *Time* in the dentist's office without their perusal being image-driven and without ingesting at least some of the images? And we're not talking about sexual lust or sex here.

Mental pollution implies that this appetite can pollute the mind. I would go farther and say pollute the spirit (Shakespeare's *Sonnet* 129). This really means we are being changed.

In sum, Susan Sontag and many recovering lust addicts bear witness to the phenomenon that citizens of industrial societies are image-junkies who have allowed their very human natures to be altered by an appetite that is essentially new to the human environment. (Comment from one reader: "We don't even have a choice; it's an absorbed consciousness. . . .") There's no value judgment here; we're just trying to look objectively at what's going on with pictorial images.

Voyeurs

> Sontag: "Taking photographs has set up a chronic voyeuristic relation to the world. . . ." (page 11)

Implications: A voyeur sees something more than the simple image of one undressing behind a lighted window shade; he sees something that isn't there, something lust creates within him. Sontag says that taking photographs has set up a new relation to reality, a voyeuristic one. Thus, what we're doing when shooting or looking at photographs—the voyeur reaction—is the very essence of what lust is. And thus the modern image revolution has created a *cultural predisposition for lusting*.

> Sontag: "Like sexual voyeurism, it [the act of photographing] is a way of . . . encouraging whatever is going on to keep on happening." (page 12)

Implications: The mere appearance of a new mode of dress (or undress) or human interaction in a photograph encourages or gives legitimacy to that act. Thus, our new image connection shapes my personal world, and because it is shaping the personal world of millions of others, it is shaping our world, which includes our sexuality.

Copulation

> Sontag: Photography is a promiscuous way of seeing, a voracious way of seeing, copulation with the material world, psychic intercourse with everything. (pages 30, 31, 129)

Implications: Before this new image appetite erupted on the scene, promiscuity was referred to as being in the physical dimension. Now, there's a new dimension to promiscuity—psychic (read *spiritual*) intercourse. And again, we see that *when we have acquired a different way of seeing, we have altered our human nature*. Again, there's no value judgment involved here; we're simply talking about spiritual evolution—spiritual mutation. But when we add *lustified content* to pictures flooding the human psyche-scape, such intercourse has far-reaching effects on our sexuality. Millions of us are being changed, with untold thousands going under. The numbers involved in the aids epidemic are minuscule compared with this forced mass-mutation of the male human psyche and sexuality across the board. Lust kills the spirit. AIDS brings only physical death.

It is not photography that is the new promiscuous way of seeing, but the new appetite within man that shoots or uses the photograph. Man is preeminently a spiritual being; man is what he is subjectively. Just as the physical component of the sex act is driven by the "chemistry," the spiritual component is driven by either love on the one hand or lust or other forces on the other. The spiritual component in sex can be either a positive or a negative force. Therefore, since we always and under any circumstances have sex both physically and spiritually at the same time, we cannot separate these two aspects of sex. Thus (and here I would go further than Sontag), it is copulation not only with the material world but with the spiritual world and cultural mind-set that is the essence of our relation to pictorial images. Infinitely more serious and life-altering.

On rereading the above Sontag quote recently, I was reminded of a fascinating scene my wife called to my attention. A captive male killer whale loved to swim by the cetologist's underwater office and ogle a black and white photograph of another killer whale the man had hung on his picture window. Viewing the unreality of a photograph was captivating, even for the whale.

Demise of Moral Boundaries

Sontag: "Much of modern art is devoted to lowering the threshold of what is terrible [read *acceptable*]." It changes morals by getting us used to what formerly we could not bear to see or hear. "The camera . . . annihilates moral boundaries and social inhibitions." This produces not a liberation but a subtraction from the self. Pseudo-familiarity reinforces alienation. (pages 40, 41)

Implications: Image addiction lowers the threshold of what is doable, wantable, desirable, thus creating new desires and changing morals. My image connection and the changing culture were catalysts in my changing morality and sexuality.

Subtraction from the self must mean that I become less me and less human. (No wonder some critics railed against Sontag.) Thus, in the sexual area, image-connection—sex energized by pictures—produces a subtraction from the *sexual* self. This equates to what we are calling pseudosexuality. In spite of the progressive "freedom" of my acting out history, mine was a progressively diminishing sexuality. Lust kills love.

It follows that for recovery, though living necessarily in an image-dominated world, we must sever our spiritual *mis*-connection with images, whatever works against sex and lust recovery. And we'll have to reverse its effects, just as we must sever our spiritual and physical misconnections with persons and reverse those effects. This is so tough it takes a community of those who are desperate enough to have to have it.

Changing Reality

> Sontag: "Photography is the reality; the real object is often experienced as a letdown." "The pictures have a reality for me that the people don't. . . ." (pages 147, 121)

Implications: Ask any recovering luster what this means and you'll get an eye-opening commentary. Better yet, ask the wives or female or male friends of lusters what it feels like to try to measure up to the image but always be the "letdown." They can never win! Why they keep on valiantly trying so long and so hard is a mystery. Don't they know that we are incapable of seeing and connecting with the *person*? The revolution Sontag's book might well have spawned was the women of America rising up against the image-driven lust of their men. But is mere refusal of sex—as in Aristophanes' ancient play *Lysistrata*—a potent enough weapon against the havoc wrought by the new lust, when the new virtual sex is everywhere and so seductive? Who needs women? Or does male lust have such an irresistible payoff for women that they're willing to sell *their* souls for it?

> Sontag: Our era prefers images to real things because the notion of what is real has been progressively complicated and weakened. (page 160)

Implications: Cultural forces working in our society, especially since the Industrial Revolution, have helped drive the *weakening* of our notion of reality. We'll be tracing some of these in subsequent chapters. But without cooperation from within ourselves, these cultural forces themselves do not produce such internal psychic change. The significant thing in the study of this history is man's choice—the fact that although we are powerless over what happens in our culture, we can nevertheless choose our attitude toward what is happening. Why do so many, if not most of us, so willingly follow where the forces lead? This brings us back to the basic question, What is man?

> Sontag: "Instead of just recording reality, photographs have become the norm for the way things appear to us, thereby changing the very idea of reality. . . ." (page 87)

Implications: Sontag describes the reality shift very well here. Can you see the implications for lust? I programmed myself, through picture-woman-lust coupled into masturbation, so that the brain's reference, or norm, for perceiving women was image-woman. Lustified photographs of women became the norm for the way women appeared to me, even though this was a perversion of reality. Lustified photographs of women conditioned the way my *wife* appeared to me. That programming would not allow me to see the person. My first-glance perception sees an image that is in jarring contrast with the lustified-image neural networks hardwired into my brain. *That's* what women have to measure up to in the mind of the lust-oriented. Every initial glance at every single woman is automatically measured against that "norm." (Ref. Appendix 3, "The 'Feminine Religion' and the Tyranny of the Beauty Cult.")

I NEED HELP By Vic Lee   February 28, 1998

But that perverted norm was normal for me! I might justifiably say, "My way of looking, of seeing women, is just the way I am. I'm incapable of doing otherwise. That's my identity. That's *me!*" Imagine trying to tell the lusting male, who feels he's God's great gift to women, the quintessence of masculine mystique, that his orientation is not really heterosexual at all, but pseudosexual. You'd better duck! This is where we discover the bronc-bucking burr under the saddle of Marlboro Man. No wonder he's getting bucked pretty badly these days.

All of this takes us back to the fundamental questions, not what is sexuality, but what is truth, what is reality, what is *Man*? And man may very well need a Reference outside himself before he can know the truth about himself. That's what I needed.

Eye Candy

> Sontag: "[E]very subject is depreciated into an article of consumption . . . ." Photography is acquisition, surrogate possession of a cherished person or thing, "and a potent means of acquiring it, of gaining control over it." (pages 110, 155)

Implications: Sontag sees clearly the spiritual ingestion (consumption) involved in our relation to photo images, carrying the idea deeper and more powerfully as acquisition and possession. We saw this clearly in the "Anatomy of a Look," in chapter 4. This is what makes image-masturbation so powerful and addictive—what's going on inside! We feel we actually *have* that woman or man! We possess something spiritually. We have truly connected! But with what? Another spirit? Some split within ourselves? Unfortunately, scientists don't try to comprehend this subjective component of sexuality; they are content to "count and catalog" and look at mere physiology and biology. The "biology" of the *psyche* is the controlling factor here.

> Sontag: Photography "turns people into objects that can be symbolically possessed." (page 14)

Implications: Images can be ingested, much as though they were some kind of sustenance, addictively ingested like food. But *possessing* a person's spirit communicated via the image goes deeper than that. Humans have become *materia lasciva*—the material, or "stuff" of lust.

Erotic Relations Programmed by Photographs

Sontag: ". . . [I]t is more common for the erotic relation to be not only created by but understood as limited to the photographs." (page 162)

Implications: Stop the music! My erotic relations were *created* by my image connection with photographs? No wonder I became a relational cripple. And for years in recovery, my erotic relation was limited by the programming from that former life of image-connection. What a tragedy for a person to be lost to the human, lost even to one's self. And how liberating to be found, and set free!

Possessed

Sontag: "One can't possess reality, one can possess (and be possessed by) images. . . ." (page 163)

Implications: How is one possessed by an image? The image is "out there" somewhere, so what possesses me? What gets inside me that was not in there before? An image impressed on the retina excites whole systems of neuronal networks. But that's a "neutral" image. Ones and zeros; brain cells turned on or off. Where does the "heat" come from, that elusive but very powerful Lambda factor—lust?

That heat can come from either or both of two quarters: from the spirit of the model the photograph captures, as that spirit interacts with mine and triggers lust, or as lust within me rises and overpowers the reality of that neutral printed or screened image. In either case, the heat itself, the lust-intensification, comes from within me. This accounts for the great payoff, the hit, of ingesting lustified picture-women or picture-men. (ref. "The Anatomy of a Look" in chapter 4.)

An important question is, Can photographic images be toxic in themselves? That's like asking if a tree falling in the forest makes a sound if there's no one there to hear it. Of course, it's exposure to humans that qualifies the thing. But I suppose many of the previously lust-oriented would say, Yes, for me there are pictures that are toxic in themselves. We learn an avoidance reflex like encountering a live wire, hot stove, or rattlesnake. We have much to learn in recovery.

I don't know about Sontag's statement of our not being able to possess reality, but I do think we can *experience* reality. And for recovery, we lust-oriented *must* experience reality, or we'll continue connecting with the pseudo- or anti-real. But what is reality and how do we experience it? What was our lust really looking for? That's the ultimate question. Recovery is chancy and incomplete for us unless we find that. The amazing thing is, that we can.

Lust

> Sontag: Our relation to photographs "can inspire something akin to lust. And like all credible forms of lust, it cannot be satisfied: first, because the possibilities of photography are infinite; and, second, because the project is finally self-devouring." (page 179)

Implications: My lust was inspired by photographs. This gave the immediate gratification of seemingly being satisfied (filled) but always wanting more. I get this self-devouring feeling watching even innocent movies. I go away seemingly filled, but oh so empty! Always needing another "fill." If image-reality is finally self-devouring, what gives such a false feeling of life must really be "a subtraction from the self" (Sontag, page 41). And image-driven lust compounds this effect.

Summation

If not always easy to comprehend, every sentence in Sontag is nevertheless dynamite! She was once asked, after she had given a staged reading, why there had been no revolution after *On Photography*. Even she was at a loss for words. And the above excerpts are a minute fraction of similar insights on almost every page of her little book.

But it's impossible to live without seeing photographic images today. And there's nothing wrong with photographic images! The problem is inside us. The fact is, today's humans need addictive escape, and every new addiction comes with its own built-in "necessity" and means of perpetuation. Think of the impact on that Civil War soldier viewing his first picture "for bachelors" or on a boy's first encounter with a nudie. We simply have to admit that we humans are prone to disorder, that we can misuse (*pervert* came to mind first) any new innocent tool. We seem to have a built-in proclivity for allowing—even encouraging—the liability inherent in each new tool to surface and continue working against our best interests.

It is difficult to exaggerate how pervasive the influence of visual images is in the modern human psyche—even images with neutral content. Every thinking person should read Sontag's book. When we get to moving pictures, this influence becomes incredibly magnified. And when we add scenes that stir the feelings and emotions to the highest degree—sex, romance, and violence—there's simply no defense against total brain, system, and psychic involvement.

. . .

We might pause here and ask some critical questions: Does mankind's new relation (addiction) to images help force us into losing or diminishing the spiritual aspect of life? Is it more difficult for today's image consumers to experience the spiritual and interpersonal realities for which we are suited by nature? And how does all this bear on my sexuality and yours? On religion? Has the image connection become the direct pipeline to the collective unconscious? If so, what does that mean?

These are difficult questions. The describing organism can never fully describe itself; there's always a blind spot. And since we are immersed within our own culture-field, we cannot step fully "outside" to see it objectively. We need all the insights we can get. So let's take this mystical image-connection business a step further into the captivating world of moving pictures, where these questions will take on even more relevance.

"NICKEL MADNESS"—
THE MOVING-IMAGE
CONNECTION

Seen on a T-shirt:

CINEMA—'sin-e-ma—The motion picture

industry. A motion picture theatre. The art of

making movies.

REALITY ENDS HERE

In 1894 the first Edison nickelodeons debuted in New York City for a nickel a show. By 1908 the "flickers" are showing to 200,000 daily in New York City, with over 4,000 new films being released annually. By 1914, "nickel madness" has become the first true mass amusement in American life. Appreciating the culture-transforming power of this new force will help reveal the relation between the film-viewing connection and pseudosexuality.

One might suppose that moving images affect us in the same way photos do. (And we had no idea how powerful that was before reading Sontag!) After all, are they not merely a number of snapshots strung together in a row? If even a little of what Sontag says is true of the still photo, regardless of content—and we sense intuitively that she is right—the impact of the moving image on humans must be vastly more complex and potent.

For one thing, the psychoneurology of film watching is more involved. Have you ever tried *not* watching an in-flight movie, even when you had no ear phones? The eyes automatically track any motion in the field of vision and are captive to motion, just as our head turns to track sounds. We are physiologically captive to motion in the field of vision, regardless of content.

There may be evidence for the fact that the frequency of images, or flicker rate, appearing on the screen (from 20 to 96 frames per second for movies, to give the illusion of motion) in itself creates a neurological condition where suggestibility increases. Early movie makers found that they had to increase the flicker rate. While watching those silent films, certain otherwise normal people had seizures, called photic epilepsy. Now we hear of epileptic seizures of those watching video games.[109] With all the hullabaloo over sex and violence in film content, have we yet fully plumbed the impact of the moving images themselves?

There is also a similarity between the film-watching state and what is called the hypnagogic state, that state between sleep and waking in which we are peculiarly vulnerable to dreams and hallucination. Merely watching a film—any film—puts me into a state where I am more susceptible to the power of suggestion.[110]

Moving images take us even deeper into the reality revolution than do still pictures. They take us into another new psychic state. Compare a single photograph—say the one mentioned in chapter 2 of the model showing off the new shoe style—with a film of that same model giving the effect of motion. Infinitely more is communicated than in the one still shot, regardless of how alluring that photo was. The viewer now experiences a veritable barrage of images pouring into him, with a combined sensory and emotional impact far exceeding that of the still photo. The impact of that rush of images into the brain, regardless of subject matter, is neurologically overwhelming, even without sound, which today, is overpowering in itself. The entire brain—and hence the entire *person*—is involved and affected. Add romance, sex, lust, or violence, and we'll see that we have the most powerful instrument of psychic propaganda yet devised.

Moving Pictures

If it took 4900 years to get from writing to printing, it took only some fifty years to get from the camera to movies, another perfectly innocent tool. Interesting from the standpoint of impact on human ecology is the fact that the advent of silent movies roughly coincided with the advent of cheap illustrated newspapers.[111] The world began going visual in a big hurry, and that's when it started spinning faster.

The work of many inventors led up to the motion picture camera and projector. On the 28th of December 1895, in the Salon Indien of the Grand Café in Paris, thirty three spectators attended the first public projection of Louis and Auguste Lumière's "Cinematographe."[112] With films made in Thomas Edison's Kinematograph, Thomas Armat used his Vitascope to project a few trite scenes in a vaudeville show at Koster and Bial's music hall at Herald square in New York City on the night of April 23, 1896. This marked the beginning of the commercial career of the screened motion picture.

Such was its instant success that the clamoring appetite (shall we call it lust?) for moving pictures of *anything* exceeded the ability to feed it. By 1916, only twenty years later, there were 125,000 silent moving picture theaters in the world, with a *daily* audience of thirty million. (See chart.) It took less than twenty years for the entire world to become evangelized and converted. But in individuals, the new appetite was aroused instantaneously, as we all became immersed in a dream reality no one had ever imagined before. The Dream Machine conquered the world as nothing and no one had ever done before, and captured the psyche—or was it the soul?—of humanity.

Note that each new appetite promising reality transformation— reading and photography, for example—takes hold instantly, as soon as people hear about it and can connect with it. This instant creation of new human appetites has to tell us something about ourselves and human nature. It is not by accident that authors write about what is now called our addictive culture.[113]

The Rise of American Film Houses and Attendance [114]

1888   The kinetoscope is invented by Thomas Edison.

1894   The first Edison nickelodeons (peepshow machines) debut at the Holland Brothers Kinetoscope Parlor, 1155 Broadway in NYC, April 14. The first public motion pictures for a fee.

1896   The Armat projector makes its vaudeville debut April 23.

1900   There are 97 licensed nickelodeons in NYC, mostly immigrant areas.

1902   "Hundreds of short films" ("shorts") have been produced and are shown all over the urban North.

1908   There are 550 movie houses, storefront theaters, and nickelodeons in NYC, with none seating over 400. In Harlem, there are as many as five in one block. The "flickers" are showing to 200,000 daily in NYC. Over 4,000 films are now being released annually.

1908   On Christmas Day police close down all 550 on the NYC mayor's and police chief's orders "in order to avert a public calamity" and not "corrupt the minds of children."

1909   Sunday attendance in NYC is half a million.

1910   There are 20,000 nickelodeons in the northern cities of the East, their numbers increasing daily. In the average poor neighborhood in NYC there are 20 dance halls, 100 saloons, and 20 nickelodeons.

1912   About 100 small firms are producing films. Movie houses now seat 1000 or more at one time.

1914   "Nickel madness" (movies) has become the first true mass amusement in American life, with 18,000 theaters and an estimated 7,000,000 daily admissions

1916   There are 125,000 silent movie theaters in the world with daily attendance of thirty million.

1927   There are now over 800 cinemas in NYC, averaging 1200 seats each, or one seat for every six persons in NY—. While the NYC population doubled between 1910 and 1930, the number of seats in movie theaters increased more than eight times.

1928   There are 28,000 movie theaters country-wide, with 20 to 30 million in weekly attendance.

Film critic Richard Griffith calls the primordial film experience, "the most powerful experience of its kind ever known, as its immediate world audience attested."[115] This critic's conclusion that even silent film was the most powerful experience of its kind ever known gets your attention when you try to think of what other experiences humans may have that rival it. The only comparably impactful experiences that come to mind are reports of religious ecstatic experiences, hallucinogenic drugs, and certain music. We are unaware of the spellbinding power of movies because they have become so much a part of the "normal" human ecology. It would take a long period of complete abstinence from all exposure to the moving image, and then re-exposure for someone to even begin to discern the effects. I found this to be true for lust. Sexual sobriety and progressive victory over lust allowed me to begin to discern its true nature and power.

Munsterberg on Silent Film

My interest here is not so much the content of film but how the film-viewing experience itself—the moving-image connection—may make us more amenable to pseudosexuality. As odd as the question may sound, *Is there such a thing as cinematic predisposition to pseudosexuality?*

Interestingly, Hugo Munsterberg, a German psychologist at Harvard, who was called in his time "the father of applied psychology," was one of the most ardent converts to the silent film experience. He was in love with the new flicks. I suspect he may even have thought film to be the superb art form. Yet he is the one who most perceptively has given us insights into the impact of moving pictures on humans. And he was speaking only of the silent film. Only a careful reading of the whole of Munsterberg's thin volume *The Photoplay: A Psychological Study* can provide an adequate understanding of that aspect of film psychology we are grappling with here.

Why do I use Munsterberg and not a more contemporary work on the impact of film? In his perceptive introduction to Munsterberg's work, film critic Richard Griffith, in 1969, says,

> Those whose ordinary business it is to nail down such insights—
> to secure and organize the evidence, and draw conclusions from

it—have conspicuously failed to take the hurdle, and this includes experimental psychologists as well as film theorists. There has evidently been some sort of block to further investigation— perhaps the feeling that its results might have disturbing philosophic implications.

Disturbing *philosophic* implications? Blocking further investigation? *Of movies?* Intriguing. Another reason for my choosing Munsterberg is that his analyses come at the beginning of the moving picture era. If we can see the "disturbing implications" inherent in the silent black and white film experience of 1916, it should be easier for us to discern elements of the present day impact of the moving-image connection on the human organism, and hence on the new lust and pseudosexuality.

The following excerpts from Munsterberg's 1916 work that are not in quotation marks are my paraphrases or condensations, for brevity. Page references are to the 1970 Dover paperback edition. Comments in brackets are mine. As we discuss these excerpts from Munsterberg on film, note not only the parallels but the direct correlations between the psychology of lust we examined in chapter 4 and the psychology of the film experience. Quite amazing, if we think about it. How might these two psychologies correlate? What should become apparent is how the film-viewing experience may not only set us up for predisposition to pseudosexuality but may actually help shape our sexuality.

Mind-Bending

Munsterberg: The massive outer world loses its weight, is freed from space, time, and causality, and is clothed in the forms of our own consciousness. The mind triumphs over matter, and the pictures roll on with the ease of musical tones. It is a superb enjoyment which no other art can furnish us. No wonder that temples for the new goddess are built in every little hamlet. (page 95)

Implications: Note the correlation with the drug addict's experience! And the luster's. Don't all addicts wish to be freed from space, time, and causality, with mind triumphing over matter? That fits me to a T. And "temples"? "goddess"? Yes, there's a new religious connection here. Never mind our attraction to the sensuality and sexuality imbuing those early silent films; what is that spiritual power they have? All from the flickering nickelodeon, without sound and color!

Psychic Tsunami

> Munsterberg: The movies have become the most popular entertainment of the world, and their influence is one of the strongest social energies of our time. (page 93)

Implications: Mass entertainment is new in human history, requiring the mass media, a revolution in itself. And mass entertainment implies mass soul-set, a power shaping us collectively in every aspect of our lives, including sexuality. This is why film is *social energy* driving humankind. Munsterberg sees the power of that social energy since he himself admits to being affected. The power of this energy must lie in a force operating within us, so we may say that film is one of the strongest *spiritual* energies of our time. But of what kind, and to what effect?

> Munsterberg: As soon as the moving picture show had become a feature of the vaudeville theater, the longing of the crowd for ever new entertainments and sensations had to be satisfied if the success was to last. The mere enjoyment of the technical wonder as such necessarily faded away, and the interest could be kept up only if the scenes presented on the screen became themselves more and more enthralling. (page 8)

Implications: This principle continues to this day: For us to keep attending cinema, our longing for ever new sensations must be satisfied. A new appetite is created, an article of consumption is put on the market, and the supplier has to keep stimulating demand for the product by whetting the new appetite. But this product stimulates its own demand.

This sounds suspiciously like the tolerance principle in addiction, where more of the drug is required to maintain the initial effect. And this *longing for the enthralling* seems to have its own kind of "lust" written all over it. The craving is for more and more as our appetite becomes jaded. Today's shockers and "breakthroughs" are soon passé, and we let ourselves in for more with all the promised intensity of a new drug.

Munsterberg makes the observation that even in his day, 1916, "the camera men of the moving pictures . . . are always haunted by the fear that the supply of new sensations may be exhausted" (page 54). We could say the same about advertisers and pornographers. The point is that both movies and porn are image-driven, have become mass addictions, and therefore must supply increasingly varied and potent forms of the drug.

I suggest that the history of film reveals that it not only parallels and reflects but helps drive both the sexual and pseudosexual revolutions

Induced Propaganda

Munsterberg: "If we really enter into the spirit of the play, our attention is constantly drawn in accordance with the intentions of the producers. . . . [W]e must accept those cues for our attention which the playwright and the producers have prepared for us. . . . [A]ll play on the keyboard of our mind and secure the desired effect on our involuntary attention. . . ." (pages 32–36) It is as if that outer world were woven into our mind and were shaped not through its own laws but by the acts of our attention [controlled by the intent of the camera and film editor]. (page 39)

Implications: This involuntary attention principle might be called *the induced propaganda effect.* A consciousness alien to my own can be induced into me without my voluntary control. Now that's an expert psychologist speaking! And it can work for good or ill or whatever, depending on one's susceptibility. This is an incredibly powerful force affecting the human psyche. No wonder Munsterberg gave it religious power—"goddess" and "temples." If this isn't a religious force, what is it? It requires faith and risk, has its own gods and goddesses; is consciousness-changing, consciousness-inducing, life-changing; and commands and receives commitment and devotion.

Soul-set transference, more powerful than mind-set, is another way we might describe the psychology of the film experience. The soul-set communicated in the images is transferred directly into the viewer, without the viewer even realizing it. The most effective propaganda the world has ever known.

> Munsterberg: "The soul longs for this whole interplay . . . ." (page 45)

Implications: This longing of the soul is interesting terminology for a psychologist. Munsterberg's implication is that we can be hooked on things other than substances or behaviors. When I ask myself precisely what it is that I am hooked on in movies, I'm hard put to figure it out. This longing must be for something spiritual, but I don't know what it is, unless it might be substitute Life. The substitute is that which provides the feeling of "life" without the reality. Just like lust.

> Munsterberg: "A suggestion, on the other hand, is forced on us: The associated idea is not felt as our creation but as something to which we have to submit. . . . The spellbound audience . . . is certainly in a state of heightened suggestibility and is ready to receive suggestions." (pages 46–47) "The fact that millions are daily under the spell of the performances on the screen is established. The high degree of their suggestibility during those hours in the dark house may be taken for granted." (page 96)

Implications: Munsterberg uses the analogy of hypnosis to illustrate this concept of suggestibility. Are we dealing with something like the hypnagogic state here? Hypnagogic reverie is a dream-like state that can be induced by having the patient listen to the amplified sounds of his own breathing, for example. This trance-like state is characterized by heightened suggestibility.[116] Psychic lock-on occurs automatically; the person has no choice.

The director of the movie *JFK* tells us that, "We want to . . . get to the subconscious . . . and certainly seduce the viewer into a new perception of reality. . . ."[117] We need to think through the implications of such intent, such propagandizing. There seems to be an increasing awareness—and acceptance—of the power of film over the subconscious. It's almost as though we want to be changed by the experience. Hence the religious connotations, which we will look at later.

Just how much of our sexual attitudes and behavior is affected by the suggestibility inherent in the spell of the film experience? Are the addiction-prone like myself more susceptible, or are the effects simply felt more deeply than what "normies" would experience? Insights gained from withdrawal from the film experience may prove informative, as we shall see in the next chapter. The question is, do we realize the awesome power of a tool that has such direct access to the subconscious?[118] We are being targeted, affected, and changed—and of course, that includes our sexuality—*in an evolutionary progression of imperceptible increments over time.* I'm old enough to be a walking history of that evolution.

In a brilliant comparison of film and stage, Munsterberg summarizes the film experience:

> Munsterberg: "The color of the world has disappeared, the persons are dumb, no sound reaches our ear. The depth of the scene appears unreal, the motion has lost its natural character. . . . [T]he objective course of events is falsified; our own attention and memory and imagination have shifted and remodeled the events until they look as nature could never show them. What we really see can hardly be called any longer an imitation of the world, such as the theater gives us." (page 59)

Implications: If not an imitation of the world, what can film be called but a new reality, a manufactured reality, and thus a pseudo-reality? But doesn't all art create a new or pseudo reality; what's wrong with that? Nothing, unless it gets to the point where the human no longer has control over the involuntary suggestibility and is changed without his knowledge or will, where human freedom is lost. And who is to know when that happens, when such lines are crossed? That's precisely what happened in my sexual devolution.

Munsterberg's analysis of the film experience quoted above bears an uncanny resemblance to what goes on in lust in the "Anatomy of a Look" (chapter 4), as shown in the following paraphrase of his last quote, above:

> Details of the scene have disappeared, no sound reaches the ear. The depth of the scene appears unreal; motion has lost its natural

character. The objective reality of that person (the sex object) is falsified; the attention and memory and imagination have shifted and remodeled that reality until they look as nature could never show them.

What a perfect description of the subjective lust event! The film experience and lust event track perfectly! The point I am making about the human still- and moving-image connection is that regardless of the extent of our involvement, *all* of us are affected. This is irrespective of the content of what we happen to be watching or our value judgments; the content just takes it all further. This has special relevance to those of us who may try to recover from PS, but who will want to hear it?

Addiction

Munsterberg: "The work of art aims to keep both the demand and its fulfillment forever awake." (page 68)

Implications: Keeping demand and fulfillment forever awake is what lust and addiction are all about. They never satisfy. In our time, both the still and the moving-image connections seem to have come to the point where demand and fulfillment—sexual and otherwise—are kept forever awake. That was true in 1916; much more so now. This means that *fulfillment* keeps moving farther and farther beyond our reach.

In seeing how demand and fulfillment are kept forever awake, there's no better resource than *Communication Arts* magazine, the industry standard for "the very best in photography, illustration, design, and media." James Hilman Todd calls it "the style guide for people who manufacture desire" (Amazon.com, March 7, 2003). Perusing the whole range of back issues is to take a quick course in seeing how front-line image makers are the designers behind the whole advertising world. Competition within that image-communication industry spurs the ever-escalating manipulation of image to create desire, sell it, and keep it forever awake. The half-life of technique in these areas of photography, illustration, design and media keeps getting shorter and shorter as Lust seeks ever-new forms and faces.

Munsterberg: "This heightens the feeling of vitality in the spectator. He feels as if he were passing through life with a sharper accent which stirs his personal energies." (page 94)

Implications: Today, we call this a "high." Movies and lust both heighten the feeling of vitality. They give me a shot of "life," a great payoff. Pseudolife. Immersed in either, I feel more "alive" than at any other time. But that feeling is induced, simulated; it does not come out of reality. Instead, I seem to wind up with a *subtraction* of life (Sontag). The drug downer?

Psychic Infection

Munsterberg: "The intensity with which the plays take hold of the audience cannot remain without strong social effects. . . . The associations become as vivid as realities [I would say *more* vivid], because the mind is so completely given up to the moving pictures. . . ." There is strange fascination. ". . . [S]uch a penetrating influence must be fraught with dangers. The more vividly the impressions force themselves on the mind, the more easily must they become starting points for imitation and other motor responses. The sight of crime and of vice may force itself on the consciousness with disastrous results. [If he said this in 1916, what would he say today?] The normal resistance breaks down and the moral balance, which would have been kept under the habitual stimuli of the narrow routine life, may be lost under the pressure of the realistic suggestions. At the same time the subtle sensitiveness of the young mind may suffer from the rude contrasts between the farces and the passionate romances which follow with benumbing speed in the darkened house. The possibilities of psychical infection and destruction cannot be overlooked." If scenes of vice are shown with all their lure and glamour, the moral devastation of such a suggestive show is not undone by any moral social reaction tacked onto the film. (pages 95, 98) "It is not the dangerous knowledge which must be avoided, but it is the trivializing influence of a steady contact with things which are not worth knowing. The larger part of the film literature of today [1916] is certainly harmful in this sense." (page 97)

Implications: Whew! Whenever I read this passage I am struck. Sounds like he's talking about today's films. This describes the very essence of pseudosexuality. Images becoming as vivid as realities. Again, I would say *more* vivid than reality. The mind completely given up to it. Strange fascination. A penetrating influence. Impressions forcing themselves on the consciousness, starting points for imitation. Disastrous results. Normal resistance breaking down. Moral balance lost. Sensitiveness of the mind suffering. Psychical infection and destruction . . . Moral devastation.[119] Considering all this, may it not follow that one's film *connection* can in fact engender or foster predisposition to pseudosexuality?

> Munsterberg: The mind suppresses the ideas which are contrary to our secret wishes and makes those ideas flourish by which those "subconscious" impulses are fulfilled. (page 98)

Implications: If I understand him correctly here, Munsterberg is saying that we humans have secret wishes, subconscious impulses, which we normally keep under check, but that movies create a situation within us where inhibitors to those subconscious desires are lifted so that those secret wishes can be fulfilled. In other words, Munsterberg comes right out and says that movies are potent sources of subconscious (do we dare say spiritual?) *programming*—soul-set—something more change-inducing than mere propaganda.

PS paraphrase: *The film experience suppresses those personal sensibilities that would inhibit the sexual suggestions being shown and makes those ideas flourish that can fulfill them.*

Preachers, psychiatrists, and politicians would give an arm and a leg to have such power over humans as Munsterberg attributes to the *silent* film. Film is an instrument that facilitates changes in our thinking against whatever mores and morality we may bring into the theatre. Thus, whatever good there is that film portrays (and I suppose it must be capable of imaging the very best of humanity), it is also an infection carrier. A meme creator and meme carrier. It not only reflects the human condition, but *carries and induces* the human condition, of whatever sort, right into the unguarded soul of the viewer. *Induced attitudinal change.*

There are forces in our culture that are changing us.

The film experience, like lust, is a unique state of consciousness, artificially induced, with mood-altering and mind-altering effects. What we are seeing on the screen seems to bypass that which in the normal waking state of real life would be a conscious filtering mechanism, and what we see then becomes our own consciousness. The film experience is thus *an induced consciousness*. Well, sexual thinking is part of our consciousness—and is being changed!

Munsterberg the psychologist affirms that there is a part of human nature that is hidden, suppressed as it were by the conscious. In recovery we progressively discover hidden disorders of the self and see that that's where the work of recovery really lies, for that is what drives the conscious behaviors that seem so inexplicable. Munsterberg the discerning psychologist can be a great help to us here. Recovery from PS is more than we ever imagined. Who would want it but those who are hurting?

God-players

Those who have been moved to reflection as I have by Sontag's and Munsterberg's analyses are likely to be so affected as to start thinking about their own image connection. I would hope so. I was recently in a position to watch a film being made nearby over several days. I had no idea what a tedious and disjointed process film making is. Any given scene is made up of many different camera-angle setups. To show someone walking into a bedroom and reclining on a bed, for example, could have a sequence of many different takes: focusing only on the feet moving, then only on the clenched hands, then on the expression in the eyes of the actress while walking, then a shot from the bed looking up, then a shot from the ceiling looking down, etc. All transpiring in one fluid sequence on the screen. In a real situation, a human observer would be in only one place, viewing the actress walking to the bed from one angle, in one continuous motion. Not so film, with its infinite possibilities. Infinite is god-like.

The various camera shots are put together by director and editor to produce the desired effect on and in the viewer. The result is *super*-natural, creating something that transcends the natural. Author, director, cinematographer, cameraman, and editor are thus "Creators," with god-like power over the scene. And this puts the viewer in the seat of the gods, both high above it all and deep within it all. We are seeing things impossible to ordinary mortals. We experience god-like transcendence over the normal human limitations of space, time, and motion. And instead of the experience being a product of say, hallucinations, dreams, or ecstatic religious experiences, it is perceived as photographic "reality." No wonder the film-going experience is so mesmerizing! God-like control over the woman is exactly what our luster was doing in "Anatomy of a Look" (chapter 4). Power! Or rather, pseudo-power.

Question: Can the moving-image connection create not only predisposition to PS but induce it directly?

The history of film not only parallels and reflects but helps drive both the sexual and pseudosexual revolutions.

The Magic Dream Machine—Injected Consciousness

> Many people have noticed that watching a film is like having a dream. . . . The viewing conditions in the theater (such as the darkened room and the relative sense of isolation) are reminiscent of our solitary existence as dreamers alone in the night. The overpowering images on the screen sometimes frighten us and make us feel the same kind of paralysis we know in nightmares. In addition, films seem "real" in the way dreams do. . . .[120]

Robert Eberwein goes on to describe how our experience of film permits us to return to the infantile state where perceiver and what was perceived were fused as one. "We discover that *our* dream screen has been the site of another's dream screen. . . . that we have been linked to another consciousness. . . ."[121]

We now know that dreaming is a necessary part of normal learning, living, and coping; that we sleep in order to dream. In movies, however, it is not my own dream but another's. I have another consciousness "injected" into me without any defense against it because I'm in that dream-state. Thus, movies mess around with my subconscious and directly affect my own psychological, spiritual, and hence sexual processes and development. This is just the opposite of what I experience in good human relations in my PS recovery—an integrative *finding* of my life—my life.

In the moving-image experience, I'm letting myself be affected by an alien consciousness, by whatever the spirit is that is being communicated. And this is what seems to carry the most imprinting, an invisible effect of which I am unaware and against which I am rather defenseless. To me, this spirit is often not in tune with what I have come to want for myself, even when the subject matter of the film is benign. I get the feeling that for me this whole experience creates a *spirit-set* in some direction other than what my natural recovery wants to take—that my moving-image-connection is part of my problem.

. . .

Can you now feel the emotion behind creation of the T-shirt slogan on cinema opening this chapter? Even a judgmentally neutral observer will have to admit that whatever else there is, REALITY ENDS HERE. Thus there appear to be direct correlations between elements of the lust/pseudosexual process and the psychology of the still- and moving-image experiences. And the moving-image connection is another factor involved in inducing predisposition for the lust/pseudosexual process.

THE NEW IMAGE RELIGION

"If mankind be itself God, the appearance
of the idol is then inevitable."
Karl Barth[122]

Had Hugo Munsterberg been around when television appeared, he would have been the first to observe that the "temple of the goddess" had moved from the movie theater into the home.

Television

> *... [T]he problem of the twenty-first century is the problem of the image. ... Everyone knows that television is bad for you and that its badness has something to do with the passivity and fixation of the spectator.[123]*
>
> *There are roughly as many studies showing that television rots the mind as there are studies showing that junk food rots the body or that cigarette smoking rots the lungs—as if we needed studies.[124]*

There are those who have asked why I didn't hit television harder. But it should be obvious that everything we've been saying about the moving image connection applies to television. One statement from a *Time* magazine essayist, suggesting decriminalization of drugs, speaks volumes: "Then there's TV, the addiction whose name we can hardly speak—the poor man's virtual reality, the substance-free citizen's 24-

hour-a-day hallucinatory trip. No bleary-eyed tube addict, emerging from weekend-long catatonia, has the right to inveigh against "drugs."[125] Listen to a reviewer talk about a modern play about television:

> Just as we stare in horror at the chain-smoking habits of Hollywood's 1940s movie stars, future generations may look back at our television-obsessed behavior and gasp, "Didn't they realize it was killing them? Couldn't Americans at the end of the 20th century see that TV is physically addictive?" . . . Like victims of the quiz show hoaxes, we're still reeling from the power of an unknown new God called television.[126]

The answers to life's problems aren't at the bottom of a bottle. They're on TV![127]

The Unreality Industry

A book with a highly intriguing title came out in 1989 called *The Unreality Industry, The Deliberate Manufacturing of Falsehood and What It Is Doing to Our Lives*. Its thesis is that the deliberate creation of unreality is one of the most pivotal social forces shaping our time. "For all practical purposes, reality has lost out. A pervading, powerful sense of unreality infiltrates the land. Unreality has become in effect our primary mode of reference."[128] Evidence is produced to show that our energy as a modern society is drifting into the mass proliferation of unreality and that television is a potent force in this national flight. "The primary purpose of TV is not to inform or to educate, and even strangely enough not to entertain, but to keep the viewer from switching [channels] by holding his or her attention. But to do this requires a never-ending series of quick, almost totally unrelated, attention grabbers. . . . The result . . . can be devastating."[129]

   While still a slave to television, I remember an interview between Eric Sevareid, premier news analyst for CBS, and Robert Maynard Hutchins, one of the great thinkers of our time, president and then chancellor of the University of Chicago, editor of the *Great Books of the Western World*, and author of such books as *The Higher Learning in America, Education for Freedom*, and *The Conflict in Education.*

The interview was on the impact of television. I remember one of Dr. Hutchins' statements verbatim: "Television is making us what we are."

Eric Sevareid then asked Dr. Hutchins if *he* watched television. Dr. Hutchins hesitated briefly, then admitted that yes, he did watch it. Sevareid smiled discreetly as though thinking, Well, you too, eh!

The modern *image-connection* is making us what we are.[130]

Apparently the moving-image *connection*—whether television, movies, videos, or cyberspace—is an undisputed way of life for increasing millions. One comment from a cable television installer sums it up:

> I could have gone in there and muddied their new carpet, beat their dog, and broken their favorite piece of china, but when they saw all those 37 channels come in, they'd have thanked me for it.[131]

One reader who thought I was too hard on movies asked, "Are you saying that when I walk out of a movie theatre I'm toast?" No. What I am saying is that when I walk out of a movie theatre or watch television I feel gratified and filled! I've partaken of a hearty repast, consumed something highly satisfying. But I'm also saying that while under that influence, I've been subjected unawares to the most powerful propaganda process known to man. I don't have answers for anyone, including myself. What I'm trying to do is see what's really going on. So let's briefly look at all this from some other angles.

It is said that evolution now has shifted from random genetic mutation to being man-made and media-driven. If true, that is incredibly powerful! What is the teleology of this new evolutionary force; that is, where is it going, that evolving image of psychic man? Where is it taking us? If we are made in the image of God, in whose (what) image is man remaking man?

Splinters to the Brain

In the cartoon shown below, Calvin feels that one of the characteristic phenomena of our mediated existence is a "barrage of non-linear free association."

CALVIN AND HOBBES By Bill Watterson   March 22, 1993

In the history of movies, for example, it seems to me that the interval between shots (a shot is a unit of action constituting a single camera view) has consistently decreased so that to linger on any shot for even ten seconds is now passé. In television commercials, movie previews, MTV, and movies like *JFK*, instead of one shot every several seconds, we now often get several shots per second! The impact on human suggestibility may be why the ad makers resort to it in their commercials. For myself, I can't tolerate this rapid shifting of images. It is immediately unsettling. No wonder people are beginning to wonder where attention deficit disorder comes from.[132]

The director of *JFK* calls this rapid shifting of images "splinters to the brain," a very apt designation. But even the highly precocious Calvin misses the real point here. The question is, What effect does this have on human psychology and the human spirit?

It is obvious that this hyperkinetic technique in no way reflects life or reality. Life does not proceed in millisecond jumps. Life is analog, not digital. It flows. What Calvin calls the "barrage" is a deliberately induced neurological state preventing our switching channels and keeping us glued to the tube. But it's more; it keeps the mind in the *trance state*, with reason and intelligence shunted out so we are more suggestible.

The New Voyeurism—Peepers Welcome

Behind all of this is something even more potent: such voyeuristic glimpses lower the threshold of what is unacceptable to us (Sontag).

Suppose I'm watching a movie preview—"approved for all audiences"—a teaser to get me to buy the picture. In being neurologically attached to that image-barrage, I am unwittingly seduced into quick peeks into the "forbidden." The peek technique itself—regardless of the image on the screen—tells me it is forbidden. And there's no way I can avoid it, because I don't know what's coming! I'm peeking at something I normally would not unabashedly look at or drink in. Thus, the peek technique in the media seduces me into opening myself to the unacceptable. Without warning, the screen flashes the crotch of someone we thought was a woman. We initially are shocked that she is really a man, but days, weeks, and months later we find ourselves replaying that peek with less and less inhibition. In street parlance, a "peeper" is a peeping Tom.

Since I saw it portrayed in the public temple of the goddess (Munsterberg's term for the movie house), I'm given religious permission to peek; it's no longer unacceptable to think about it, and my mind toys with the idea entertainingly. (Isn't that what entertainment/advertising is?) There is a psychological principle at work here that is powerfully effective in "inventing desire."[133] Today's moving-image connection is the great leveler of the so-called religious and sinners alike. There are no saints in the movie theater! Or on the TV couch. We are all voyeurs.

Look at the preview's rapid succession of shots—quick glimpses of the leg show, sex shots, violence, or whatever. So quick it's like what we lusters do when conning ourselves: "I'll take only the quickest glance to see if it's something I shouldn't be looking at." Voyeurs in spirit if not in letter. Venial instead of mortal. In Susan Sontag's words, our relation to photographs is setting up a "chronic voyeuristic relation to the world." And with moving pictures, we have no choice but to peek because it's the camera that is doing the peeking, and *we're captive to whatever the camera is peeking at!* We don't know it's coming and can't help seeing it! Without conscious intent or even awareness, we are forced into being peepers! What my conscience would not normally let me gaze at, can be allowed for a split second. *But that split second lowers the threshold, and that's me letting it in in that split second!* Induced voyeurism.

At our next movie, we might as well cast a playbill heading over all of it in flashing neon: WELCOME PEEPERS ANONYMOUS! We're going to be peeping in on some of the most private and intimate scenes men and women will ever experience and many no one wants to experience. And it's not only all right, it's why we're all sitting there in the dark. We don't discover life—or sex—on life's terms any more, naturally, experientially, slowly, in life's own time and pace; we're force-fed it all at once, often against our will. And how we love it and beg for more! This is pseudo-life. How can our sexuality not be affected?

Seduction of the Subconscious—The New Fascism

The movie *JFK* initiated a storm of controversy. Seldom had there been such a flood of editorial opinion expressed, both pro and con, on a new film. A Rutgers professor of communications observed

> [The co-author and director of *JFK*] is quite direct about his intention and his ability to massage our minds in whatever directions he chooses. "What's interesting about the movie," the director says, is that "it's one of the fastest movies. . . . It's like splinters to the brain. We have 2,500 cuts in there, I would imagine. We had 2,000 camera setups. We're assaulting the senses . . . in a sort of a new-wave technique. We admire MTV editing technique and we make no bones about using it. We want to . . . *get to the subconscious . . . and certainly seduce the viewer* into a new perception of reality. . . . [emphasis added]"[134]

By now the words "get to the subconscious" and "seduce the viewer" should be making us squirm. We're far beyond confining the issue to whether art reflects or molds the culture, or vice versa; we're talking about psychic surgery, or worse yet, psychic contagion. Can we begin to see even some of the role all this has in propagating the lust virus and driving the PS revolution?

The film director goes on to say that "Ultimately, *JFK* is not really a political film. The ultimate questions are philosophical ones: Who owns reality? Who owns your mind?"[135] That's the film director talking. These are awesome statements that should raise a flag in the mass consciousness! Is there any question as to whose minds this film maker has tried to own, whom he wants to seduce? Are these idle boasts, or is this new tool capable of such soul-infecting power? Has anyone psychoanalyzed these producers and directors? What are they up to? These may be extreme cases, but the techniques and intent are common to all. It's the nature of the beast.

This director knows better than most of us what is possible with this modern propaganda tool. His new wave has already hit and will probably keep advancing. His television debut mini-series was described as "mind-bending mayhem." It was called "disorienting" and "a paranoid dream play that bombards us," "a consistent mood of subtle menace." The director himself said, "I like the concept of television taking over our reality. . . . I like the concept of a man who does not recognize his reality anymore, who sees every prop in his reality removed and deconstructed. . . ."[136] Psychic fascism.

This "seduction of the subconscious"—can we limit it to Oliver Stone-type movies, or is the principle an intrinsic characteristic of the moving-image experience? We would do well to ponder the ramifications of such direct access to the subconscious, its seduction of the viewer, and how this affects all human attitudes and behavior. And we're not even talking about sexual content here. What we are talking about is human freedom. Spiritual freedom. Or lack of it. Today's moving-image generators are Meme Machines, churning out templates for the viewer's subconscious. I for one want the freedom to be me, and I'm more and more willing to pay the price for it and find something better. But it's too tough trying to do this alone; it would take a recovering community.

The New Propaganda

I think Hugo Munsterberg would have said that film is the superb art form, surpassing all others in capability and expression. But by virtue of that fact, it is also the medium most suitable to communicating, transferring, and injecting practically any state or condition into the human psyche and soul. It is thus the most effective vehicle for propaganda, influencing changes in attitudes and behaviors and affecting personal, cultural, and sexual mores. And our sexuality itself.

How do we really know if or when we're in control of our innermost defenses? What has more control over my subconscious, the movie or me? This is where Sontag and Munsterberg hit a nerve.

It seems film can drive me to change negatively, but can it not also drive me to change positively? I don't know. I have felt uplifted by "good" movies. Is there not healing mediated therein—human parables, storytelling that makes me look deeper into a reflection on the human in very positive ways? Cinema certainly produces these *feelings*. But have I really become any better? I think not. For me it was just like walking out of many a religious service, *feeling* all inspired, ennobled, and uplifted. But not changed! As a matter of fact, I see now that my pathology was being covered over, hidden more deeply! I only temporarily *felt* good.

Question: Can even the feeling of transcendent goodness short-circuit our slow, natural, pain-driven growth toward real goodness that recovery pulls us toward? As one reader put it, *"Becoming a voyeur of goodness does not make me good."*

Moving-picture art—are we sure that's all we want to call it now?—no longer merely reflects life; it is the most powerful tool in human history to shape life. It is difficult to grasp the awesome significance of the fact that the expression of just one person's inner soul—that which communicates his or her weird form of lust, for example—can be captured via these media, intensified through fantastic technology, and injected right into the soul-set of millions, with life- and culture-changing results.

Idolatry and the New Paganism

Is there a connection between pseudosexuality and idolatry? An idol is thought by the believer to have power over her or his life. The icon is honored, done obeisance to, offered sustenance. And the believer gets something in return that confirms his commitment and keeps him coming back. Some ancient has said, *"We worship what we cannot live without."* There is no secret about what we do obeisance to today and cannot live without. Just imagine the millions of Americans who are this very hour sitting passively before their television, movie, or monitor screens, with their souls open to the spirit of the age, all the while feeling they're just being entertained. That's the new paganism underlying American life today, in both the religious and the secular.

There's a false-worship revolution going on—with both irreligious and religious bowing to the same altar!

This idolatry is not limited to the sexual experience. Vastly more insidious and pervasive is the influence of the mediated personalities, lifestyles, and attitudes that take the place of and shut out the real Life connection. Whatever else today's image connection is, it has become a religious ritual mediating the new religion of Pseudo-Life.

Ours today is not only the image illness, it *is the image religion.* The director of *JFK* and *Natural Born Killers* himself says that ". . . [T]he new god is 'image.'"[137] This is a new and universal religion, with more power over us than anything we normally call religion. The Higher Power that is served has the power to give us transcendent feelings of change on the inside—"highs"—and give us what we want: escape; to medicate; surrogate experience of the strange, the new and unattainable; and the freedom to desire, want, have, and take. The medium is the message. And the Gospel we surrender to is salvation by the baptism of psychic immersion. We exchange Life for the spirit of pseudo-life.

CALVIN AND HOBBES By Bill Watterson   October 8, 1990

As a religious force, this requires faith and risk, has its own gods and goddesses; is consciousness-inducing, life-changing; and commands and receives commitment and devotion. Due to its marvelous effectiveness, entertainment value, and consciousness-changing magic, we sit captive in the pagan Sanctuary of Image and Sound, seduced to feelings of transcendence and pseudo-life, which hide our true condition and great loss.[138]

At this point, the reader may ask, "What about truly good shows and movies? Seeing some films can be a very positive, constructive experience. Why just look at such-and-such." I've been there too and feel the force of this. I'm not disputing the possibility of real value in the moving-image encounter. Film can be truly artistic, educational, and profoundly affecting, leaving one with a *feeling* of transcendent goodness. *The Red Shoes* comes to mind. They reflect the true human condition in an uplifting manner and are universally acclaimed. One could list many examples of the finest of movie fare.

But I'm not evaluating movie content or value; that speaks for itself. I'm simply taking Munsterberg one step further. I am trying not only to assess the impact of the moving-image experience on the human organism, but especially its role in predisposing individuals and the culture to pseudosexuality. I am asking the hard question, even when content is totally innocent and ennobling: For many of us, is there a hidden price to pay, not for watching movies, but for our personal moving-image *connection*? Not just the effects that the subject matter may or may not have, *but the very Connection itself*—the life-connection we've established with this medium.

I am asserting that there appear to be direct correlations between the psychology of the moving image experience and the psychology of lust. *There is every reason to believe that the new image-connection across the board may create not only a predisposition to the new lust and PS but can induce attitude changes and soul-set supporting them.*

To illustrate the power of this connection, let's see how all this theory plays out in a personal experiment.

A PERSONAL EXPERIMENT

My own experience with television and movies as it relates to recovery is checkered—but very informative. By the time I had graduated from high school in 1945, I had seen only two or three feature films. When I was a boy, we went to a Sonja Henie film once, since Mother had always wanted to ice skate. All I remember of that film was the final scene where Sonja and the male star retreat to the bedroom and the door closes behind them. That aroused me and stuck with me. Even though I didn't know what was going on in there, the scene had FOR-BIDDEN written all over it—intense desire. Imprinting.

A vampire movie at high school graduation was the only other one I remember. Although we were not made aware of it, we were raised in poverty, and besides, it was during the Great Depression. I think I began going to movies more in the sixties, and resorted to them regularly from then on. They became part of my "liberated" lifestyle. Both before and well into recovery, I even sought out the avant-garde in movies, including underground and student films, shown after midnight at the end of the regular playbill. I thought every bold new film experience was "life." This is where it's really at, I thought.

Some years into sex and lust recovery, however, my reaction to watching both television and movies began getting my attention. In looking back over my journals, I see that I started agonizing over how I was being affected by them. Periodically I tried stopping both and discovered that I felt better abstaining. Then the on-again-off-again cycle got to the point of "swearing off," just like alcoholics do with alcohol, and as I had done so many times with lust-sex. Becoming more aware of withdrawal symptoms over the years eventually convinced me that

I must be hooked on both movies and television. The late renowned film critic Pauline Kael used to say, "You have to be open to the idea of getting drunk on movies."[139]   That fits me to a T, a movie-show junkie. Frankly, driving by one of those movie multiplexes has more of a pull on my insides, even today, than passing a strip joint. Eventually, I stopped watching television, but continued the on-again-off-again affair with movies. Finally, I also stopped watching movies.

For some reason, which I don't recall, after some years of total abstinence I began going to movies again; at first, occasionally, then more often. It turns out I had unwittingly been performing an experiment. I had gone through complete moving-image withdrawal (television, video, and movies) for a long enough period of time so that my system had been "cleaned out" (*detoxed?*) and I never thought about it any more. Then, letting it back in, I could see and isolate the effects within me that the experience produced. Perhaps moving-image abstinence helped in discerning its effects, just as sexual abstinence had helped in discerning the nature and effects of lust in the "Anatomy of a Look." Delving into the subconscious and penetrating the psyche's own defenses was part of a searching and fearless inventory I found necessary for my own awakened self-interest. I found there was honest data waiting there that I could get in no other way.

Without realizing it, I found myself in the same position Hugo Munsterberg found himself in 1916, having to look inside his own psyche and see what was really going on. This may help shed additional light on the role the moving-image connection may play in facilitating and driving PS.

I speak only for myself, one with an addictive personality, one who has discovered through experience how susceptible he is to the effects of various cultural forces. What leads me to include this is hearing hundreds over the years share how they too are discovering their need for recovery in this area. I'm still wrestling with my own solutions and seek dialog with others seeking theirs.

Here are some effects I jotted down after having watched a PG-rated movie once I began resorting to the flicks again. I did this long before beginning the research that led to this book and before reading Hugo Munsterberg. (Comments in brackets were added in subsequent editing.)

- Watching gives me a sense of life. Whether it's gazing into the image of a pretty woman or just being captive to the stream of sensations, I somehow feel "better." But it is artificial life; it's not my own. The sense of life is comparable to taking an "upper," such as caffeine or sugar. But then I'm let back down and wind up wanting more.
- I feel as though I have actually *lived* what I was watching. I feel it is happening to me, that I am relating to this woman, that I am being chased by the bad guy, that I am vindicated in the end and win. Often, I feel good, energized. I have the *feeling* of really living life, of being *alive*. But it's not real. I always wind up with my own emptiness, needing to resort to the flicks again to fill the lack. Like eating certain foods; they taste so good, but I'm hungry again soon after.
- The simulation displaces the real. Yet I feel I've gained the reality of "life." But this feeling passes away; I've gained nothing. That's the great delusion, because it *feels* so real, more real than real experience. After a while, that immediate feeling of gain turns into a feeling of loss. I'm loving something contrary to me. [The one thing a PS like me cannot afford to do is separate himself from the reality of himself. That's what used to happen during masturbation.] More and more in recovery—not always—I want the abiding reality of myself, the serenity of just being me.
- This experiencing of another reality gives me the feeling of having "found" myself, whereas afterward I feel as though I've actually lost something of my self. What price Entertainment! But wait a minute— I go supposedly for entertainment, but for me, read that as *escape*. But this isn't escape; it's just the opposite. This is being held captive to something, the influence of which is impossible to escape and that changes me, affects me in ways I don't want to be affected! What kind of escape is this?
- Watching movies, I have the experience of actually possessing it all. I feel I wind up actually taking that world into me somehow. I'm experiencing the world as I never would be able to otherwise. It is not my world, but I feel as though I'm actually *having* that world. [But as with Sontag's observations on still photos, am I not being possessed by it?]

- I don't just watch as a disinterested investigator or observer; I seem forced into it or captive to it, even when I don't like and reject what I'm seeing! [I envy movie critics who can apparently (?) escape this effect.]
- Apparently I've developed an appetite for this moving-image-reality that must be fed. If this is a new appetite we humans have created [Munsterberg], then I've got it. I see now that I misuse it; I seem unable to do otherwise, but I keep trying to "control and enjoy." [Like a compulsive overeater or alcoholic.] This is but another indication that this may be addictive for me. The drug effect or "high," or whatever, tapers off in a day or so, leaving me wanting it again. I see now, writing about this two days removed from the last movie, that this feeling of wanting to go to a movie again—any movie—is my simply *wanting another fix*. Often, even brief exposure automatically sets up the craving for more. Even when I'm fully aware it is happening. Does that exposure access and trigger conditioned responses related to my social intercourse with others? But there's nobody there! I'm still all alone. Am I being cheated? What kind of mentality am I developing?
- This seems to be some sort of ingestion. How can ingesting *images* make me feel nourished? But what am I really getting? I notice when channel surfing on television, that I seem to be trying to connect with something that satisfies. The only way I can describe the effect is that it's some kind of spiritual *connection* I'm getting. An ingestion of the spirit? But it doesn't really satisfy because I keep having to repeat it, looking for "more." [There's something *pseudo-* going on here.]
- Watching often seems to induce anxiety. And then, more of the drug is sought to decrease the anxiety! Why anxiety? Typically, I find myself wanting to keep eating something. Does this suggest that my viewing really is an ingesting, and therefore "craving circuits" have been triggered or enabled? [The television viewing and eating connection is well recognized.]

CALVIN AND HOBBES By Bill Watterson   June 23, 1993

- Watching shuts out all my own feelings and thoughts—like a drug, a sedation, like the nirvana or dream state I experienced when I first started masturbating. Only now, my feelings and thoughts are replaced by those induced from the movies. No wonder I don't want—can't tolerate—any distractions while in that trance! [I'm downloading something into me.]

- Watching for me does seem to be a form of "copulating with the world, psychic intercourse with everything" [Sontag]. Why is my soul so open to moving images, especially in a darkened theater? Can it open me up to lust, even when the images are not erotic? For me, I think it can.

- I seem to want a periodic dose of that world—the sensate, the forbidden, the larger-than-life, the un-God. What does this tell me about my lack of real Connection?

- That evening and the next day I felt separated from the inner peace and Presence [I don't realize that until it is gone]. There's a feeling of sad loss. A substitute presence has filled me. I'm full of the images I've ingested that have become part of me and gave brief satisfaction. During meditation that evening and the next morning my mind is full of the images and keeps drifting back to them, whether those images are benign or not. I am powerless over keeping them out of my mind. They keep playing back. [The same happens with certain passages of music. And here again, I speak only for myself, trying "clinically" to see what's going on inside me.]

- I feel sullied and unclean, even though I haven't lusted sexually, and not necessarily because of the subject matter. Just being exposed to that alien world seems to have such a lingering effect within me. Why? Even when all the images in a movie are totally benign, I still feel something has gone out of me, that in being possessed by those images, I've been cheated of myself and filled with something foreign.

- Why does being filled with the spirit of even a good person or scene up there on the screen later feel like loss ["subtraction from the self," as Sontag would suggest]? Could it be because the experience is playing tricks on my nervous system? The moving-image experience stimulates those sensory areas and programmed neuronal networks of the brain to produce the sensations of real experience *without the live encounter of real personal experience*. The simulation of life is more than perfect; it is super-real. Even feelings of goodness can be elicited—but without the goodness itself! I'm not a better *person* as a result.

  The simulation of reality is part of the burgeoning pseudo-reality in our world. Is it simulated spirit? Counterfeit spirit? Am I a double loser, not only having deprived myself of real human intercourse, but having been tricked into the sensation that the substitute is the real? And is my capacity for knowing and having the real diminished?

- [I felt myself coming down with a virus and made the decision to "watch TV." I channel-surfed from 6 P.M. to 12:30 A.M. Friday night. I went to bed feeling I'd been in a mad house: unrelated and disconnected snatches of scenes, commercials, and sounds. Kaleidoscopic dismemberment. A mind having lost all grip on reality and thrown into chaos. And very addictive. I didn't want to stop. What happens when we spend more time absorbing the spirits we open our souls to than in real human intercourse of our own choosing? How are we changed?]

When I look at the evidence of my own experience and hear the stories of increasing numbers of others, I see that this innocent tool has also become the most potent *carrier* of the PS virus—the virus that disables our immune systems and leaves us diminished and crippled at the heart of our interface with others. We need identification and conversation here. If you've ever wondered about what the moving-image connection may be doing to you, why not try the experiment on yourself? We need more case histories from those who wrestle with this whole issue.[140] (Ref. Appendix 6, Image-Connection and Our Relational Capability.)

. . .

To summarize Part III: We should now see that what we have in today's total Image-Connection—whether still or moving, large screen or small—is one of the most significant forces shaping our character and sexuality and driving the PS revolution. The stark realization may begin to dawn as to why pseudosexuality and our addiction to lust are so widespread and all-encompassing, have become so much the very fabric of our lives, and are seemingly so impossible to overcome. This is a significant factor in keeping many of us from the deeper life that is our birthright as humans and what increasing numbers of us in recovery crave.

PART IV
OTHER FORCES DRIVING PSEUDOSEXUALITY

In Part III we have been talking about predisposition to pseudosexuality mediated by mankind's new image-connection; but this is merely the visible tip of the iceberg. We now turn our attention to a few other, less obvious factors. These will represent but a fraction of those that might also be considered, such as the technological, advertising, and entertainment revolutions; the population explosion; the medicalization of society; globalization and personal mobility; consumer capitalism; the American Dream; momism;[141] popular music; and City as a force all its own. Volumes could be written on how popular music and popular novels not only reflect pseudosexuality but help drive and shape it.

And what of modern man's audio connection, his audio ecology? Even with only three percent of our brain's neurons processing sound, there's an incalculable impact that the sonic media have upon us—radio, records, tapes, CDs, etc., not to mention the whole new sound experience tied in with the moving image. We're immersed in a world of unnatural sound. This is not to mention factory and traffic noise, airplanes, household appliances, and the omnipresent 60- or 50-cycle hum permeating our electrical world. What is the effect of the constant barrage of sounds in which we live, first the effects of the sounds

themselves on the human organism, and then the effects of their content? And lest we fail to see it, the audio media are also carriers of
the psycho-spiritual force field and lust virus. Increasingly we cannot
seem to live without immersing ourselves in the audio-visual womb of
World-System.

Is there a price we're paying for this? My life without media-ted
sounds not of my choosing is too precious. Just today I had to spend a
few hours proofing typesetting at a design agency and found the background music was too distracting. After enduring it much longer than
I should have, I finally asked them for a quiet room so I could concen-
trate. Try to limit the unnatural inputs to your life and you may begin
to appear to others as a freak.

We will bypass these and many other important topics and focus
on the reality revolution (continued), great ideological shifts from
Darwin to Kinsey; the death of father; and the death of God—all powerful forces helping to set the stage for and to drive pseudosexuality.

FROM APE-MAN TO *PLAYBOY*

The most significant thing in the last half-century has been the dramatic expansion in personal freedom and personal mobility, individual rights, the reorienting of culture around individuals.

John Q. Wilson in Time, August 23, 1993

The Shift to a Self-Centered Center of Gravity

The center of gravity of man's encounter with the realm of mystery and danger has shifted from nature—his wonder of earth and sky—to the self. "Not the animal world, not the plant world, not the miracle of the spheres, but man himself is now the crucial mystery."[142]

This shift to an anthropocentric center of gravity has had increasingly dehumanizing results. Individualism has its flip side; not all is well with the American Dream. When we lose our connection with the rest of the cosmos, we get lost inside ourselves and actually lose part of our humanity. Today science and psychology are racing into man with increasing speed. As knowledge about man increases explosively, it becomes too much for anyone to comprehend, much less bear, and the concept of man becomes fragmented into a thousand scientific specialties, so that in our expanding universe of knowledge about man, we have lost *Man*.

185

That searching after God by the prehistoric and ancient peoples is now the pursuit of Science, though she may not admit to such, where there may be as much or more awe and reverence for the creation than will be found for the Creator behind

stained glass organ choirs
and pulpiteering vanity.

The paradox is that when we seek and see only ourselves, we lose ourselves. We become self-centered and self-obsessed. Our sexuality is directly affected, because *self-centered sex is pseudo-sex*. Self-obsession could well be the name of our societal as well as personal and sexual sickness. Self-obsession—addiction to the self—is one of the symptoms of pseudosexuality. And it leads to the disintegration of man.

. . . [I]t was never meant for you to live in the consciousness of self,
and no man can live in that, but must go mad, but must turn in
and in upon himself until he goes mad or goes out of being.

George MacDonald

Reality Shifts, Continued

In Part III we touched on the reality revolution involving reading, photography, and the moving image, forces directly bearing on cultural and personal predisposition to pseudosexuality. But of course that's only part of the story; reality seems to keep shifting, dragging us along willy-nilly. Appearing in the midst of the ongoing industrial revolution—the most impactful in the history of the human race and now accelerating more than ever—are ideological revolutions of such power that they have changed the very concept of reality and shattered man's concept of himself. To get a feel for these intangible revolutions within the revolution, let's take a brief glimpse at the work of only four men, Darwin, Freud, Einstein, and Kinsey, whose ideas struck our world as gigantic asteroids from outer space, altering the ideological atmosphere and driving changes in man's spiritual, social, and sexual evolution.

Darwin. Charles Darwin died in 1882, but his revolutionary *Origin of Species* hit the world in the middle of the 19th century like a cataclysmic earthquake, more like a planet-wide shift in the tectonic plates. All the ideological fault lines loosened. What would later be called "evolution" claimed that "species originate by descent, with variations, from parent forms, through the natural selection of those individuals best adapted from the reproductive success of their kind." We are still experiencing the aftershocks. The effect of this sea change in man's concept of himself is that he is perceived as diminished and powerless, just another element in the infinite gradation of species stretching back into the past millions of years and forward into a changing and unknown future. Man is relative to a blind force called natural selection that he can neither see nor comprehend, yet which is inexorably driving him along an uncertain path to Anywhere. Which really means Nowhere.

Freud. Sigmund Freud died in 1939, and although psychoanalysis may not be as popular as it once was—psychological knowledge is in continual motion too; small wonder, considering the subject—his view of man had revolutionary impact. We and our sexuality will never be the same. Evolution reduces man's biological being to the product of unseen forces acting over mind-boggling eons of time; and now his psyche—his very inner self and identity—is reduced to "systematic structures involving the relation of conscious and unconscious psychological processes." You mean all I really am is the interaction of conscious and unconscious processes, genetically driven at that? Can you see how we begin losing our concept of self, and because of that loss, shift to our *selves* all the more?

Of special significance is Freud's impact in the area of sex and morals. He concluded that a basic cause of much of the world's neurosis was repressed sexuality, and the way to be emotionally healthy and be rid of crippling inhibitions was to express our sexual instincts freely.[143] ". . . Freudian theory pervaded the advice of newspaper columnists, the creation of advertising campaigns, the training of social workers, and the everyday lives of millions who came to know an unresolved Oedipus complex, a 'Freudian slip,' or an anal character when they saw one. . . . What really won popularity was Freud's pansexualism, translated into religious terms by Americans like G. Stanley Hall (1844–1924)."[144] (Hall is credited with being most influential in establishing the new science

of psychology in the United States) Pansexualism is the theory that all
human behavior is based on sexuality.

Freud's concepts infiltrated the middle-class imagination: the
notion of infantile sexuality, the drama of sexual conflict in the family, the case histories of female patients who seemed to suffer from the
denial of their sexual desires, and the idea that the sexual instinct per-
meated human life and might change the course of civilization. (Some
would argue that the course of civilization has thus been changed.)
Above all, Americans absorbed a version of Freudianism that presented
the sexual impulse as an insistent force demanding expression.[145] It is
interesting to note that Freud himself, however, voluntarily went into
total sexual abstinence at about the age of forty, which apparently continued until the end of his life.[146] Paradoxically, Freud viewed masturbation as "the primary addiction," "the great sin," "the original sin" and
admonished his own son against it.[147]

Freudian psychology paved the way for not only the Kinsey
report but also the sexual revolution. What was changing because of
Freud was man's concept of himself. The question, What is man? was
answered in the post-Freudian world by the new concept that man
is primarily a sexual being, the product of unconscious psychological processes. Freud opened the sex door in modern society. Popular
conception of Freudian thought is that physical sexual pleasure, or satisfaction, is critical to human happiness.[148] The self is sexual; man is
subject to blind instinct.

Einstein. Albert Einstein died in 1955, but the mind-set he created lives
on. His concept of the relativity of space, time, and mass has already
affected every branch of human endeavor and knowledge. The more
we delve into subatomic physics, astrophysics, and quantum mechan-
ics, the more we sense an uncertainty principle underlying everything.
What is space? What is time? What is matter? What is light? What
is *life*? The more we know, the less we know about the most fundamental questions of human existence. The universe of knowledge is an
expanding universe.

> Could no one see or guess that there is no end to knowledge as
> Technique? The Ultimate Tool! That it leads man deeper, further,

on and on? There is no end to splitting the atom; there is no end
to comprehending the universe. And there is no end to man!

Knowledge itself is the expanding universe, racing outward
at the speed of light, pulling man on, beguiling him, teasing him,
tempting him, dangling its fabulous fruit ever beyond reach but
seemingly ever more within reach. Because each bit of knowledge
is another tool with which man can gain more knowledge, to give
him more tools to gain more knowledge, so he can— So he can
what?! Lust, Professor. Man lusting after the fruit 'Of that forbidden tree. . . .' trying to sustain himself on the fruit of his own
Ego, the Tree of Knowledge, the great Lure of the universe. Not
knowledge in itself—man's unique and glorious birthright—but
Knowledge as Savior, man's nemesis! . . . .

Man, racing into Knowledge, the great escape mechanism, the ultimate ego addiction. But racing from what? From
himself![149]

We're up against the relativity of all knowledge—the enticing illusion of knowing everything, but the impossibility of *knowing* anything.
We shall never comprehend the universe. And we shall never comprehend man. We move farther away from reality rather than closer. And
Man is demolished, a strange quark, a lost particle appearing for an
instant as a vanishing trace on the cloud chamber of life.

Today, the mystery of man himself is gone, atomized into a particu-
laristic infinity. Demolished Man is his name. So why not *dis*-integrate?
With nothing higher than ourselves, and obsessed with ourselves, our
sexuality and relationships fail to outgrow masturbatory adolescence. We
remain trapped in an aborted and pseudosexual adolescence. My story.

Kinsey. The strongest assault on sexual reticence in the public realm
emerged not from the pornographic fringe, nor from popular culture,
but from the respectable domain of science. The publication of Alfred
Kinsey's reports on sexuality of the human male and female in 1948
and 1953 respectively propelled sex into the public eye in a way unlike
any previous book or event had done.[150] Kinsey's conclusions pointed
to a vast hidden world of sexual experience sharply at odds with publicly espoused norms, and his use of statistics pushed his agenda that

cultural values surrounding sex needed revision to match the actual practices of Americans. The stated implication was that sexual norms should not be those set by moral code or law but those practiced by the public at large. In other words, what's right is whatever people are doing. If bestiality is normative for farm boys because they see animals having sex, then why should incest not be normative when it is part of a family's history? (In fact, this argument has its proponents; witness the society that wants to legitimize incest, for example.)

The Kinsey studies, as much as pornography, shaped the context in which the Supreme Court responded to the obscenity issue. The Warren Court progressively contracted the domain of obscenity, in large part by affirming the appropriateness of sex as a matter for public consumption.[151] *And sex as public consumption became the hallmark of American pseudosexuality.*

Kinsey's concept of "sexual outlet" is an assumption pervading his entire work: he maintains that sexual outlet for the male is not only natural and normal but necessary. As far as I can tell he never examined or tested this most fundamental of his presuppositions. But his research also unwittingly shows that sexual outlet is directly proportional to "erotic stimuli," and where these decrease, so does the incidence of sexual activity. He cites war and prison as two examples, examples going against this very presupposition. The authorities at boot camp never did put "nitrate" in our coffee to lessen our libido, as the scuttlebutt had it. We were more occupied with survival.

Alfred Kinsey died in 1956, but Kinsey, *Playboy*, and the Pill ushered in the sexual revolution of the 1960s. The Kinsey revolution turned our ideas of sexual behavior—what is normal versus abnormal—upside down, opening the door wide into sexual and moral relativity. This revolution was as significant in the area of sexual attitudes and behavior as Copernicus's in astronomy, Darwin's in anthropology, and Einstein's in physics.

Listen to the lead actor in the movie *The Crying Game* answering an interview question about the impact that a male actor playing the female lead had on the film crew:

> [T]he men on the film crew were attracted to Jaye because he
> looked like their notion of a woman. . . . Well, if you are attracted,

why not deal with it? It is only a piece of meat, only flesh, and there are all varieties of flesh. If you are so inclined.[152]

This is a logical extrapolation of the sexual relativity revolution. We've all been born into a world with rapidly changing, mass-mediated pseudo-sex.

Male Identity

How does all this affect our intrinsic identity? The broad features of the evolution of man's self-concept might be outlined as follows:

The man-over-the-animals self—prehistoric primitive hunters
The tribal self—primitive communities
The sin-awareness and God-seeking self—religion
The civic self—rise of cities
The individual self—"life, liberty, and the pursuit of happiness"
The self-centered self—consumerized citizens
The genital self—Freud, Kinsey, *Playboy*, Masters & Johnson, etc.
The pornographic self—the new lust
The self as "orientation"—personal identity in terms of sexual orientation.

Self as orientation? That should give all of us pause. But that's where we are. There has been a progressive change in man's self-concept. The new consciousness underlying and pervading our masculine identity is that which is mediated via the culture. But has Man changed? I think not. We get into big trouble if we think and live as though he has. Man is damaged—yes!

. . .

In sum, four of the most fundamental aspects of human existence— man's biology, his psychology, his cosmology, and his sexuality—have been relativized. Man is a mere transitional life form in an infinite gradation of species, lost to the blind forces of evolution, lost to the blind forces of his own psyche, lost to the blind forces of the entire cosmos, lost to the blind forces of libidinal energy and lust. This means man has no identity, unless it is the sexual, and increasingly, the pornographic.

Today—just since yesterday—man is floundering on a sea of relativism. All the absolutes are gone. Science does not have The Answer, and long ago lost The Problem. Science has failed us as Father. And religious institutions have failed us as Mother. Suddenly the props are knocked out from under us; we feel lost and infinitesimal, and we create and resort to the vast new pharmacopoeia of escapes to stop the world and ease our pain and cosmic loneliness.

Thinking people are beginning to ask, How do we get reality back? "So persuasive is Neal Gabler's thesis that entertainment has overtaken reality, you wonder how to get real life back."[153] To recover from pseudosexuality will require a profound and all-encompassing change of attitude and life, one that connects us with a Reality transcending all relativity. That change of attitude—required for recovery—is supremely difficult to accept and make because it requires a shift in the grounds of our being, from the tangible to the intangible, from the sensate to the spiritual. Plus, it requires our coming to the end of Self. For the pseudosexual, it is nothing less than *counter-cultural.*

THE DEATH OF FATHER

CALVIN AND HOBBES By Bill Watterson

November 4, 1993

The scene in this simple cartoon captures the tragic essence of our times. This father is incapable of seeing and understanding both his son's need for him and his own need for his son. Why? How did he get that way? It took a revolution. And the great vacuum in the heart of that boy *must* and shall be filled. But with what?

There's a hole in the soul of Calvin's father—and probably most American adult males. At its worst, this hole is a void inviting a host of demons pressing for entry from every quarter. At its best, this spiritual vacuum seeks connection with others—*mis*-connection. What is this hole? Where does it come from? And how does it contribute to the great havoc in our sexuality and human relations?

Men Without Father

One of the most significant effects the industrial revolution has had on males is that it separated father and son. The "death" of father must figure prominently in the constellation of forces creating the new sexuality. This is captured in the arresting English title of a book by the German psychiatrist Alexander Mitscherlich—*Society Without Father*. Robert Bly, poet and leading figure in the men's movement, in a fine introduction to the English translation, has given us a lucid summary. (Emphases are all added.)

> The father society has collapsed. . . . the image of the working, teaching father has faded from the mind. An image that has existed brightly in the mind for thousands of years has faded. . . . and the implications are so immense—that we really turn our heads away, we can't take it in. Because he no longer teaches as he works, we in our rage call him a nuisance, a curse, a survival from archaic times, an enemy or a virus, some persistent strain in the bloodstream. . . . the father as a positive force in society has fallen, or been exiled. For all practical purposes, he is not. . . .
>
> Industrial circumstances took the father to a place where the sons and daughters could no longer watch him . . . as he fumbled incompetently with hoes, bolts, saws, shed doors, plows, wagons. . . .
>
> In 1900 about 90 percent of American men were self-employed, most on farms, which meant they dealt with objects in full view of their children. Now 50 percent of men work either for the government or for the Fortune 500 corporations. . . . As when a photograph in an album fades . . . so young women and young men look inside their souls now and see a remote father, an ascended father, a rejecting father, an indifferent father, an unknown father, a desperate father, even a thoughtful, caring father, but they do not see that old image . . . of the father who fumbles and works with things before their eyes, and then stops and teaches them how to hold a nail or a calf. . . . 49 percent of the divorced fathers never see their children again after the divorce. . . .
>
> *But . . . if the sons do not have constant association with their fathers in a human way, if they do not see the father when he is working, failing, laughing, complaining, pleased, weeping, hurting, stupid,*

fooled, then a hole develops in the son's psyche. It doesn't remain empty long but soon fills with demons. . . . When such demons invade the son's or daughter's psyche, then the sons and daughters feel virtuous if they tear down buildings that "the fathers" have built . . . they replace old meaning with a masterful emptiness. . . . That mood began to show itself during the sixties . . . and the mood extended itself to attacks on all codes that limited pleasure. . . .

Under these circumstances it is difficult if not impossible to learn renunciation, which . . . can only be learned in the presence of a person who loves you. The practice of accepting renunciation of immediate pleasure for the sake of a goal to be achieved later . . . is no longer viable. . . .

Two distinct types of pre-Oedipal sons develop. The first type is characterized by *passive lingering in an inarticulate fantasy world.* The second is characterized by ruthless aggression under pressure of which the world is imagined as a jungle . . . 'Both types of abandoned individuals are parasitical and unproductive . . . *a state of instinctual chaos'.* . . .

In the absence of the teaching father men have lost ground. For some the loss seems virtually beyond repair. *The anonymous quality of their lives, the lack of joy, the openness to despair, isolation, and self-destruction is desperate.*[154]

Sad to say, that's my story too. This whole description could be taken directly from the case histories of lust-oriented men—it fits me and hundreds of others I know personally. And the two last paragraphs say it all. This anonymous quality of our lives, so fundamentally a part of male pseudosexuality, is nowhere better illustrated than in the escalating wave of anonymous sex. And the more anonymous sex gets, the less it matters who or which gender it is with.

Robert Bly's insightful use of the Mitscherlich work has given us much food for thought; someone needs to analyze it for the impact on our sexual attitudes and behavior. Much of what he describes can be attributed not only to the forces he cites, but to the modern male's plunge into pseudosexuality. Remember the Boys at Duke (Chapter 1): what filled the vacuum left by the absence of the father-connection was the pseudo reality of countless sexualized image-connections and their resulting *mis*-connections with girls.

The Boy Next Door

This subject of society without father is new to me; I was the ghost father of my own children but had no way of knowing that, since I never had a father relation (he died when I was five). Today, I am beginning to see how very powerful this drive is in boys. Some years ago I made friends with a precocious five-year-old who seemed to be instinctively using me to fill this need Mitscherlich describes so well.

Since I write at home, I'm here most of the time, and this fact was important to him. Practically every day he would come over and want to make contact—spiritually. As soon as I open the door, he looks me square in the eyes and takes an instantaneous reading of my mood: will it be accepting or rejecting? Am I glad to see him? That's what he needs to know. Will I open my soul to him, take him in, even if it's only to look him steadily in the eyes, smile, say Hi! and call him by name?

I can be standing at the opened door, without saying a word, and either take him *in* (open my heart to him) or shut him out. And without fail, whenever he knocks, I'm at the computer working hard, not wanting or expecting any disturbance. When he senses this preoccupation, the lad is not satisfied. I have taken him in enough so that he has experienced intimations of emotional-spiritual union with me. So he goes after that invisible connection. He will stand there until I meet that unspoken need and take him *in*, making the spiritual connection. This is real intercourse; I should do it more with my wife, children, and others. Taking them in through the eyes, inviting them into my life, in that moment, into my soul. The real connection.[155]

The boy needs to know where I'm at and what I'm doing behind these closed doors. So many times, I'll stop my work and bring him inside and just let him look around and ask a million questions. I can see where suspicion begins when a son cannot do this. The lad has a need to see me at work, in the house, hiking, playing, eating, etc. My life is larger than his, and he's reaching up to it. I was surprised to discover he had remembered the nights we're not home when we were square dancing. If I'm not here when I'm supposed to be, he's got to know why, or apparently it is somehow threatening to him.

On some occasions, I've been inside the house, otherwise occupied, and when my wife told him I was shaving in the bathroom, for example, he asked if he could come in and see. When she refused, he couldn't understand why and kept after her until she relented. It was simply to see what I was doing in that particular behavior and time and place and situation. This must be how he grows up inside—spiritually. Our relation seems to give him a frame of reference, a psycho-spiritual foundation, a settledness, a serenity, a fulfillment, a sense of belonging, a relation with a larger part of himself that is still outside, a part he does not know yet, only senses intuitively.

Robert Bly would be glad to know that the second story I started reading to the boy was Bly's translation of Grimm's fairy tale, "The Story of Iron John." The boy loves it! And he's absorbing it, little by little, making me go over the first part again and again. We go on a hike, cross a tiny stream with a small pool of water, and the next thing I know, he's looking to see his reflection and pulling out a hair and dropping it in the water to see if it will turn into gold!

Society without father—Guess what other demons fill that hole in the psyche in increasing millions of us American males? I see not only Suspicion but Fear filling the hole in the boy's psyche when the father connection is absent. Then Resentment comes in, with its twin brother Anger. Then the shadowy ghoul Lust gains easy entrance and takes over. And then the lust to "kill" the father; (the origin of violence is spiritual). It's easy to see how all this creates a predisposition to both anonymous and "nonymous" sex. Pursuing person-connection to fill up the deficit—heterosexual, homosexual, or whatever. The misconnection in order to fix the disconnection.

"Please connect with me and make me whole,"
we cried with outstretched arms. . . . Lusting after the Big Fix,
we gave away our power to others." [156]

The Father Deficit and Pseudosexuality

There is a remarkable convergence of ideas between Mitscherlich's concept of absence of father leaving a hole that must be filled and certain analyses of homosexuality. Some psychologists argue that the relational difficulty in homosexuality is, paradoxically, a difficulty in relating to the *same* sex. They urge that because of this same-sex relational deficit, the capacity for same-sex love should be seen as a legitimate developmental drive, and as such should be facilitated and not blocked; adding, however, it should be fulfilled non-sexually. The statement of a contemporary feminist lesbian historian is of interest here: "Widespread homosexuality is one of the results of a weakened family structure, not a cause."[157] How about widespread pseudo-heterosexuality being the result of weakened family structure?

However, such psychologists imply that the heterosexual does not have these particular developmental deficits. Wrong! This misses the whole point made by Mitscherlich. They fail to see the pathology of today's so-called heterosexuality, which is what we're trying to uncover in this book. Man without Father helps produce the deficit—the hole—that helps drive *both* heterosexual and homosexual pseudosexuality. I believe our analyses of lust imply that the deficit-driven pseudo-heterosexual just happens to act out with the opposite sex; what he is really doing is trying to make a connection with Person, which he never had. In the process, I perverted the reality both of woman and of my own identity. How can this be any different for a lust-driven homosexual? If we could but see this, it would help eliminate some of the existing polarity tension, since *we who are caught in pseudosexuality are all suffering from the same thing*, even though we express it sexually in different ways.

Society without father has opened the window of the empty and desolate male soul for the legion of addictions to fly in and take possession. It has created a vast and growing demimonde of sexual misconnection: boys and men seeking image-women, and boys and men seeking image-men—all desperate to fill that abhorrent black hole and connect with Life.

The effect this father deficit has in the development of male sexual attitudes and behavior is incredibly deep and far-reaching. This involves our very identity as males and men and husbands and fathers. I'm still growing too slowly into maleness, manhood, fatherhood, and husbandhood. It is incredibly demanding and difficult, but I wouldn't miss this adventure for anything!

THE DEATH OF GOD

The death of father goes hand in hand with the death of Father. This is why one of the factors enabling our predisposition to pseudosexuality has been the virtual death of God in our culture. God is effectively dead, but the devil is alive and doing very well. That may be why it is easier for someone like Robert Bly to speak of demons than of God.

God is dead in most areas of our lives today: science, education, business, politics, the arts, the media, and . . . religion. It is not the fault of science, education, philosophy, the media, or even religious liberals that God is dead. It is the fault of multitudes claiming to be true believers, even "keepers of the flame." Religion is affected and shaped by our culture just as our sexuality is and suffers from all the forces driving the pseudosexual revolution. What is harder to see is that the religious mind-set can actually be another factor in driving and supporting the pseudosexual revolution.

I get the feeling that God has also become increasingly dead in the rapidly proliferating Twelve Step movement. However, we must be careful to distinguish the movement from those twelve recovery principles themselves. Compared with its origins in 1935 New York City and Akron, that experience seems increasingly lost today. In the proliferation of organizations patterned after AA, what increasingly takes the place of spiritual awakening promised in the Twelfth Step is *socialized spirituality*. The results show it, not the least of which is the dramatic drop in success rate when compared to its origins. Popularization, commercialization, medicalization, and professionalization have affected its quality and are rendering the movement increasingly devoid of power for the powerless.

The greatest enemy of the truth is not that which questions or opposes it but that which pushes it, carrying high the banner of Truth, preaching its Word in all appearance, but denying the power thereof. And the twin demons of believism and covert legalism are having a field day. Truth without Life is *pseudo*—the great Lie . . . but also an extremely potent drug serving religious addiction.

A View from the Pew

A man is sitting in church between his wife and young son. All three are holding hands. It feels good to be in the house of worship, together, with their child. They've left the cares of the marriage and the world outside and have entered a different world, a sanctuary: the hushed tones of the organ as the minister prays . . . the ritual order of service . . . the light coming through the stained glass . . . the choir . . . listening to God's very word . . . A sanctuary from—in this man's case, a hoped-for sanctuary from the self.

But alas, the man has brought his self with him, though he made a valiant effort to keep part of it outside this house of God. Holding hands with wife and child in the very temple of God would surely certify that resolve. They've just recited the Apostles' Creed and prayed the Lord's Prayer, and suddenly, there it is! Just a glimpse out of the corner of his eye. The hair tossed with a quick glance over the shoulder, temptingly trying to connect with someone's radar. The subtle body language. His radar, always scanning, connects. Fear strikes in an instant, for he knows he has to drink. And drink he does, taking a quick snatch. The wife feels a stab of pain and quickly suppresses it. Consciously, she denies she even saw it; subconsciously, she knows, and dies a thousand deaths. It's been eating at her insides ever since she began dating her husband-to-be. But she's in denial too. The problem does not exist. It *cannot* exist.

The eight-year-old son catches the flare of the lust-snatch. He turns to see what force has captured his father so, and it indelibly registers that there's something very powerful going on here between his father and that image. Imprinting. In the son! *"The sins of the fathers . . ."*

The programmed ritual of the church service keeps flowing hypnotically on, preventing both the man and woman from listening to that still small voice inside that would be crying out SOMETHING'S WRONG! The organ's dulcet tones coax the congregation into singing "a hymn of lofty praise to God." And as the preacher continues to "minister" over the carefully designed "service" in soothing cultic phrases, the false reality of the dream state is sustained—not unlike the passive state we get in front of the flickering screen.

This pious husband calls himself a Christian; he has, some years ago, "accepted Christ." Of course, even before that he knew he should not want to do what he's doing. But he can't stop. Turning up his willpower to white-knuckle intensity, he forcefully keeps his head from turning again. *Not here!* his conscience cries out—as his eyeballs, controlled by a more powerful force, strain out of their sockets for another drink.

What this man brought with him to the service, along with his wife and child, is what increasing numbers of religious carry secretly inside themselves all the time—a lusting heart. Whatever else he may be, this upstanding-appearing male is unwittingly, while singing that lofty hymn and taking the Holy Communion, engaged in the unholy communion of lust and false worship.

Notice that his belief system does not save, but actually helps cover up his problem. His religious system has intensified a law of moral commandments he cannot keep, and has become a curse. And all his believing in God and Christ isn't helping him one bit. As a matter of fact, his belief system—that's what it is, a system, and System shuts Life out—helps keep him under the curse of that very law. For this man, ostensibly worshiping God, is in fact an idolater, doing obeisance to the spirit of Lust. This is my story. I was that man.

The point here is not what was taking place between the pews, or how prevalent such a scene might be, but how I may have been allowed, even encouraged by the religious mind-set, to persist in my salvationless believism and hopeless legalism. Have we created a religious atmosphere where there is neither the revealing light of God's presence to expose lust nor the gracious remedy by which to overcome that next temptation?

I suggest there is a whole false religious system in place—primarily *within* us—which not only lets this pseudo-religion happen but actually helps drive it and thus helps drive pseudosexuality. A false faith is faith that is not working and is merely religious propaganda—which validates, supports, and perpetuates all propaganda, including the sexual.

Pseudo-relationship at the religious personal center of one's life validates, supports, and perpetuates pseudo-relations of all kinds.

There are those who are beginning to call for a positive alternative.[158]

Unreal Religion

We have to get rid of the plague of the
spirit of the religious age in which we live.
Oswald Chambers, 1935[159]

Much of our religious world is unreal today. Can we expect anything else, considering we live in an escalating reality revolution? Much more than our sexuality has been affected by modern cultural forces. No wonder each stage in the pseudosexual revolution always winds up being blessed, tacitly or overtly, by the religious institution. As an example, consider the rise of situational ethics in the 1950s and its blessing of pseudosexuality across the board. And note the following ex cathedra proclamation:

Masturbation, a means of self-pleasuring,
is generally appropriate and healthy.
Lutheran Report on Sexuality

The world knows that much of today's religious environment is unreal; that's why it has lost respect for it, lip service notwithstanding. That's also why religion is increasingly becoming politicized.

Religion of this sort won't do for recovery from lust and PS. It did not work for me. And it did not work for alcoholics in 1935 who comprised the fledgling AA fellowship and who could be overheard telling new prospects, "Find God or die!" We would do well to heed Oswald Chambers (above) and be willing to discern what the spirit of the religious age in which we live is, and then seek Remedy.

The Death of God and Predisposition to Pseudosexuality

This religious mind-set we are calling the death of God creates a societal predisposition to pseudosexuality by helping create the existential vacuum that drives the need for interpersonal mis-connections and opens the door to lust. Society without father is a society without Father. Since our earthly father- and family-connection is faulty or absent, we experience the deep incompleteness of our lives—the "hole in the soul"—and *must* seek ful*fill*ment.

My religious addiction inhibited my recovery. And close personal experience with many others in recovery reveals this is true for large numbers of religious lusters—perhaps even most of them. This should help us discover why and how it helps drive pseudosexuality. Pseudo-faith keeps us from recovery by keeping us from seeing the reality of ourselves—and our wrongfulness—by keeping us from the real *saving* Connection, and by keeping us diverted into religious forms and belief. *There is such a thing as religious predisposition to pseudosexuality.* But there is also such a thing as recovery from it and finding the gracious Life-Connection and joy!

. . .

So, we look into our collective condition and see ourselves as man without father, man without roots and God, displaced man, industrial man, city man, isolated man, lonely man, man as idolater striving to make the real Connection—but failing. Man instead connecting with the Image, the substitute, the ersatz, and in the process trying vainly to regain his lost maleness and manhood. Pseudo-man seeking pseudo-woman or pseudo-man, both becoming progressively more lost and unreal in the process.

The Great American Dream turns out to be a delusion—The Great American Tragedy.

On the positive side, perhaps history in the long run will show this to be a beneficial side effect of the pseudosexual revolution, that in exacerbating the spiritual void, the resulting pain will eventually force us to seek the Father of our spirits and *Life.*

Perhaps as we get through experimenting with all the substitute connections, the whole pharmacopoeia of chemical, entertainment, sexual, relational, therapeutic, and religious substitutes and escapes in our addictive culture—misconnections of every sort to fill the hole in the soul—those of us hurting the most will be driven slowly to despairing of them all and finally, with nothing left to resort to, cast ourselves upon the unseen but only real Connection with the saving Source of our lives. In recovery Fellowship with others doing the same.

PART V
WHERE DO WE GO FROM HERE?

For those infected with the lust virus who may have read this book, identify, and sense the seriousness and pervasiveness of PS both within themselves and the culture, there may well up a rising tide of despair. "It's overwhelming! What can a person do? How do we get reality back? Our spiritual immune systems have been disabled, literally shot to hell. And we're captive to a power overmastering our affections and worship. Is recovery from lust and PS possible? What would it entail? Could I survive it?"

If this doesn't apply to you, read no further.

As the malady has progressed worldwide and more and more men and women have been seeking help, increasing numbers of books and programs address some of the various symptoms of PS, especially the sex addiction aspect, but not PS recovery itself. They speak for themselves. It is best that I speak only for myself.

IMPLICATIONS FOR RECOVERY

The Malady

As its title implies, this chapter has more to do with what kind of recovery pseudosexuality (PS) requires than a traditional "how to" treatment. It summarizes in broad terms what I've had to do for my own recovery. The principles of recovery are included in the Steps and Traditions of the relevant recovery fellowships. This chapter will never be "finished" as long as there are men and women who are entering recovery; also because recovery itself is never "finished." Mine always seems to be at a new beginning, for which I am very grateful.

Considering all that we've learned about PS in previous chapters and the author's story, supported by the experience of growing numbers of others over the last thirty-one years, let's first try to form a composite picture of the malady itself—from a seasoned look-back point of view. Without an appreciation of the complexities of the malady, we're liable to minimize what is required and cheat ourselves from deeper recovery. What might appear from this "diagnosis" as too daunting and overwhelming, turns out to be a joyous prospect of healing and life. It is because recovery from these symptoms of the pathology is possible and is being experienced that they *can* be so identified!

So let's step back, try to look at the data clinically, and list some of the more obvious symptoms of what we're calling pseudosexuality. I've come to be able to identify these symptoms by being hit in the face with them in recovery and by becoming willing to acknowledge and change. Though difficult at times, this has been a most wondrous and rewarding odyssey. What a relief to see and acknowledge the truth, one symptom at a time. So, speaking objectively for myself, whatever we may call the malady, it

Increased the man's demand for sex but robbed sex of its fulfillment,

Turned demand into escalating addiction,

Required ever-escalating forms of experimentation and expression,

Diminished his maleness, manhood, and sexuality,

Diminished his husbandhood and fatherhood,

Damaged his sexual response, even to causing functional impotence,

Perverted his sexual and personal identity,

Perverted sex into something *pseudo*-sexual,

Increased his susceptibility to other addictions,

Degraded his character,

Polluted his spiritual well-being,

Distorted his personal reality,

Polluted the very spiritual air about him,

Perverted his concept of self, woman, and man;

Fostered personal isolation and alienation, leaving him a relational cripple,

Weakened his capacity for interpersonal relations and intimacy,

Induced self-obsession,

Induced anti-social attitudes and behavior,

Created a soul-set of violence, generating self-hatred and rage within,

Enslaved him to gross idolatry, making him more susceptible to evil, and

Emasculated his ability to know, receive, or give love.

What Do I Need to Recover from That?

Being in this lust-sex and PS recovery for the last thirty-three years, let me share what the process of my recovery has been telling me that

I needed and continue to need. There's no way I can put these in any order; this is how they just came out at first writing. Of course, I could see very little of this in the beginning. I've come to be able to identify these needs because they are being fulfilled in my life, if at times glimpsed only from afar. They are gradually distilled out of the spiritual awakening being brought about by the attitudes and actions experienced in the fellowship of the Twelve Steps. Thus, these needs also amazingly represent the promise and joy of recovery.

- I need help from without, since I am captive from within. This outside help must be persons who understand the problem *from the inside*—those who have "been there and back." Two-way spiritual intercourse must be established where the one reveals and the others identify and share their own recovery process.
- I need release from isolation, self-enthroned egoism, and self-obsession, without which it is impossible to recover.
- I need release from the obsession of judgmentalism and resentment—by-products of the addiction—which come out of my being god in my world and keep me isolated and *against* others, which is really being against my real self.
- I need to learn to connect honestly, intimately, non-sexually, and selflessly with the same sex. This comes first. Very difficult.
- I need to learn to connect honestly, intimately, non-sexually, and selflessly with the opposite sex. More difficult.
- I need non-sexual, non-lustful *socializing* with others, both men and women, to take the place of *mis*-connection with others and the false super-ecstasy of lust-sex that kept me from normal healthy social interaction. We lusters tend to be a grim lot and need to laugh together.
- Since my normal adolescent interaction with girls and boys was aborted or misdirected by lust-sex, I will need to go through "adolescence" as an adult. Painful, scary, slow, awkward, stumbling. And the only way I can do that is with *people*—having intimate relations with both men and women. *There's no other way to grow into manhood.* To achieve manhood means to *grow* into manhood. It takes time and work

and others. And making mistakes. We learn by doing. I need
people. I need to be *part of* a continuing intimate personal
fellowship of absolute honesty of the spirit. So I can learn the
reality of Person and myself in relation to others, both men
and women.

- I need to amend the wrongs I have done to others and forgive
those who have wronged me so I can be forgiven.
- I need forgiveness. Aside from the Law, or whatever that religious entity may have been in my past, there's a law written
within my own members that has been accusing me, the one
I kept running from, covering it over with lust and self-will.
That's the law whose accusations I have to face honestly, whose
transgressions need forgiveness. And face it fully I must. That
means a continuing searching and fearless inventory of myself.
- I need to connect with Life, the larger reality of all living
beings, because PS is anti-life.
- The only way I can connect with Life is by letting life in, letting
people in. Those with PS can't let anybody *in* because people
are real, and we've been programmed to and misconnected
with the unreal. Recovery will take major spiritual surgery, in
the context of accountability with others. Dogs help too; they
can accept us just as we are. They're easier to let in.
- I need a reason to *live*, because lust and PS kill Life and engender spiritual death.
- I need joy, within myself. This is different from happiness. Lust
is pseudo, false, promising and delivering only ecstasy, but followed by the Let-Down, and always wanting more. Joy comes
from surrender, sobriety, changed attitudes, and living rightly
with others; and it wants no more.
- I need peace and serenity from within, because lust created
inner disturbance, conflict, anxiety, and fear.
- I need to learn to give—by *giving*—because giving satisfies,
while lust is *taking*, and not only never satisfies but robs me of
my very self.
- Since I've suffered from the father deficit, as most men have, I
will need to be father to others. That's the only way to fill the
father deficit that helped set me up for PS. The endless search and

hope for the perfect father or brother by seeking pseudo-fathers or pseudo-brothers didn't work for me. Helping others recover from PS is a form of fathering and brotherhood that does work.

- To be a man, I must be rightly positioned under and related with the Father of my spirit. (See *The God Players,* by Earl Jabay. This little paperback (1970) is out of print and increasingly difficult to find.)

- I need Family, to be *part of,* only now in the spiritual realm of a safe haven of honesty-in-confrontation, self-disclosure, conflict resolution, and mutual help, where character defects and sin can be revealed and healing and growth continued—together.

- Do I need sex? Am I "deprived and lack nurturing" without sex? You'll be surprised at the answer to that one. Sex is totally optional now. Lust or demand for sex would change that.

- I need love, especially taking the actions of *giving* love, which means giving of myself to and for others. Because I was one who demanded and tried to *take* love. I need to learn to care about someone other than myself. Giving to others takes *time,* my time. But there's no better payoff.

- I need to learn how to *receive* love. That seems to come slowly as I break out of the prison house of the self so I can let God and someone else *in.*

- I need nothing less than a resurrection from the dead on a continuing basis, a resurrection from my death of aloneness, separation, and disconnection from Life that was negating my own life. And resurrection *in and from* each temptation!

- I need to be released from the *power* of the hardwiring in my brain and the programming of my soul.

- I need to recover from those elements of the culture supporting my PS. This is the "gotcha!" Where and how do we even begin? Slowly, as more is revealed. For me it began with stopping lust-image intake—"cold-turkey"—and moderating all image intake, both still and moving, in accountability with others. I'm still learning.

- I need to find what my lust was really looking for, a spiritual connection taking me outside myself, transcending my Self.

Yes, I need self-transcendence—the right kind. I used lust, sex, and media for the pseudo-transcendence they promised.

- I need connection with the Source of my being, discovering that it is not in myself, and that it is also the breath of Life in other human beings. To have this, I will need to be released from any religious bondage keeping me from this personal Connection.
- I need the love of the One who, knowing exactly who and what I am in the thoughts and intents of my heart, is willing and waiting to take me in, just as I am, in the very moment of temptation, trial, or need—at my very weakest and worst.
- I need *cleansing*. Plus, all those toxic memories need detoxifying.
- I need a fellowship of men and women who also strive to have these needs fulfilled. Part of me is still missing until I am more a part of that. *All this and more is recovery from pseudosexuality.*

That's a Tall Order; How In the World Does One Go About Getting That?

It's really an "impossible" order; that's why it takes "impossible" means. For me there is no easier, softer way. The following actions did not come easily; it's what I've *had* to do. Sometimes kicking and screaming. What I describe below is only the distilled essence of three decades of personal experience, driven as much or more by failures as by successes, both in myself and in my experience with others in the recovery movement to date. For any 12-step "program people" who might object to anything other than the "suggested" approach, I refer to page 131 in the AA book *Dr. Bob and the Good Oldtimers*, where, in the first five original steps, there are seven "musts." That's how it worked in 1935–1938, when the fire struck, and that's what works for me and a growing number of others today. (A fuller description of my early recovery appears in other literature.) Here again, this list is looking back in hindsight; thus I hope it may have value to others at various stages along their recovery path. And remember: recovery from PS is much more than recovery from sex addiction.

1. The very beginning: I had to *want* to stop acting out sexually. And I had to *want* to stop acting in. (Acting in includes lusting and fantasizing and all the associated attitudes and actions.) I didn't even know I was acting in until I stopped acting out. Nobody and no fellowship or program could make me want to stop either acting out or acting in. It had to come from my own self-interest.

    Getting initially sober from acting out tended to give me a false sense of accomplishment. But the time finally came when I *wanted* to be released from the power of the obsession to lust. And this desire came in progressive stages as I remained physically sober. (Those lust-recovery stages are still advancing; I hope it never ends because lust gets increasingly discovered in other guises.) Call this a change of heart, repentance, or whatever. Terms don't count; surrender does. Giving up. If life hasn't brought you to this point yet, even meetings or religion probably won't. "Half measures" do not work for me.

2. I had to actually *stop* acting out sexually and *stop* acting in, resorting to images and fantasy. Of course, trying to stop the acting in is what forced me to keep finding a solution, because it proved so impossible at first. This led to an open-ended period of total sexual abstinence with my wife and the willingness to never have sex again, if that was to be my lot. Nobody and no fellowship did the deciding or stopping for me; it's an inside job that came out of my own desperation. But I did not stop and apparently could not stop until I entered a fellowship where others were stopping. That's the magic of coming out of isolation—and the gift of God.

    Recovery did not start until I made the decision to stop acting out and then *stopped*. That's when I discovered the real power the addiction/obsession had over me, how impossible it was to stop the acting in. Physical sobriety merely took the top layer off so what was inside could start being revealed. That's when I discovered I needed to take the actions of recovery spelled out below. I could not begin to recover until I actually stopped deliberately resorting to the "drug." As the AA saying goes, "You can't stop drinking until you stop drinking." Yes, I know; that's the threat of death, isn't it? (Ref. Appendix 7, What Makes Lust So "Impossible" to Overcome?)

3. I had to unconditionally give up—surrender to God in continuing accountability with others—my right and desire to lust and

act out, my right to sex itself, my concept of sexuality, and what it means to be a man. These did not come all at once. Surrender is in stages too, which become apparent over time. I wish someone had told me about this surrendering my concept of my sexuality when I first came in. I'm convinced that facing this up front as soon as we come in can improve our chances of recovery. This kind of deep surrender allows us to stay sexually sober *so we can begin the process of PS recovery.* This also means ruling out all forms of solitary sex, including self-fondling without orgasm, and all forms of deliberately resorting to lust, including pictures, fantasy, the written word, and dreams. And yes, I discovered that it is possible to find freedom from sex and lust in dreams. Most difficult of all and slowest in coming was giving up the badge of my heterosexual identity—that pseudo-manhood I carried with me—and admit I was a *pseudo*-sexual, in the same boat as others across the whole orientation spectrum. It took me years to see that. The sooner we realize this, the better. Third Step surrender is a total life-involving process; it is trivialized far too often. More gets revealed if we stay sober.

4. Regardless of what meetings I went to, I had to become part of a close-knit spiritual fellowship with others who were surrendering to God their lusting, their acting out, their sexuality, and their right to sex. I could not recover through my own solitary resolve.

    Problem: Here we're up against the passing trends and limitations of the recovery movement in its various current representations, both secular (professional), spiritual (Twelve Step), and religious. To my knowledge, there is no organization or fellowship formally addressing this full-recovery issue—recovery not only from sex and lust but from PS—though some offer various portions of it. In fact, simply attending some meetings can lead to compromising recovery. As a student of one group's dismal recovery history puts it, "Once a newcomer attends his first meeting here, he has been inoculated *against* recovery." Sad but often true. The burden will be up to you to find or help create such a fellowship. And find it you must, even if you have to start with one other person who wants it. In my early recovery meeting experience I found one person at a time with whom I could have such fellowship. I *had* to find them. *"Man's extremity is God's opportunity."*

What I am *not* talking about here is starting another organization. Start from the inside out, wherever you're at, not from the outside in.

5. I had to "be there"—be available to identify with and help others who wanted out. I eventually *wanted* to "be there." This continuing fellowship of accountability and mutual support is the very heart and soul of recovery. Solitary recovery by simply going to meetings failed me after over a year of "sobriety" because it was from the outside in, instead of from the inside out; and it was self-centered. I could not keep what I had without giving it away, so I not only lost it, I became worse off.

6. I had to begin and continue incorporating into my way of thinking and living the spiritual principles of recovery embodied in the Twelve Steps in and with such a fellowship. Recovery simply never happened until I began living out these principles. (More about this below.)

7. With all that said and done—all preparatory to this—I had to experience the One who would set me free, free from the obsession of lust, the tyranny of Self, and mis-connections with others. Meetings supported physical sobriety from the outside, in; but enduring recovery from the inside out only came through the spiritual awakening—discovering the love, care, forgiveness, cleansing, and presence of God in my life. This did not come about without experiencing items 1–6, which opened the window, and then the door, for the sunlight of the Spirit.

8. I had to progressively come to terms with my relation to those elements of the culture described in this book that were part of the larger problem surrounding and helping drive my PS. Then I had to change my relation to them. Talk about "separating the men from the boys"—this is where I balked, learning the hard slow way. I had to learn, through honestly being accountable, about what activities were shutting out the sunlight of the Spirit in my life. For example, I progressively saw that I could use any of the various media as medication to shut me off from the reality of my life with others and God—whether radio, television, movies, or even newspapers and

magazines and work. I then had to give up my right to resorting to them *in such a manner* and be accountable to others who identified. Tricky business. It's still progressing.

Likewise, I had to stop resorting to religious activities that were opposed to the personal and inter-personal spiritual fellowship I came to need and crave. The same with entertainment. This kind and degree of recovery is counter-cultural; the world-spirit out there militates against it. But recovery from PS means nothing less than recovery from mis-connection with this world-System, including religious System. On the plus side, I am forced to seek and find something better, more real, and more fulfilling: serenity, joy, people, and life! Crucial to this aspect of PS recovery is *fellowship* with those who want that very thing. *"Seek and you shall find."* It's amazing how others—admittedly very few—come forward and identify after I've shared like this in meetings. There's hunger for this deeper PS recovery, and they can't do it alone either!

9. I had to put recovery first over every other aspect of my life. Yes, even over marriage, family, parents, friends, job, religion, and sex. "Whatever it takes." Religion without recovery for me turned into religious addiction, paradoxically shutting God out. And sex in the marriage was not only part of the problem; it *was* the problem. The lust-sex connection had to be broken, and that was not possible for me without going into total open-ended sexual abstinence. More than once. What a beneficial experience that turned out to be! Both the place of lust in sex and the demand for sex were broken. Sex is optional now. Sex happens. Sex is good.

10. Considering all of the above, we do not need a new organization. What we do need is a real *fellowship of PS recovery*—men and women who are actually recovering from PS. We *can* discover this from the inside out, especially since the organizational infrastructures are already in place.

These are the simplified boiled-down hard facts of life, as proven time and again in my experience and increasingly that of others. And increasingly apparent from the *failed* experiences of multitudes trying to recover. Not for everybody! But as Happy Jack, used to say, "Nobody says it's gonna be tiptoeing through the tulips."

So What Are Those "Notorious" Twelve Steps?[160]

I thought it would be interesting to look at the Steps from another per-spective. They are so familiar, and we hear them so often in standard format, that we tend to overlook what they really mean. So I tried to distill the essence of the Steps and boil them down into action words representing changes in attitudes and actions required of me. Note how these shift from being Steps that are "taken" or "worked"—and then left behind—to becoming part of a changing inner disposition of the heart, resulting in a continuing process of attitudes-in-action. Again, this comes from long hard years of discovering why the Steps are necessary and how they really work.

> **Dying** (to self)   Admit I am powerless over pseudosexuality—that my lust, sex, sexuality, orientation, manhood, and relational and cultural misconnections are disordered and that I can't fix the mess.
>
> **Needing**   Know I need a Power greater than lust and greater than myself to restore me to sexual, personal, and relational sanity.
>
> **Surrendering**   Unconditionally give up my life, my right to lust and sex, my sexuality, my badge of "orientation," and my relation-ships over to the care of God.
>
> **Seeing**   Discover and disclose the truth of myself, in the light of those who are recovering, in written moral inventories of myself.
>
> **Exposing**   Reveal this inventory to others who identify, under-stand, and give support.
>
> **Cleansing**   Continue bringing each wrong and defect of char-acter being revealed into the light of others and God until I am released from its power over me.
>
> **Changing**   Make direct amends to all persons I have harmed, except when doing so would injure them or others, and con-tinue looking at where I am wrong and promptly admitting and amending it.
>
> **Forgiving**   Ask for the willingness to forgive all persons guilty of real or imagined wrongs against me and forgive each one.

Receiving   Receive the presence of God into each fantasy and temptation to sex, lust, misconnection, judgmentalism, resentment, fear, etc.—into the very temptation itself; instead of acting out or thinking out—letting God in.

Giving   Join with others in helping other pseudosexuals find a fellowship of recovery and the One who is saving us from our lust, from PS, from ourselves, and from the spirit of world-System.

Praying   Seek through prayer and meditation to help others and improve my connection with others and God.

Living   Make these principles a way of living, taking the actions of love—especially when the feeling of love is absent—to improve my relations with others.

From Dying to Living! That's the story of my life. And my recovery. Thank God! And I've barely begun! I need and want more of the same.

Note: While the above twelve words were inspired by the Twelve Steps of AA, they are not really an adaptation. Rather, as noted above, they were boiled down to represent continuing attitudes and actions. AA, which is a program concerned only with recovery from alcoholism, is not in any way affiliated with this publication.

"God as we understood Him"

As I proceeded in recovery, the higher power concept began taking on changing significance. And I think this is typical. It is obvious from the above and to most careful students of the history of the AA Twelve-Step program that, as originally experienced, it was "a God program." The words "God as we understood Him" appear in Steps Three and Eleven; and in Tradition Two, it is "a loving God as He may express Himself in our group conscience." That's why the word spoken to those hopeless and helpless alkies in 1935 in Akron, Ohio, the crucible where the program was forged, was often, "Find God or die!"

Often, if we are religious, we may be too quick to affirm the God-centered essence of the program, not realizing there's something drastically wrong with our own relation to God that took us to where we were. That's what I did. But it took only a year and a half to discover that my "believism" did not save me. So I'd like to share the "understanding" of God I have come to as one recovering from the malady delineated at the beginning of this chapter. Having experienced the ravages of PS for some forty years and then having progressively discovered through continued necessity the presence and working of the Higher Power in my life, *"God as we understood Him"* for me became *"God as I have come to need and actually experience Him."* Thus, for me this entity

- Must be available within me—as close as the thoughts and intents of my heart and soul, lusts, fantasies, and memories.
- Must be available at the moment of temptation and utter powerlessness.
- Must be an intelligent personal entity to comprehend me and what's going on in there and be able to discern my lies, and denial strategies.
- Must be a spiritual entity, since my spirit is the playing field of the malady.
- Must understand and identify with human emotions—my emotions—lust, resentment, fear, etc. (Think about this attribute; the implications are enormous.)
- Must be able to *connect* with me at my very worst, regardless of the evil that's in there, any time any place.
- Must be able to recognize my lust, resentment, fear, fantasy, etc., for what they really are—my death—even if I don't see them as such.
- Must be able to take the transfer of these diseased attitudes from me so I can be released and free of their power.
- Must *want* to take that transfer—anytime, any place.
- Must be able to *raise* me out of that self-destructive spiritual death and bring me to life.
- Must be able and willing to direct my life better than I.

- Must offer forgiveness and cleansing from my wrongs, guilt, and shame.
- Must be more real, more powerful, and more satisfying than my lust or fantasy.
- Must be holy to reveal and deal with my pollution.
- Must be and give me something better than what my lust, fantasies, and misconnections were looking for—unconditional redeeming love.

I came to progressively discover these attributes because I was getting what I needed! What an incredible journey! These experientially required "musts" that come out of my needs and desperation are what I am actually experiencing. It can't be true; but it is. And so much more. Thank God. He has never failed me whenever I've despaired of self and abandoned myself completely to his mercy and grace—in temptation after impossible temptation, trial after impossible trial, and fear after impossible fear. I only speak for myself; but if I do not so speak, I fail to share my experience, strength, and hope.

What Kind of Fellowship?

Let's Be Realistic About 12 Step Recovery Meetings. Below are listed first some potential negatives, seen over the years, and then some countervailing positive hopes:

Some potentially unintended aspects of meetings:

- Meetings can reinforce focus on and obsession with the self, putting personality before principle.
- Meetings can promote or reinforce isolation, notwithstanding the pseudo-togetherness we feel.
- They may not give God and the Twelve Steps and Traditions their rightful place.
- Meetings that rely for the most part on the "talking cure," as in therapy. One responds to the passage read in a book study or to the question raised in a topic meeting or to the sharing of others in participation meetings by whatever triggers one's

mental association at the time. The result can be avoiding or covering over the recovery principles in the 12 and 12, blocking the healing grace of God.

- Meetings can act as a religious confessional, making us feel better, even without sobriety or lust victory, and without revealing what may be shutting out the sunlight of the Spirit. We may still be acting out or consciously resorting to lustful media, but still act and talk like we are okay.

- Meetings can unwittingly promote lack of recovery through an atmosphere of pseudo-democratic people-pleasing and pseudo-fellowship (the "club" mentality). "Keep coming back" (no matter whether you've ever surrendered your right to act in or act out or even want recovery). Thus, there is implied license to support the malady. This can be more prevalent than we would like to admit due to the manifold difficulties in lust and PS recovery.

- Attendance at meetings can devolve into what has been described as "addiction to meetings and socialized spirituality," where the good can be the enemy of the best.

Some ideal meeting qualities:

What if you could go to a meeting where there was a "critical mass" of sobriety?

Where sober people are actually learning how to live free from lust, resentment, and unforgiveness?

Where people are walking and talking in absolute honesty?

Where focus is not self-centered, as in a therapist's office?

Where we reveal the deepest thoughts and intents of the heart, and where that is carried through to forgiveness, victory, and joy?

Where you are finding what you hoped for but could not find in other meetings, religion, therapy, or medication?

Where spiritual awakening comes to life in helping others?

Where both the lingering trauma of the sins of others upon us and the burned-in stigmas of our own sins are not only forgiven but cleansed and healed and turned into avenues of healing for others?

That's a Tall Order; How Do We Get That?

"A man's reach should exceed his grasp, or what's a heaven for?" You
don't get it handed to you, unless you're unusually fortunate. You have
to want it, and you have to work for it. That's what you get when the
12 and 12 are realized in the group life and consciousness. If you want
it badly enough, you may have to find another who wants it and cry
out to God together for it and then work for it. The original promise is,
"He will show you how to create the fellowship you crave" (*Alcoholics
Anonymous*, p. 164). In whatever group you happen to be in. Keep at it,
and try lighting a candle instead of bemoaning the darkness. And let's
remember that it's better to give than to get; that it is by giving that we
receive. I also believe in the power of a collective Eleventh Step experience, praying for this *together* in the light of the Second and other
Traditions.

PS Recovery and Orientation

Recovery for any pseudosexual, regardless of orientation, should *not*
begin by focusing on the orientation. That approach is from the outside in, instead of from the inside out and doesn't work. Recovery must
begin with the heart of the problem—the disposition of the heart. This
work begins with *sobriety*—sobriety from the addiction and from
obsession with sex and lust. This is because our cancerous malady
radiated outward from our inner diseased attitudes, through lust and
sex, and then out into every aspect of our lives and relations. Recovery
can only begin once the foundation of sobriety is established regarding
sex and lust. It can't begin with the drug still in the system. Only then
can recovery begin dealing progressively with the rest of the symptoms
of the malady.

Although our sexual acting out and acting in exhibit gender pref-
erences, lust itself is asexual; that is, lust is not gender-specific. Lust is a
non-sexual spiritual force within us, which happens to use sex—or eating or drinking or resentment or money or power or entertainment or
the media or whatever. *Thus, the problem is not the gender we lust after,
but lust itself.* The problem is not our so-called sexual "orientation"—
that situation in which life and experience find us—but the spiritual

attitudes that have shaped and driven our fantasy or sexualizing. This was especially difficult for me to see, that even though my lust focused on the opposite sex, I was still perverting my sexuality.

Part of me thought I was God's great gift to women—the quintessence of sexual masculinity. I *had* to believe that, since my sexuality was really damaged; but I was blind and could not see that. Before I entered recovery, all of my sexual fantasy and most of my acting out was with the opposite sex. However, lust corrupts the natural reality of the person or picture we happen to be looking at into something to suit what has come to be our "need" (read *demand*). Lust perverts the innocent reality of that person or picture into something I take, ingest, and consume spiritually. This happens regardless of whether or not the lust is sexualized or remains pure fantasy. Lust destroyed my ability to see and relate to the person, and instead, saw only what was there to be taken or used, for whatever need, however "gentle." It is this taking, ingesting, consuming, and using that is the real spiritual force at work within me. Lust. This was the force possessing more and more of me as it finally mastered me and I become powerless over its power over me. This is the asexual force that has become hardwired into my body, brain, and soul. This is the force from which I must be saved—*and am being saved*—in recovery. And this is where the program of the Steps is worked and is working.

For me, the so-called "heterosexual," this was the most difficult part of recovery, because it was impossible for me to see it from within that lifestyle. First, it means I must change my way of perceiving my sexuality. Then, how I perceive the object of my sexuality. (Or, maybe it's the other way around!) But those faulty perceptions are intrinsic to my basic personality and character! I must thus surrender my whole learned relatability to Woman, my right to women, my mis-connection with women. And how can one change that?! It also means I must give up the core of my sexual identity, my very sexuality, because that sexuality was twisted, self-centered, and perverted—thanks to lust, and whatever other spiritual sins I nourished! Deeper yet, this means I must give up the right to my very *personal identity*! (This must be the same terrifying dilemma same-sex people face if they ever think about "changing.") I had to give up the Big Lie about my heterosexuality before I could recover from my pseudo-sexuality.

How can this be otherwise with lust-addicted same-sex persons? Must they not thus surrender their whole learned relatability to Man, their right to men, their *mis*-connection with men; be willing to give up the core of their sexual identity, their very sexuality? That's why we're in this together as pseudosexuals.

Give it all up, but how? Left to myself, this is death! That's where the Third Step surrender to God comes in. And "one step at time, and *"Without God, I can't; without me, God won't."*

Please note: No one told me about this sexual identity aspect of recovery when I came in. But what if they had? What if they had already learned about PS and shared with me? So I could see what lay ahead and find some hope? Maybe I could have slowly understood, especially hearing them identify. It's taken me years of progressive recovery to be able even to begin to see this on my own. This may be why recognition of deeper surrender is usually so slow in coming. Maybe that's why it's taken more than a quarter century of sexual addiction recovery history in the movement before we could even begin to write about this. But what an opportunity we have now to share experience strength and hope with the vast numbers of those still suffering in sexual identity crisis!

This may also help explain why single "hetero" men often have such problems when they think about dating and actually begin dating in recovery, or why married men have such problems recovering in sex with their spouses, and why we proceed cautiously and stay in the light about it all. This can prove tricky, disconcerting, and most challenging. This can also explain why we seem to take such a long time before we can view women, or men, with even the beginnings of a recovered "male gaze." Recovery means growing up, and that takes time.

If we can see and understand this most difficult aspect of our illness in opposite-sex recovery, we can begin to understand the dilemma we have with our same-sex recovery. It's the same dilemma; but can we see or admit that? Recovery for us lust-aholics means "stepping outside the box" into unexplored territory. This is why we must chart our own way and be careful not to get caught up in the shifting cultural mind-sets concerning our sexuality. In recovery we know more about lust (the problem, at least) than what is put forth in those culturally mediated mind-sets. And we must follow what recovery dictates for us—*what works for us*—not what the changing world out there says about it.

> **Note Well:** The fantasies and temptations are still in the framework of the old mis-orientation, but recovery is being set free from the *temptation*, one temptation at a time and being released from the power of the obsession. *This contradicts any misconception that recovery means* temptations *must stop, change, or shift to the other gender.* This is very, very important and sadly misunderstood. Many may be stuck with the shame and guilt that the temptations are still with the gender involved in their lust or acting out. But that's the very place we bring God in. That's where the Remedy takes place. The only place.

PS Recovery—the Media, Entertainments, Etc.

Recovery from lust is counter-cultural. Recovery from PS is counter-cultural. We have no choice but to face that fact. Progressive recovery places escalating demands on us to assess the role various elements of the culture have on our recovery and spiritual growth. That's why it's not for everybody; most of us will try to get by with "half measures." Until we're forced to admit they don't work. We've seen how the new lust and pseudosexuality are *mediated*; that is, how the media propagate the virus and shape our sexuality. The result is that *we* are mediated. And the question then becomes, Must we not become *un*-mediated to recover? What does that mean? And how do we even approach the subject?

This is an area we should face and talk about together. It's too tough alone. We all have common problems here that affect us deeply. And it's very difficult to find solution in isolation. Speaking for myself and the checkered history of only my image mis-connection, I can honestly say that trying not to be *mis*-connected to movies and television, for example—that is, being free *not* to watch either—is a continuing challenge. I am free not to watch today, if I so choose. That did not come easily; it took years of trying to "control and enjoy," as indicated in chapter 12. But I can easily lose it, as I have many times in the past. For me, the solution to the moving-image connection seems either that I have to abstain, or, from within the freedom *not* to watch, choose only what is non-medicative. The latter "easier softer way" is very, very tricky and loaded with temptingly easy excuses and denial. Basically, the solution should be very simple: BREAK THE *MIS*-CONNECTION. Easier said than done! That's why we need to work this out together in deeper fellowship and start asking and working toward something better.

I've come a long way, but I'm still not where I'd like to be in this very personal aspect of recovery. I want something better than mediated life, and that means *people*, those who are no longer satisfied with the pseudo-real. I desire fellowship with those who want more of the same freedom, finding that which fills the real need. I hope for such dialog and accountability with others. Where this really counts is when it comes down to evaluating how we and our recovery are affected by all the media, entertainment, and avenues of escapism and "medication" in our world.

As we grow in recovery, we feel the need for dialog and accountability with those who come to realize their own personal dilemmas in these areas of modern life. It takes sobriety and *time* for such realizations to develop, we're all very young in this. There's more powerlessness and addictive behavior in this area of our recovery than we might care to admit. How about at the next recovery meeting or convention asking for a show of hands from those who admit to addictive powerlessness just with television alone, or just with movies or games alone, etc.? You'd be surprised.

Those of us who have tasted the freedom in this area and then slip back need a fellowship of others desperate enough to seek *together* what our Image-Connection was blinding us to and keeping us from. There's no doing this alone; the new Image Religion is designed to serve and foster that very aloneness! To escape this prison-house of pseudo-life, we need something better. We need to experience Life; and that means *people*, real human intercourse, being part of the family of Life.

So let's be absolutely honest, open-minded, and willing in all of this—*together*. If we could not recover from the tyranny of our lust-sex obsession alone, by ourselves, how can we expect to recover alone from the effects of these most powerful forces shaping our pseudo-sexuality? We need the identification and support of others—others who also identify and long for something better. This doesn't get dropped in our laps. If we're desperate enough, we take action, start sharing honestly about it, and seek others who identify. We might be surprised what a continuing practice of the Eleventh Step on this can produce.[161]

PS Recovery—Personal Union

CALVIN AND HOBBES By Bill Watterson   January 21, 1993

We have seen how recovery for the lust and sex addicted only begins with stopping the sexually self-destructive thinking and behavior and continues with deeper PS recovery. Escaping the prison-house of lust and sexual bondage is so liberating, we are often supremely happy just to be free. Free *from*, yes, but free for what, free *to* what? Free to begin the personal, human recovery that we so tragically lost in pseudo-sex and pseudo-relationships. Free to experience what was aborted—that normal process of emotional growth *in relationship.*

Unfortunately, being caught up in the work of the recovery movement kept me from seeing such needs for too long a time. For me, the relationally impaired, recovery means freedom to begin seeing myself and people in their own right, improving interpersonal relations and communication, and learning how to give and receive love. I had no clue as to the amount of effort such relational recovery would entail. Actually, it's the toughest part of my whole recovery.

It is marriage and family that have afforded me the opportunity, like no other, of learning how to experience what it means to be a male, a man, a husband, and a father. This is a tough proving-ground, and not for everyone, but one that offers what nothing else can. And what is helping me in marriage, family, and interpersonal relations is the follow-on endeavor of applying the Twelve Steps directly to the characteristics of co-dependency that I've discovered in myself as I strive to recover from those characteristics with others:

Denial Patterns:

I have difficulty identifying what I am feeling.

I minimize, alter or deny how I truly feel.

I perceive myself as completely unselfish and dedicated to the well-being of others.

Low Self-Esteem Patterns:

I have difficulty making decisions.

I judge everything I think, say or do harshly, as never "good enough."

I am embarrassed to receive recognition and praise or gifts.

I do not ask others to meet my needs or desires.

I value others' approval of my thinking, feelings and behavior over my own.

I do not perceive myself as a lovable or worthwhile person.

Compliance Patterns:

I compromise my own values and integrity to avoid rejection or others' anger.

I am very sensitive to how others are feeling and feel the same.

I am extremely loyal, remaining in harmful situations too long.

I value others' opinions and feelings more than my own and am afraid to express differing opinions and feelings of my own.

I put aside my own interests and hobbies in order to do what others want.

I accept sex when I want love.

Control Patterns:

I believe most other people are incapable of taking care of themselves.

I attempt to convince others of what they "should" think and how they "truly" feel.

I become resentful when others will not let me help them.

I freely offer others advice and directions without being asked.

I lavish gifts and favors on those I care about.

I use sex to gain approval and acceptance.

I have to be "needed" in order to have a relationship with others.

The Patterns and Characteristics of Codependence are reprinted from the Web site www.CoDA.org with permission of Co-Dependents Anonymous, Inc. (CoDA, Inc.). Permission to reprint this material does not mean that CoDA, Inc. has reviewed or approved the contents of this publication or that CoDA, Inc. agrees with the views expressed herein. Co-Dependents Anonymous is a fellowship of men and women whose common purpose is to develop healthy relationships and is not affiliated with any other 12 step program.

The first time I saw these characteristics, while meeting with others who identified, I immediately identified with most of them. I feel I've barely begun recovery in this area and that "more will be revealed." But I'm very grateful for the results already realized and the promise to which they point. I sense that many, if not most, of us in sex, lust, and PS recovery, need such a follow-on focus in recovery. As we stay sober and thereby get to understand more of the complexity of our malady, we need all the help we can get.

In such a recovery context, true spiritual and marital sexual union find their fulfillment in companionship and love. Indeed, God gives us what we need, and more, if we are honest, open-minded, and willing. The prospects are open-ended and wondrous, nothing less than finding what our lust was really looking for all along.

"Eye hath not seen, nor ear heard,
neither have entered into the heart of man. . . ."

. . .

This whole concept of PS recovery is a new Promised Land. It promises deeper unity, a unity based on *full-breadth recovery,* from the darkest depths of lust to the most profound heights of victory, peace, joy, and love in relationship. Very few seem to realize the depths recovery must penetrate for those of us infected with the lust virus. As we see this and allow recovery to penetrate this deeper dimension of being, we can discover the God of Recovery together in a deeper way. What a marvelous prospect. And it is happening! There is a recovery infrastructure in place, and a core fellowship of sexual sobriety and lust recovery is in process. Even the Berlin Wall of orientational apartheid is being dismantled.

Rays of light are breaking through here and there. Growing numbers are finding what they hoped for but could not find in their other Twelve Step meetings, religion, therapy, or medication. Not in great numbers, but it is happening. Personal spiritual awakenings (Step Twelve) are being manifested in reaching out and helping others. And yes, the lingering trauma of the sins of others upon us and the burned-in stigmas of our own misdeeds *are* being forgiven, cleansed, healed, and turned into avenues of healing for others.[162]

For this we shall never be sufficiently grateful.

APPENDIXES

WHAT *IS* LUST?

*"Lust is the craving for salt of a man
who is dying of thirst."*
Frederick Buechner

The following question was printed at the top of an otherwise blank sheet of paper and given to a group of twenty men in a meeting for recovery from lust and sex addiction: *"Considering lust's power over me, and what lust does to me, in me, and through me, What IS lust; what kind of a thing must it be?"* Their written answers are given below. The average age of the group was about forty. Length of sobriety from the sexual addiction varied from none to several years. Spelling errors were corrected.

"For me lust is spiritual. A spiritual drug. This drug for me is absolutely tied to violence. Lust is an act of violence for me. This drug of lust is rooted in my violence, for myself and others, esp. women. This drug of lust seems to be the way I calm myself from my fear of violence; the medication I use to come down from my fearful, anxious and angry/violent states. A big lust trigger for me is to be threatened in some way!"

"Lust is an escape—a drug. Lust lures me in and folds around my body like a soft pillow. Lust is dangerous and destructive, causing spiritual and emotional death—the path to a spiritual wasteland."

"Lust is the spirit of the age."

"Lust in my life is a desire to see, smell, touch and feel women. Lust causes me to look at any woman and find something sexually desirable

233

about that woman. Lust is fantasizing about women and a desire to have any kind of sex with them. Lust is a constant desire to be needed by any woman and to prove to her that that need is justified and can be sexually and emotionally filled by me. Lust is an overwhelming feeling that takes over and controls all aspects of my life and especially interferes with my rational, logical and moral thinking."

"Lust is an obsession to look and drink in a female's form, sexual fantasies, thoughts and to seek sexual encounters. All of this separates me from God and leads to guilt and remorse, leads to isolation. 'A thing'—lust is the most forceful disease that is of Satan."

"Experientially it's an exciting experience/sensation that occurs when seeing/relating to attractive women. It's a desire or appetite pulling on my will driving me to act and receive sexual gratification in some way. Just as greed is an abnormal perversion of the natural good desire to succeed and be financially ok in life, lust is an abnormal perversion of the need for love and faithful sex."

"As I think about it, it is a *state of mind* that begins with (because my problem is self-gratification thru masturbation) my ritual of first making sure that I am alone and will not be discovered. Then it is becoming totally withdrawn to the pursuit of finding the right stimulus and then the self-gratification of the climax and ejaculation."

"Lust is a power that affects my way of thinking and my behavior. When I am in lust, all reason, all rationality goes out the window and I, instead, rationalize that the feeling of the power of lust within me isn't so bad, in fact it actually makes me feel good, or I desire the effect of its power within my mind and body. Lustful thoughts fill my mind and my entire consciousness and I can find no peace until I act out. Even prayer has no deterrent power once I have embarked on the path of lust."

"What It Does for Me Now: craving for self-satisfaction, fantasy, desire for physical stimulation with no emotion or price, no emotional connection, pure escape from reality, no reprisals or judgment, numbing anger, resentment, emotional pain relief, power illusion, acceptance illusion. Results: Regret, fear!!! loss of self-confidence, loneliness, isolation, depression, procrastination, negative emotions, anger."

"First of all when I see an attractive female, I begin to imagine all kinds of sexual fantasies and after however long I let the lust thoughts stay in my mind, I feel guilty because I allow myself to be controlled by these lust looks and fantasies. It makes me bored of the whole matter and women are just objects to me. I go back and forth with this battle."

"Lust, in my opinion is an instinctual and completely natural feeling that I believe all humans possess in some degree. I believe we have this feeling to help man reproduce. It's a sexual attraction. It's the force that attracts us to someone or something sexually. I believe the problem I have with it is I let it become so important and so exciting to me that I became obsessed with it. I let it control my behavior therefore controlling me."

"Lust to me is the inability to control my need to speak with other women either on the telephone or on the computer. The need to feel that I am needed. Lust is a power much stronger than I, because I know without this program and my attempts to let God into my life, it eats me up and spits me out. Lust is a habit. Lust makes me lie. Lust is making my life miserable. Lust makes me *angry*. Lust is filled with guilt. *Lust is destructive.* Lust is shameful."

"Lust is desire which overpowers and defeats my will. I can possess and control desires, but lust possesses and controls me. I have no ability to control lust, but I can only lift it up to God's hands to defeat it and gain victory over it for me. Lust is very attractive and deceitful and seeks to destroy me. Perversion, controlling, deceitful, destructive, spiritual, escape from reality."

"A *sexual* or other type of fantasy that once triggered takes over my mind and "makes" me respond to the "impulses" in a physical way even though I don't really want to do them. But they give short term physical pleasure followed by overwhelming guilt."

"Lusting for me is seeing a provocative appearing woman and then imagining what it might be like to be with her—I should say that that is the way it was, but that feeling still breaks through at times even though I do not want it to. Also, lusting for me is to allow my anger to break through and control how I act and what I say without regard for how it affects those around me. It is an evil thing that controls my spirit."

"It's a built-in self-destruct mechanism, a reflex to punish myself for my wrongs. It's a God pointer to who's taking my place in being punished and destroyed."

"When I'm lonely I use lust as a way to feel wanted and loved. When I'm angry and seriously hurt by someone else I use lust as revenge and a way to prove I'm valuable. However, lust is really always lies. It is a way to escape from reality, a way to avoid difficult decisions and feelings and a method to feel better right now but at the cost of tomorrow. Lust makes me feel numb and distant from my wife."

"Lust for me is an adrenaline rush. A chemical change. It takes me out of whatever I'm doing. It puts me in a trance. It is powerful. It gives me short term medication, taking away whatever pain I'm in. But there is a price. It is spiritual noise. It prevents me from having meaningful relationships with myself, others, or God. Lust today can bring depression/self-criticism/guilt. Lust keeps me lonely. It allows me to live in my head. I don't have to have outside contact. It's also a habit, a conditioned response to pain. Acting out today will not relieve the pain."

"Lust is my addiction, my compulsion and certainly a power that has control over a great deal of my day-to-day behavior. It makes me angry, allows or forces me to lie or not be honest with myself and others. It drives me inward toward isolation and I become distant from both family and friends. It does not allow me to develop personal relationship with other people including my wife. It is a power (dark) that I personally have little control over. I must continue to 'give it up to my higher power.' It is my relief, my way to release stress in my life. It makes me feel so good but so bad. It feels good when acting out only to have anger and resentment after the act."

"Lust is a force inside me that wants to kill me. It's a Deceiver and Liar because it offers me one thing, promises me life, and gives me the opposite, spiritual death. It's a seducing spirit that is cunning, baffling and powerful and comes in many disguises. Lust is a perverter of reality. Lust is anti-male. Lust is an anti-God spiritual force. Lust is ME—apart from God!"

When I read these few comments today, I wonder, Why did I have to write this book? It's all here! These give eloquent testimony to the fact that recovery from whatever this is that we're calling lust involves so much more than we could ever have imagined when we first set out on this journey. It also implies that recovery will need the intervention of something or some One not only more powerful than what is described here, but who can fulfill whatever it is that lust is really looking for.

2

PSEUDO-WOMAN AND FAIRY QUEENS

This season fashion is outrageous, sexy and glamorous, full of slick fabrics, tight miniskirts and dangerous stiletto heels. Spring's baby doll has become Fall's vixen, intent on showing off legs, hips and breasts. Hair is coiffed, lips are dark, nails are lacquered midnight red. Fashion hasn't been this blatant since the '70s. The message: Dress up. Provoke. . . .

Los Angeles Times Magazine [163]

This is a *woman* talking. Trying to look and act like a prostitute. It is no accident that this has been called "call-girl chic."[164] And this evangel is heralded to America's young style-conscious women via one of the country's "greatest" newspapers, with circulation approaching one-and-a-half million. And provoke? Provoke what? Lust? From men? From women? In herself? It sounds like some kind of lust is active in the woman writing this. Lust for what? Wanting to be lusted after? Where, how, and why did this aping of the prostitute image begin, and what does it tell us about pseudosexuality?

> **prostitutize** \pros-te-too-tize\ *vt* — to impart or imbue with the appearance or demeanor of a prostitute; to turn into a prostitute.
>
> (From the author's *Pseudo-Dictionary of Fabricated Words*)

237

Some 28,000,000 immigrants came into the United States between 1840 and 1910, with the influx peaking in 1910. This population tidal wave crammed millions of single or unattached young men and women into tenement districts in the large urban centers. These, together with migrations from within the American farmland, constituted a whole stratum of urban society cut off from homeland, roots, and families and thrown together in highly unnatural living and working conditions. Prostitution became very widespread about the same time immigration was peaking, running rampant in the cities, bringing an epidemic of venereal disease.

Demand for prostitutes was so great that there arose a large-scale traffic in recruiting and importing "white slaves," with the resulting "white slave panic" of the years 1908–1914. And the word "slavery" was not hyperbole; what went on was unspeakably villainous and degrading. Prostitution, even under the best of circumstance and time, is never what it is made out to be in the movies. Take it from someone who's been there. In 1912 there were over 1,800 "vice resorts" and an estimated 15,000 prostitutes in New York City alone. This situation gave rise to many "vice commissions" and "committees of fourteen," and the Mann Act (White Slave Traffic Act) was passed in 1910. Between 1910 and 1918 the U.S. Justice Department obtained some 2,200 Mann Act convictions for trafficking in women.[165]

Apparently the most available men—the as-yet unassimilated into the new country, language, and culture—were the ones resorting to the prostitutes. Prostitution was in the air. City herself had become the Seductress, beguiling the crowds with her newly electric-lighted streets and rituals of pleasure, amusement, and escape. What was the effect of this phenomenon on city women and girls? What went through their minds when they encountered this prostitutized atmosphere for the first time? And what was the effect on men?

Is it possible that to connect with men, women may have come to seek the same access to men (or power over them) as their sisters in scarlet and rouge? Perhaps it was no coincidence that the new "fashion" was born at this time to emulate the image of their sisters on the street: makeup, hairdos, dress, mannerisms, and their manner of relating to men, especially since this was now being advertised and legitimized in the new illustrated media, and especially in movies.

Valerie Steele, professor at New York's Fashion Institute of Technology and author of the scholarly *Fashion and Eroticism*, says, "All my research has led me to believe that the concept of beauty is sexual in origin, and the changing ideal of beauty apparently reflects changing attitudes toward sexual expression."[166] Changing sexuality reflected in changing fashion? Powerful. Pseudo-sexual.

The prostitutizing of female beauty went hand in hand with the new showy element in the culture, the ethnic sensualism in the "dance craze" and music, and the cabaret scene, most typically in New York City. All of this was in an environment where men could increasingly "pick up" women without the stigma of vice. Movies—where the new modes, sexualities, and behaviors made their appearance and were made attractive and okay—were the prime catalyst in the acculturation of this prostitutizing and prostitution of the female image.

Remember the comment from one of the boys at Duke when asked what the nudie magazines taught them to look for in girls? "The image of beauty—large breasts, thin waist, model-esque features. . . ." That's just externals, surface stuff. Practicing lusters would say that what the boys were really looking for was lust triggers—"prostitutized" image-woman. The awesome Goddess.

Emergence of the Feminized Male

It is not just a striking coincidence that at this very time and in this very cultural nexus in New York City there arose not only the cult of female "beauty" and the feminine religion but the cult of men imitating the new female image. Drag queens emerged in New York City and other metropolises—men dressed and made up to imitate the new highly stylized female image in appearance and demeanor. The drag queens at the Hamilton Lodge balls in New York City, for example, largest of the balls, where hundreds of the queens paraded and danced together and audiences of thousands watched, were competing in doing renditions of what feminine demeanor was purported to be (the pseudo-feminine). Thus, at the time when the new morality and fashion revolutions were taking off around the turn of the century in the manufacturing of pseudo-woman, pseudo-*man* was appearing on the scene.

We are told that in New York City of the twenties and thirties "it was at the drag balls, more than any place else, that the gay world saw itself, celebrated itself, and affirmed itself." "The image of the fairy [in the twenties and thirties] was so powerful culturally that it influenced the self-understanding of all sexually active men. . . ."[167] George Chauncey, historian of the gay culture and author of *Gay New York*, is on to something here; he too apparently sees that there is a commonality underlying the genesis of both today's homosexuality and today's heterosexuality.

George Chauncey writes that the fairies' style was not so much an imitation of women as a group but a "provocative exaggeration of the appearance and demeanor ascribed to prostitutes." As a result, many men seem to have regarded fairies in the same way they regarded prostitutes. This may have made it easier for them to use fairies for sexual purposes in the same way they used female prostitutes. And once a man makes even this disguised male-to-male sexual connection, must not a corresponding imprinting take place within him? It did with me.

This is where we begin to see cultural forces dramatically shaping today's sexuality and orientation. Did the new lust bring more lust into being? Did the mass-market idolization of pseudo-woman, sending the new lust into the air, lead to the desire of some *men* to be lusted after? Does glorification of media queens of glamour somehow call forth queens in drag?

I came upon George Chauncey's analysis of "fairy" sexuality in New York of the twenties and thirties long after I had come to see the pseudosexuality in myself. It is very revealing:

> . . . [M]en did not just use different categories to think about a sexuality that, despite appearances, was fundamentally the same as that of men today, for those different cultural categories governed and were manifest to men's everyday social practices. Even in the terms of the late-twentieth-century hetero-homosexual axis, in other words, it would be difficult to argue that the "normal" men who had sex with fairies were really homosexuals, for that would leave inexplicable their determined pursuit of women sexual partners. But neither could they plausibly be regarded as heterosexuals, for heterosexuals would have been incapable of

responding sexually to another male. Nor were they bisexuals, for that would have required them to be attracted to both women as women and men as men. They were, rather, [pseudosexual] men who were attracted to womanlike men or interested in sexual activity defined not by the gender of their partner but by the kind of bodily pleasures that partner could provide. (Interpolation added)[168]

Note: This conclusion of Chauncey's really illuminates my pseudo-sexuality thesis. Our modern attempt at pigeonholing human sexual orientation has a false ring to it.

The historical congruence of these three cultural phenomena—the rise of widespread prostitution, the cult of female beauty, and the fairy queen phenomenon—points up the power the image of pseudo-woman was achieving. It was not chance coincidence that this was the time when the new mass media were taking over. When both women in the fashion revolution and men in drag are aping the appearance and demeanor of prostitutes, we sense something very powerful—*and pseudosexual*—is going on. At the bottom of this is nothing less than the new lust in action. Valerie Steele brings up a sobering thought:

Men act and women appear. Men look at women. Women watch themselves being looked at. . . . The surveyor of woman in herself is male; the surveyed female. *Thus she turns herself into an object* [emphasis added]. . . .[169]

Pseudosexuality in a nutshell!

In the industrial age, does the new lust start with women? To connect with men? To latch on to a man? Does she insist on playing out the "curse" of Eve? "Your desire shall be for your husband, and he shall rule over you."[170] Woman lusting after beauty, after a pseudo-image, after her self? Wanting to be lusted after? Who knows? Does the "sacred feminine" come in here somewhere?[171] On the other hand, it was man who sought out and had to have substitute pseudo-woman. Yet a lust inside woman seems to come autonomously into play—media driven. Whatever the answers, how could all of this *not* greatly affect our sexuality, yours and mine, in any and all of its expressions? For example, think about possible implications for sexual "orientation" in the concept Valerie Steele describes: "The surveyor of woman in herself is male." What's going on in this *surveying*? We know so little about lust.

. . .

Pseudo-woman will never satisfy—either herself or anyone else. And pseudo-man will never satisfy. The forces at work shaping our sexualities are incredibly powerful forces. All this begins to look like mass-addiction. Both men and women. And this is why recovery is so seemingly impossible for the lust-addicted and why our relation to the media is such a crucial part of it. We need to experience the reality revolution in reverse. Whether we want to face it or not, as President Clinton once implied, we need to recover from our very culture itself.[172] Recovery from pseudosexuality is counter-cultural.

THE "FEMININE RELIGION" AND THE TYRANNY OF THE BEAUTY CULT

In the early 1900s, the French Comtesse de Tramar wrote books on feminine beauty with deliberately religious titles. She compared the feminine rite of beautification and adornment with the sacred rites of the Catholic Church and wrote that this feminine rite

> ... is, in effect, an essentially feminine religion, which woman will practice across the centuries, a devotee of this cult, of this ceremony, which creates her happiness, placing in her soul infinite ecstasies.[173]

Gloria Swanson, the major movie star of the 1920s, said beauty was her career ... for "the world holds no place for a worn looking woman these days, and admiration is so necessary for a woman's happiness."[174]

When was the last time you walked through the feminine beauty aids section of your local drug store? Did it ever strike you how disproportionate was the percentage of space given to this section? I am advised that roughly one third of the dollar volume income in drug stores such as Longs or Sav-On in Southern California comes from feminine beauty aids.[175] In Lisa Loomers play, *The Waiting Room*, Wanda, the bold, fortyish, street-smart contemporary woman from New Jersey who is searching for physical perfection through cosmetic surgery, says, as her enlightenment begins to dawn upon her, "I sat down with a pencil and paper and figured out I've spent 6,750 hours of my life—on my hair." Something pseudo is going on.

> The modeling world is a fickle place. Waifs are out and glamour
> is in—again. Fashion writer Maureen Sajbel looks at *the ever-
> shifting notion of what the ideal female form should be* [emphasis
> added].
>
> *Los Angeles Times*, August 25, 1994

This article goes on to sketch "the Ping-Ponging changes in America's
dream girl." Strikingly thin Twiggy had everyone talking in the 1960s,
when women didn't seem to mind being called "chicks." The '70s started
with a wider range of ethnic looks with the first black woman on the
cover of *Vogue*, but by the late '70s, the "healthy blond" was back in.
Photographer Richard Avedon's Revlon ads captured the "glamazon"
look of the 1980s—bigger, taller, bustier models—"super-sexy glam
vixens." The 1990s began with the odd looks that were the opposite of
this in the form of tiny Kate Moss, androgynous Kristin McMenamy,
and the waifs, who fit the latest grunge and neo-hippie styles: tight-to-
the-body, shorter fashions, showing "more curve, more leg." Later in
the '90s, an urge for a new, idealized female silhouette moved fashion
beyond the waif, with sexier, more glamorous models. (Is there something of the addiction tolerance factor at play here too—more needed
to achieve the desired effect?)

Notice how the half-life of modeling and fashions kept getting
shorter. Economically driven, sure, but what drives the economics?
May we suggest that lust, whether active or passive, plays a significant
role? Of course, fashions have always been changing. The point is that
today, in our image-driven culture, these changes affect us more than
ever. A static lust object will never do; lust demands the new, the different, the more risqué. It's the same force driving changing automobile
"fashions." Lust-driven advertising and economics demand it.

We are told that the Barbie doll image "has been badly rat-
tled by Bratz, a line of hip, trendy dolls launched in 2001 by MGA
Entertainment. Mattel's turnaround plan for Barbie has entailed
"everything from a breakup with Ken to trendier fashions to . . .
enlisting [actress and recording artist] Hillary Duff to talk her up.
For all that, Barbie still seems stuck. She is trying 'to out-hooker
Bratz . . . .'"[176] Prostitutizing Barbie reveals how lust education and
imprinting begin very early in life.

I am reminded of Hugo Munsterberg's comments on film making, which "aims to keep both the demand and its fulfillment forever awake" and where "the camera men of the moving pictures . . . are always haunted by the fear that the supply of new sensations may be exhausted" (chapter 10). Keeping demand and fulfillment forever awake with new sensations is what fashion and modeling—and lust—are all about. They never satisfy.

Listen to a fictional description of night life at the Copacabana in the 1940s:

> Helen O'Connell has just finished a sultry rendition of "I Like the Likes of You," singing directly at Jacob King, a good-looking gangster celebrating the fact that he has just beaten a murder conviction. Then Blue Tyler makes her entrance.
>
> Poured into a black evening gown, draped with a red fox fur . . . [she] sashays into the club with a small army of bodyguards, publicists, and boyfriend of the moment . . . . "She smiled and waved at the photographers, their cameras loving her and she loving their cameras in turn . . . . Blue always in motion, posing, vamping, cooing, 'I'd walk a mile for a man who walked a mile for a Camel.' Joe Romagnola, the maitre d' produced a cigarette, offering a light from his silver Tiffany lighter. . . ."[177]

> **beatify** — \be-at-e-fi\ vt to declare a person to be among the blessed and thus entitled to specific religious honor (*Random House II*).

Is there any doubt that Blue Tyler had been beatified—declared blessed, assumed into the pantheon of "stars," and entitled to "specific religious honor"? The icon of pseudo-woman is center stage, the object of adulation and desire, a powerful force unleashed upon the accelerating cultural evolution of American pseudosexuality. How are adolescents or young men supposed to relate to *that*?

> The new economic order impinged upon sexual norms in a number of ways. Americans did not automatically respond to factory output by multiplying their desires for material goods; *an ethic of consumption had to be sold.* Advertising came into its own as an industry in the 1920s, as executives consciously strove to *incite*

desire [emphases added]. In the process, they helped shape a new conception of womanhood [read *pseudo-woman*]. . . . As one advertisement pointedly claimed, *"The first duty of woman is to attract."*[178]

Comment: Woman prostitutized and prostituted to create an ethic of consumption and male desire (read *male lust*). With woman's consent! It's still going on. And now with men. Why do we insist on being victimized? Every presidential campaign still preaches The American Dream, and every new administration pushes the kind of consumerism that helps fuel the new paganism.

The Tyranny of the Beauty Cult

The following quotes are from Albert Ellis's book *The American Sexual Tragedy*. Ellis did an in-depth sampling of mass media including radio, television, movies, and print media published or extant on January 1, 1950, then again for January 1, 1960. I do not know whether what he calls the "beatification of beauty" is still going in the direction indicated; the point is that what he described was a cultural change that apparently began with the industrial revolution and accelerated sharply since the turn of the century.

> Ellis: ". . . American women are specifically *taught* to feel physically inadequate . . . women's feelings of being insufficiently beautiful are not only family-taught but are largely culture- or society-centered, and hence present in virtually *all* contemporary American females."

Comment: Even though advertisers created such campaigns to sell products, this still sounds like a (subconscious?) male conspiracy to manipulate women's appearance. But why was it so easy to sell women on pseudo-attraction?

One reader of this book gave me the following note: "At a recent Photoshop conference, the presenter mentioned that at a top modeling agency, the first thing they do before showing the images to the models [presumably photos taken of the models themselves] is to take 3% off their weight (because even the models think they look fat) and then add sparkle to their eyes."

> Ellis: ". . . [T]he modern woman's feelings of physical inadequacy also stem from culture-centered and socially propagated influences which make it virtually impossible for any contemporary female, no matter how psychologically secure she may be, not to have a wide-ranging and deep-raging [sic] horror of several of her own physical attributes."

Comment: Note that the word used is *deep-raging*. I thought we sex and lust addicts were the only ones who had such self-hatred and rage. Lustified women too?

> Ellis: "The one thing most consistently emphasized and embellished in today's most popular publications and productions is not, as you might think, sex, nor love, nor marriage. It is, rather, the great American prerequisite to sex, love, and marriage—feminine pulchritude. In innumerable ways, female beauty is thrown in the faces of our readers, viewers, and listeners, and is made to seem a debateless desideratum not only for men to view and women to possess, but for women to ogle as well as to flaunt. Indeed, although the implication behind the modern emphasis on feminine loveliness is that it is largely for the attraction and distraction of males, beauty in its own right, beauty for the sake of female appraisal and approval, has become as much the rule as the exception today."[179]

Comment: Female pulchritude (read glorification or *lustification*) as the great American prerequisite for sex, love, and marriage—that's but another term in the pseudosexuality equation. The author goes on to say that women must be dressed romantically, fashionably, and sex-enticingly. The impossible tyranny lust has put women under! This is pseudosexuality. No wonder the women eventually revolt! Or go under.

Question: Is image-driven anorexia a form of lust for women? Let's hear what they have to say about the new lust.

PICTURE-LUST CASE STUDIES

The following are excerpts from five interviews conducted by the author with self-described lust-sex addicts in various stages of recovery. These give added dimension to image-driven lust and picture-sex and their effects within the individual. The same twenty-one questions were asked of each man, and their responses were tape recorded. "Sexually sober" means no sexual activity with himself or anyone other than his spouse. "Abstinent" means no form of sex with self or others.

M.
Single male, age 44. Two years sexually sober and abstinent; one year sober from looking at lust images.

1. *At what age did you experience images coupled with any kind of sexual thinking or behavior?* "Twelve or thirteen."
2. *Describe the scene of how that initial connection between pictures and sex (or sexual type thinking or activity) came about.* "On shelves at convenience stores. Detective magazine cover; inside more pictures of scantily clad women. Submissive women. Then more explicit magazines in the *Gent* and *Playboy* genre."
3. *Describe the image itself, what the picture shows.* "A woman posing, scantily clad, emphasizing breasts, large breasts, stockings, garters. I remember white stockings and garters, fishnets, bra and panties, women usually looking into the camera."
4. *What effect did viewing that image have inside of you? If you can, play back your feelings in slow motion so we can see the progression of feelings and impact. Another way of asking this is, What was the picture (or pose) communicating to you?* "I was particularly

aroused when the woman was looking at the camera; this communicated that she was posing for me. Looking into her eyes gave me a sense of connection with a real person and a feeling she wanted to arouse me."

5. *With the picture there in front of you, what did you do?* "Usually ended in masturbation. When I didn't have pictures handy I would close my eyes and act out to memory of them or picture a real person."

6. *Did your use of images escalate? How? Did your inner reactions and feelings change over time as you continued to resort to picture sex? Please describe.* "Yes. Began stealing magazines from stores. Acting out to pictures more often. [My] stash grew. Took my favorite pictures with me even on family vacations. Discovered hardcore pornography, films, pictures. My inner reactions, feelings: Developed more of a fantasy world. Depended more on pictures, fantasy to deal with loneliness."

7. *Did you reach a point when you would say that you had crossed the line into addiction? At what age?* "Yes. Fourteen to fifteen."

8. *Did you experience any turning point(s) in your history of picture-sex where something new was going on, either in the content of the images themselves, your behavior, or your thinking? Was there some specific incident connected with this, such as a special picture or experience? Describe the picture and/or incident.* "I had been addicted to hardcore pornography films for years. Oral sex images where the woman was looking at the camera (making me feel I was participant) were my choice. Also, every new perversion I witnessed on film made vivid extreme imprint (golden showers, bestiality, S&M), hooking me in. I remember in my early twenties reading a foreign-film pornography catalog, when I experienced a hard drool and a rush from head to toe, like something had overtaken me. This was a very real moment that I can reflect on and realize I was totally enthralled by the addiction overpowering me like a drug."

9. *What place did these pictures come to have in your life?* "When I didn't have actual pictures or films, I would still masturbate to them in my mind almost nightly. But eventually I had two Hefty bags full of tapes and would view tapes and films regularly several times a week. I flew across country binging and buying more tapes."

10. *How would you say your sexuality was influenced by resorting to images?* "I began acting out images I saw in the tapes with actual women, but ultimately preferred tapes over women (less hassle, less fear)."

11. *How would you say your personality was affected by this practice?* "Lived in my own world more—'checked out.'"

12. *How would you say your perception of and relation to women and/or men was affected by this practice?* "I viewed all women sexually (if they were okay-looking and in my age range). I feared women and the lust power they had over me."

13. *What has happened in recovery to your resorting to these images?* "I don't look at them at all. When I play them in my head, I give them up. Sometimes I still allow them to play longer than they should."

14. *What's your relation to these images now?* "When they pop up in my head they don't arouse me like they used to, but are still vivid. They don't control me and put me in the trance. I choose to let them go. I definitely feel more detached from them. When I chance upon them (TV, newspaper), I flip past quickly."

15. *Are you still tempted when you see one of them? How? What power do they still have over you?* "Rarely. It might flash through my mind occasionally what it would be like to watch a film, but it's easily dismissed. It took a couple of years of [sexual] sobriety for me to come to the point of not lingering at all on lustful images."

16. *Do you still "drink"? If so, how does it affect you?* "No, although I sometimes linger on the mental pictures too long."

17. *If you do not drink, how do you not drink?* "I just consciously remind myself I'm on a different path now, following God when I'm tempted. I just deliberately think, 'I choose God.'"

18. *What does recovery mean for you?* "Giving, not taking. Trying to look outward, not live in my head so much, staying in the moment. My relationships with people are no longer because of what I can get out of them."

19. *How would you summarize the effect picture sex has had on your life?* "I believe the seeds were there for me to become addicted to lust anyway, but pictures ignited lust sooner and helped it progress more quickly. Picture sex also definitely influenced the way I saw (as lust objects) and treated (selfishly) women. They were there to

please me (like the women in the pictures), and I didn't have to reciprocate. Picture sex also gave me an easy retreat, an easy way out inside myself. I didn't have to deal with dating or relationships if I didn't want to. Helped construct a major fantasy—playing around in my head."

20. *What would you say or have someone else say to your parents (or caretakers, educators, etc.) if, knowing all this in recovery now, you could go back in time to the very beginning of your picture-sex experience?* "Though I searched out materials myself, I wish I hadn't had such easy access to them and been able to stumble across them at such a vulnerable young impressionable age."

21. *Do you have any suggestion on how this should be handled with your own or other children today?* "Do not keep any lewd materials around the house. Be vigilant [regarding] what your children are watching on TV and buying. Perhaps send [them] to counseling if an addiction is noticeable."

J.
Age 44, married with children, sober two years.

1. *At what age did you experience images coupled with any kind of sexual thinking or behavior?* "15."

2. *Describe the scene of how that initial connection between pictures and sex (or sexual type thinking or activity) came about.* "I found *Playboy* and *Penthouse* magazines my dad had."

3. *Describe the image itself, what the picture shows. (Detach yourself from the effect the image had on you and try to communicate what's actually there in the picture. The next question will ask for the effect the image had inside you.)* "Pictures of naked women with large breasts."

4. *What effect did viewing that image have inside of you? If you can, play back your feelings in slow motion so we can see the progression of feelings and impact. Another way of asking this is, What was the picture (or pose) communicating to you?* "I immediately got excited and wanted to have sex with the women in the pictures."

5. *With the picture there in front of you, what did you do? Act out? Fantasize? Go into a trance? Etc.* "I went into the shower and masturbated while fantasizing."

6. *Did your use of images escalate? How? Did your inner reactions and feelings change over time as you continued to resort to picture sex? Please describe.* "Yes. I bought and found more magazines and masturbated whenever possible. I couldn't wait to get new ones."

7. *Did you reach a point when you would say that you had crossed the line into addiction? At what age, and what makes you think you were addicted?* "Not until age 40. When that became more important than anything else."

8. *Did you experience any turning point(s) in your history of picture-sex where something new was going on, either in the content of the images themselves, your behavior, or your thinking? Was there some specific incident connected with this, such as a special picture or experience? Describe the picture and/or incident.* "I needed more explicit pictures showing people having sex and reaching orgasm."

9. *What place did these pictures come to have in your life?* "1st place. They were more important than anything in my life."

10. *How would you say your sexuality was influenced by resorting to images?* "I became bolder with women and lusted after those that looked like the ones in the images."

11. *How would you say your personality was affected by this practice?* "Became more secretive and lied more often. Took many more risks and was more outgoing with women."

12. *How would you say your perception of and relation to women and/or men was affected by this practice?* "I looked at every woman as a potential sex object."

13. *What has happened in recovery to your resorting to these images?* "I don't look any more at the images or other women."

14. *What's your relation to these images now?* "I think they are degrading and harmful."

15. *Are you still tempted when you see one of them? How? What power do they still have over you?* "Sometimes I am tempted momentarily but I look away and pray."

16. *Do you still "drink"? If so, how does it affect you?* "No."

17. *If you do not drink, how do you not drink?* "I think of those things in my life that are more important to me now than those images, and I pray."

18. *What does recovery mean for you?* "Overcoming the desires to lust after other women and [my need of] pornography."

19. *How would you summarize the effect picture sex has had on your life?* "It has almost ruined my marriage and my relationships with my family and friends. It completely changed my priorities."

20. *What would you say or have someone else say to your parents (or caretakers, educators, etc.) if, knowing all this in recovery now, you could go back in time to the very beginning of your picture-sex experience?* "I would advise them to elect officials with high morals who would do everything they could to ban these images and keep them out of the public domain."

21. *Do you have any suggestions on how should this be handled with your own or other children today?* "I would advise them of the harmful effect it has had on many people and how degrading it is to love and sex in a marriage relationship."

R.
Age 45, sexually sober one year.

1. *At what age did you experience images coupled with any kind of sexual thinking or behavior?* "Age 8. Tinkerbell, from the Wonderful World of Disney. Some female to make me feel good. The second time was the *Playboy* magazine my brother-in-law gave me when I was twelve or thirteen. I looked at the pictures and was intrigued and gave me desire for more. I also was embarrassed."

2. *Describe the scene of how that initial connection between pictures and sex (or sexual type thinking or activity) came about.* "I remember feeling lonely and going into a fantasy world looking out my bedroom window. I think I was feeling no love from my mother or family. The Tinkerbell fantasy was wishing I could get her to do things to make me feel good. I didn't have a physical reaction, but it opened up a desire or longing to see more and even touch."

3. *Describe the image itself, what the picture shows. (Detach yourself from the effect the image had on you and try to communicate what's actually there in the picture. The next question will ask for the effect the image had inside you.)* "It was a fantasy picture in my head of a fairy type female creature scantily dressed. The picture was of an undressed woman in alluring posture."

4. *What effect did viewing that image have inside of you? If you can, play back your feelings in slow motion so we can see the progression of feelings and impact. Another way of asking this is, What was the picture (or pose) communicating to you?* "Hope, relief, comfort. Hope of feeling good, relief that I had an answer to life, combat my loneliness."

5. *With the picture there in front of you, what did you do?* "Trance and fantasize."

6. *Did your use of images escalate? How? Did your inner reactions and feelings change over time as you continued to resort to picture sex? Please describe.* "Yes. I began to integrate magazine, advertising, and TV images into my fantasies. I needed them to masturbate. My feelings at the time were of desperation to conjure up a fantasy in my head. Over time, I became numb to shame so it wouldn't interfere with masturbating and the high."

7. *Did you reach a point when you would say that you had crossed the line into addiction? At what age, and what makes you think you were addicted?* "Yes. Age fifteen or so. When I needed masturbation to relax or sleep."

8. *Did you experience any turning point(s) in your history of picture-sex where something new was going on, either in the content of the images themselves, your behavior, or your thinking? Was there some specific incident connected with this, such as a special picture or experience? Describe the picture and/or incident.* "I think women's lingerie or bathing suit pictures in print or TV that got my attention and I wanted more of."

9. *What place did these pictures come to have in your life?* "Solution to making me feel good. A possibility of a 'quick hit.' A rush."

10. *How would you say your sexuality was influenced by resorting to images?* "I wanted women who looked like the images and in my head portrayed a self-serving object."

11. *How would you say your personality was affected by this practice?* "I began to view women by how close they resembled the images. My relating to women was based on if they qualified to these images I had in my head. Relating to people was based on how their images created in me [the feeling] that I was important. If you looked like the images or were around them, I wanted to be around you."

12. *How would you say your perception of and relation to women and/ or men was affected by this practice?* "I missed having people be my friends. I don't know how to be a friend or what that means. Relations were conditional and sometimes now are still. I missed having women relations (long-term) that were loving."

13. *What has happened in recovery to your resorting to these images?* "I realize they are triggers to acting out. I stay away from them."

14. *What's your relation to these images now?* "They represent the wreckage of my past. They distort reality and dehumanize women."

15. *Are you still tempted when you see one of them? How? What power do they still have over you?* "Yes. The same solution for a 'quick hit' to feel good. The power to solve my life reality."

16. *Do you still "drink"? If so, how does it affect you?* "Sometimes. Like going over the speed limit and seeing if the CHP saw me. A lot of fear that I will be triggered. I surrender and admit my powerlessness over the drink to God."

17. *What does recovery mean for you?* "It means God is going to make a better person of me even when I can't see it. It means my life will have value to my family and all relations. It means I will live life on life's terms, not mine, and experience joy."

19. *How would you summarize the effect picture sex has had on your life?* "It began as harmless, [and progressed] to becoming a slave master and dementor [sic] of my thinking of women and relationships. It became the tool to take the drink and act out."

20. *What would you say or have someone else say to your parents (or caretakers, educators, etc.) if, knowing all this in recovery now, you could go back in time to the very beginning of your picture-sex experience?* "Learning of women-men relationships is not based on picture-sex. Please explain what the pictures are and aren't. Ask me what I was feeling and thinking when I saw the pictures. Correct any misconceptions. Get me help if I can't get the misconceptions out of my head."

21. *Do you have any suggestion on how this should be handled with your own or other children today?* "I'm learning. It is a real battle with the media and the portrayal of women [and] men and how they relate to each other. My only suggestion is be an example and tell them that the images are not real and (with discretion) how my experience affected my relationships."

M.
Age in the forties. Not sober at the time, but trying to stop.

1. *At what age did you experience images coupled with any kind of sexual thinking or behavior?* "About seven."
2. *Describe the scene of how that initial connection between pictures and sex (or sexual type thinking or activity) came about.* "My father was an excellent artist and sketched the nude body. I imitated him and sketched nude women and men and thought it was neat until an older cousin said my drawings were smut and terrible. I shamefully shrank back.

   "I began masturbating at the age of seven. At nine or ten, my sister brought a magazine into the house with photos of men and women doing soft porn, bizarre things. The woman was naked and he partially. It was absorbing me and excited me, the first connection between male and female, even though I didn't know what it was about. I would keep that in my mind over and over again while masturbating."
3. *What effect did viewing that image have inside of you? If you can, play back your feelings in slow motion so we can see the progression of feelings and impact. Another way of asking this is, What was the picture (or pose) communicating to you?* "I seemed to be preoccupied with the male and female body. At age eleven I drew a chalk female figure on the sidewalk. It made me feel good; I was occupied by it and it filled my thoughts. But the neighbor kids thought it was funny. At about 12 or 13 I would look at male body-builder magazine covers on the rack. Kept staring at the images and masturbating to them. Bought the next issue; regularly feeding on it."
4. *Did your use of images escalate?* "Yes. At the beginning it was body builders, then nude models, then men and men together in sex acts. It had to progress into more depraved stuff or in more detail. This was in fifties and sixties. Then videos came in. The force was too strong and occasionally I watched a video."
5. *Did you reach a point when you would say that you had crossed the line into addiction? At what age, and what makes you think you were addicted?* "Yes. I had to find ways to obtain those images. I wrote away to addresses at the back of the magazine for photographs, and

they got more pornographic, and then they sent me sheets of hard core male porn revealing everything. As soon as I opened it, I was in shock, staring at it, heart beating very fast, like I'd found a gold mine. And immediately masturbated to it. I'd go to any lengths to get my hands on new stuff and with each effort came a new high."

6. *How would you say your sexuality was influenced by resorting to images?* "I regret that what it did was give me direction, ideas that kids my age did not have. So it showed me what to do and how, and I became rather skillful, and with that I knew it was shameful and secretive. This led me to setting up other kids, and later to being abused by older kids."

7. *Did this ever lead to sex with real people?* "Yes. The first time was when another boy masturbated in front of me. I was molested at the age of 10, 11, and 12, and it wasn't something that offended me. At 16 my best friend of 15 had a girlfriend and needed money, so I got him to pose nude so I could photograph him. I then used these to masturbate to them, several times in succession. The man-to-man sexualizing began at 15 or 16. And everything I saw in the pictures or videos, I did with others."

8. *How would you say your personality was affected by this practice?* "In looking back, I realize that I was so absorbed in it that it became my prime hobby, and I'd spend a lot of time with this and would hide it."

9. *How would you say your perception of and relation to women and/or men was affected by this practice?* "I didn't develop the same way as other children/friends who weren't exposed to it. I think it changed me, made me self-centered, and made me feel it's okay. If they pose and if I want to look at it, it's okay."

10. *Do you detect any attitude change toward women?* "There were parts of a woman's body that frightened me. I disliked looking at women's genitals; they frightened me, didn't know why. Breasts okay. Started becoming preoccupied with the male figure."

11. *What has happened in recovery to your resorting to these images?* "This is my biggest problem in recovery. At 24 I learned about Christianity and saw that the Bible condemned such practices. So to become a Christian I had to throw out my pornography. I had started the collection at 14, saving "the best," and was now 24. It broke my heart to burn it. Felt like a good friend was leaving. I knew I had to exist without it. But frequency of masturbation increased. Before this, I

had been masturbating morning and evening. After this, I was masturbating also after school. Without a stash, I was replaying them in my mind, which gave me shame, because I recognized the moral issue, that I was using people as objects to feed on what was greed."

12. *Are you still tempted when you see one of them? How? What power do they still have over you?* "Yes. I stopped acting out with men when I became a Christian at 24. But from time to time if I would look at a magazine or bookstores; lust overcame me, and I'd be addicted again and would binge, buying it, reading it, looking at it, throwing it out. Then Internet came about and no one could catch me at it. It made it easy, and it was killing my soul. And I knew I'd have to break the habit again, so ingrained was it in me."

13. *How would you summarize the effect picture sex has had on your life?* "It was not just a slight experience; it was something that was teaching, training me, influencing me, and had a very damaging effect on me because I didn't have the proper view of men and women, didn't have a healthy view of sex. It made me live in a world of sex with sexual thoughts. Worst part of it all is that whatever I am today it's still ingrained in me; it's still part of me. If I only had someone at the beginning who said, 'This isn't right,' but nothing was ever said. So today I know the damaging effect it has, but is now a fight on my hands because it's an addiction."

14. *How did the power of picture-sex affect you and your sexuality?* "Extremely powerful! And since my personality might have been a bit addictive or compulsive, this was the worst thing for me. Parents would never think of allowing their children to swim in infested polluted waters with garbage floating around them or partake of a drink that has poison in it or food that was sitting out and spoiled and allow them to eat it and become ill, and yet, their children are feeding on pornography. It poisoned my mind. It is not healthy food. 'A picture is worth a thousand words.' Incredible power. Its damage is there because it just forced me to go keep going back. If I didn't have pornography I created it in my own mind."

15. *How hard is it to recover from picture sex?* "Extremely hard! And I don't know why. I just know that it makes me feel good, I want it, it's an expensive habit, and yet I want to break free from it. It has the strongest hold on me. I was able to stop acting out with men, but the pornography is so hard! It's getting less; I've looked more at male and

female having sex on film, but sometimes I come right back to the other. I'm trying desperately to stop it. I got on the Internet, and now I cannot cancel it, no matter how much I want to."

16. *Do you have any suggestion on how this should be handled with your own or other children today?* "I wish my parents would have looked through my room carefully to see what I was up to. And then show me the correct way. I don't blame them for it, since they did the best they could, but they didn't protect me in that area."

17. *At what age do you think such preventive education could start today?* "At any age, depending on the child."

D.
Age 39, married but presently separated. Sober 3 days.

1. *At what age did you experience images coupled with any kind of sexual thinking or behavior?* "I was 7 or 8. My first 'image' or picture was my mother."

2. *Describe the scene of how that initial connection between pictures and sex (or sexual type thinking or activity) came about.* "My mother's image was tied up in my relationship with her and her crazy, cruel, and inappropriate behavior. Her treating me as an object led my sexual development to be unreal relationship to her, and through her to all women."

3. *Describe the image itself, what the picture shows. (Detach yourself from the effect the image had on you and try to communicate what's actually there in the picture. The next question will ask for the effect the image had inside you.)* "I have a picture of my mother and myself (overweight) at age12 or 13 for me and 40s for her. She had aggressive, domineering pose; self absorbed trance; *inappropriate* sexual areas (hot pants, breast showing); so self-absorbed I was not 'there' for her—I was fat, feminized child."

4. *What effect did viewing that image have inside of you? If you can, play back your feelings in slow motion so we can see the progression of feelings and impact. Another way of asking this is, What was the picture (or pose) communicating to you?* "A dual feeling of wanting to strike out and hurt her and also one of wanting to submit to the very real force of her persona—submit in order to escape the exhaustive process of hating and fighting her."

5. *With the picture there in front of you, what did you do? Act out? Fantasize? Go into a trance? Etc.* "The overall image and spirit of my mother was present with my first masturbation (7 or 8), the frustration with her neurotic, non-participatory as my mother-nurtures; the pain of her treating me as an object; not caring for my development as a human being and a man, seeing her manipulate my father, being jealous of my father and my relationship, her manipulating him in front of me—sexual overtones—her saying, 'See; I have the power!'"

6. *Did your use of images escalate? How? Did your inner reactions and feelings change over time as you continued to resort to picture sex? Please describe.* "I started to use pictures to find a "good" mother, one who *wanted* me. This wanting me was the prime motive, to get-take what I did not get from her."

7. *Did you reach a point when you would say that you had crossed the line into addiction? At what age, and what makes you think you were addicted?* "Right from the start (7 or 8) addiction, the only way to medicate rage, anger and frustration."

8. *Did you experience any turning point(s) in your history of picture-sex where something new was going on, either in the content of the images themselves, your behavior, or your thinking? Was there some specific incident connected with this, such as a special picture or experience? Describe the picture and/or incident.* "At age 30-32 I found a magazine at work about the domination scene (males slaves). This hit me in a very significant way—the ultimate act-out—to dispel the exhaustive process of hating mother. Just give in to her and her spirit—'the ultimate surrender.'"

9. *What place did these pictures come to have in your life?* "Very large— then to act [it] out for real with my wife—[and] to some extent with others. Same theme recurring became only way to have sex."

10. *How would you say your sexuality was influenced by resorting to images?* "Completely giving in to lust, taking all humanity out of sexual contact. No caring for the other person or myself. Denying my own humanity."

11. *How would you say your personality was affected by this practice?* "More trance-like at all times. Less cognizant of reality of myself and others. More of being and treating others as objects—all others, including males."

12. *How would you say your perception of and relation to women and/or men was affected by this practice?* "As I said, more perception of people as objects, less compassion."

13. *What has happened in recovery to your resorting to these images?* "When lust occurs, this is still underlying and at times the prime emergent factor."

14. *What's your relation to these images now?* "Much more toxic! The worshipful role I take is in direct conflict with my relationship with God."

15. *Are you still tempted when you see one of them? How? What power do they still have over you?* "Yes; at times. Pulls me into trance, escape from my anxiety, from misconnection to females/humanity, and hatred for females and female behavior."

16. *Do you still "drink"? If so, how does it affect you?* "Do not drink often; really comes down to spiritual fitness."

17. *If you do not drink, how do you not drink?* "By being centered, fit spiritually and abstinence. Once sexual, I am far more temptable."

18. *What does recovery mean for you?* "To get to the root problem of hating my mother. My 'deeper' recovery means positively and finally resolving my hatred for my mother and all females."

19. *How would you summarize the effect picture sex has had on your life?* "Dominate my consciousness, the image starting with mother. Insight: the image of mother was not REAL—clouded/fuzzy by means of fear/anger TRANCE. My *drug* to medicate the sin of fear and hatred."

20. *What would you say or have someone else say to your parents (or caretakers, educators, etc.) if, knowing all this in recovery now, you could go back in time to the very beginning of your picture-sex experience?* "This society must change its orientation/focus from materialism, which obviously is not working (not many happy people) to one of recovery and true spiritual union to our Creator. 'Seek FIRST the kingdom and his righteousness.'"

21. *Do you have any suggestions on how should this be handled with your own or other children today?* "By first providing the example— talk is cheap. A child needs to see the parents' recovery to give it the guidance into its own recovery process. Then meaningful discussions on why lust and pictures are so deleterious and destructive."

THE SPIRITUAL BASIS OF
PSEUDO-REALITY

Why are we so in love with the unreal? Why are we so susceptible to pseudo-reality? Why does pseudo-reality pass so easily for or look better than reality? If we can glimpse what lies behind our affinity for pseudo-reality, it will help us understand pseudosexuality and establish the basic direction recovery must take. The line of reasoning that follows is new to me; I'm still groping around the edges of the ideas.

Let me begin by categorically stating that, all of our cultural predisposition notwithstanding, *the basis of our propensity to pseudo-reality lies not in our culture but within ourselves.*

We entertain a fundamental fallacy about ourselves. The fallacy is that we perceive ourselves to be isolated within ourselves. For example, listen to the inner dialogue of a person trying to justify not loving his neighbor:

> I can't get into another person's consciousness, and he can't get into mine. I feel for myself; I do not feel his consciousness. The world shines into my consciousness, and I am not conscious of his consciousness. I am an individual; he is an individual. My self must be closer to me than he can be. Our two bodies keep me apart from his self. *I am isolated within myself* (emphasis added).[180]

This isolation within myself is the key here. The ego-in-isolation acts as though it were a separate entity within me, requiring my absolute attention, care, and devotion. This is a phantom self that usurps the place of the rightful possessor—the Father of my spirit.

263

"For the only air of the soul, in which it can breathe and live,
is the present God and the spirits of the just:
that is our heaven, our home, our all-right place."[181]

We must be wary of giving unthinking heed to the insistent cries of some who would label as "sexist" references to God as Father. Such views and demands are what would be expected from the pseudosexual revolution we've been talking about. We can be charitably understanding without capitulating.

We are made to be fundamentally relational. The self is one only when it is one with its Father, who is Love. When disconnected, we create this isolated self within us, this "other-Ego," which demands our attention, care, and devotion. Therefore, without the Love-Presence, the self is divided and in conflict with itself, catering to this "Self" that seems to be the real me but is a usurper.[182]

"To embrace is the necessity of our deepest being." No one loves because he sees why, but because he simply loves. Love is being one with. But we attempt to fill the relation by taking instead of giving. *"The violent seize joy by force only to find her perish in their arms"* (MacDonald, "Life").

"'Connect with me and make me whole,' we cried with outstretched arms." And in our misconnection, our isolation is confirmed and enhanced.

When a man does not love, the not-loving has to be rationalized, since love is the natural state of existence. Let's say I can't stand a certain person. Actually, I may even despise her. I have no love for her at all. But since love is the natural state for the human, I will have to create a reason *not* to love that person, which is precisely what has been happening in my addiction. It turns out I am really addicted to my phantom or pseudo Self, serving its demands. This addiction to Self is what lies behind and drives pseudosexuality and lust.

Another way of looking at it: When Love is not present, there is a separating gulf between me and the person. A lust addict experiences this gulf in every encounter. Therefore, the gulf of separation is interpreted by the addict as the normal state, i.e., there is overwhelming evidence *for* isolation. But I cannot believe the ground of my isolation and separation is in *me*! I am Okay. Therefore the other person must be at fault. This is the Great Lie, issuing from pride-blindness. Therefore

I must discover what's "wrong" with her and create a phantom "her," which is nothing more than a composite of perceived wrongs or characteristics I have selected to fit my need to reject. This is how I manufacture that pseudo-person that stands in the gulf between me and the real her. I create that phantom to shut Love out. I create the "defective person" in a vain attempt to justify my absolute individuality and resentment. No wonder I am isolated within myself and hence a law only to myself.

We create a rationale not to love so we don't have to surrender to the law of Love—to God—so we can serve our own inner god. This is idolatry of the Self—self-worship. Love would demolish the phantom, and I would have an openness toward that person instead of being isolated within myself. Oneness, instead of separateness. (Do we not feel the pain when someone doesn't let *us* in? When they harbor that phantom image they have of us and shut us out?)

When the real person whom we will resent or lust after comes to our attention, we make a decision, issuing from the disposition of our heart: to negate their reality to keep the defective-person phantom or lust-object phantom alive and hence keep our Self-in-isolation "alive." We shut Love out. This has become a reflex, and is so pervasive today, so insidious, we cannot see or feel the force of it. Yet this may well be the root cause underneath not only domestic violence today, both emotional and physical, but relational and marital conflict. The origin of violence is in the soul of man.

Since the Self in isolation, our pseudo-self, cannot love, it must *take*. When I take, Self is enthroned and seems to be enhanced. I seem to be more, to get more, have more. But this is pseudo-Life, without freedom. Shutting out Love comes at the terrible price of slavish servitude to the inner god of my own making. *This pseudo-Self is the basis of pseudosexuality.*

This whole process is what lies behind many of those inner scenarios, or "tapes," we play concerning people, those scenarios having to do with our resentments and fears. We are conjuring up phantom people who aren't real so we can shut out Love and serve the god of Self. The Love we shut out is beckoning, knocking at the door of our hearts to come in in every one of these situations!

The spiritual basis of pseudo-reality is thus a willful turning away from Love, separation from the Source of our life, shutting out the love of God, which is seeking entrance in and through our relation with others.

In this condition we're all set up, ready and waiting, for phantom persons and images to take the place of Love, the Real. This helps explain our affinity toward resentment and lust and also toward the image-connection.

> But let a man once love, and all those difficulties which appeared opposed to love will just be so many arguments for loving. Let a man once find another who has fallen among thieves; let him be a neighbor to him, pouring oil and wine into his wounds, and binding them up, and setting him on his own beast, and paying for him at the inn; let him do all this merely from a sense of duty . . . yet such will be the virtue of obeying an eternal truth even to his poor measure . . . that he will yet be ages nearer the truth than before, for he will go on his way loving that Samaritan neighbor a little more than his . . . dignity will justify. . . .
>
> This love of our neighbor is the only door out of the dungeon of self. . . . The man thinks his consciousness is himself; whereas his life consisteth in the inbreathing of God. . . . To have himself, to know himself, to enjoy himself, he calls life; whereas, if he would forget himself, tenfold would be his life in God and his neighbors. (MacDonald, *Unspoken Sermons Series One*, pages 203–215)

Applying this concept to lust and sexuality, we have already seen that every lust event is a negation of Love (chapter 4). Every resentment event is likewise a negation of Love. No wonder we lustaholics are such love cripples, we have engineered Love right out of ourselves! We've done it with those thousands of instances where we have chosen to believe the Lie. Misperception of ourselves and others to serve our false self, the self in isolation. The image revolution and our image-connection make this misperception of reality immediately available because the omnipresent phantom image-woman and image-man saturate the physical and spiritual air about us now—a cultural manifestation of that which is within us. We live in the air of phantom reality, which is the negation of Love. That's why we dash so madly and so futilely after sex and love. I pray God my recovery will not stop until my false self—my ego-in-isolation—is no more.

Recovery progressively stops this ego-in-isolation process and eliminates the basis of our need to lust, resent, and fear. This is what the Steps do when each of these twelve principles becomes incorporated into a new way of living.

IMAGE-CONNECTION AND OUR RELATIONAL CAPABILITY

I venture into theory here; words fail me in trying to communicate what I sense. This at least may help us think critically, and it's important that we do so. Remember, we're the ones who have to "step outside" our world to see how it is affecting us. So, how does image-connection affect our capacity for interpersonal relationship? First, what do we mean by image-connection, also referred to as image addiction? We've seen that it is our way of perceiving and relating to reality conditioned by living in a picture-driven world, described in Part III. Beginning with the advent of photography, we increasingly live in virtual reality—image reality—which is pseudo-reality. It is this image-addiction, this image-Connection, that has affected our relation to reality, others, and God.

Humans have the very special capability of relating to each other at the deepest level of being, the spiritual level, which is deeper and goes way beyond physical, linguistic, or social intercourse. We are designed to relate spiritually, at the very core of our inner being. Let's call this our *spiritual relational capability*. Image addiction perverts this relational capability by programming it to virtual reality. Once this spiritual intercourse capability has been oriented to virtual reality, our ability to interface with Person at the spiritual level is diminished or even locked out. The person cannot *connect* with another person in this deepest and most human dimension of spiritual intercourse because his or her relations have been programmed in image-driven ways. Programmed by and living in virtual reality, we're shut out of the spiritual.

Once the spirit (soul) is set into this image reality, it's as though it cannot directly connect with the *spirit* of Person. True human spiritual intercourse is lost because the soul now lives in a different universe or dimension, virtual instead of real. The spirit-to-spirit, and hence, Person-to-Person relational interface has become obstructed, one might even say lost or perverted. This is why so many of us today are relational cripples and need (must have!) recovery in this area, once we are sober from the addictions.

And since spirit-to-spirit interface is the only means of intercourse with God, who is spirit, God is effectively dead in and to that individual. Not the god instinct or religious sentiment—everyone has that, and most everyone prays to God. The real *connection* is dead; there's no connectability. It's as though there's a sign above our souls that reads, OUT OF COMMISSION.

America's image religion has no room for the God of Life.

WHAT MAKES LUST SO "IMPOSSIBLE" TO OVERCOME?

Answering this question is what this whole book has been about. With the impact of images on the human organism in mind, let's briefly look at the connection of all this with one aspect of recovery. Men in recovery testify to the persistence of susceptibility to lust triggers, and this seems to be typical for lust-sex addicts of any stripe. "I'm sexually sober and want victory over lust; why is this craving to take a "drink" still there when I see a trigger?" This persistence of susceptibility is no respecter of "orientation" and is no respecter of length of sobriety. It seems to be one of the fundamental and virtually universal characteristics of this particular malady. Let me illustrate from an experience of my own after several years of sexual sobriety:

> I pull into the store down the street to make a phone call. Suddenly, in the corner of my eye I see the image of a woman at the bus stop. There's something about the figure, body language, emanation, whatever, that wants to grab me, a powerful magnetic force pulling at the center of my soul. I want to look and connect. I have to. The image is an overpowering trigger for my lust. I'm a goner! The compulsion to turn and take that first look is irresistible. I know that I must look—and "drink." I'll die if I don't.

The fact that I was given the freedom—the grace—not to take that particular drink is the miracle of progressive recovery. But the awesome power that temptation had is the point here. To not take that visual drink is a very real threat of death to lustaholics.

The neurology of addiction helps in understanding this phenomenon. (See Gerald May's excellent treatment of the neurological nature of addiction in his *Addiction and Grace*, HarperSanFrancisco, 1988.) Whole systems of the brain's neurons are apparently configured by conditioning to respond to stimuli as we become habituated to substances or behaviors. In other words, the brain becomes "hardwired" for the lust response, much like an automatic muscular reflex. This explanation has obvious merit and points up one of the difficulties and challenges in recovery: We must experience a power that can transcend our electrochemistry and neuronal programming so we can act against that programming. And we must do the hard work of addiction recovery.

However, this neurological explanation does not seem to satisfy the persistence problem where the new lust is concerned. Most recovering alcoholics who get sober eventually lose the craving to drink, even when in the presence of alcohol; and *their* neurological programming for the addictive chemical is also hardwired in the brain, is it not? This is true even though they are never cured in the sense of becoming invulnerable to resorting to alcohol again. If alcoholics and drug addicts can overcome their neurological conditioning so as to no longer crave the chemical, why does susceptibility to *lust* remain so potent in the lustaholic, even when one is sexually sober and/or abstinent and where sustained victory over such temptations may be in effect for a long time—as in the above example of my story. I don't think we have anything like a complete answer to this important question. Let me offer a bit of conjecture.

Lust reveals a deeper dimension of human existence, which, for lack of adequate vocabulary, we call the spiritual. The fact that denying myself the drink in the above incident felt like the threat of death reveals such a spiritual aspect of my being because the threat of death had nothing to do with my *physical* existence. Knowing I would die if I did not drink tells me I have created within me a spiritual connection with the spirit of Lust. It means I have been having spiritual intercourse with Lust and have become one in spirit with it. It means Lust has been my god, my object of worship, the life-giver without which I cannot live. Thus, through a religious-spiritual addiction, I have created a perverted soul-set. And thus, my spirit-to-spirit interface has become diseased, changed, programmed. Not just neurological programming, *soul programming*!

Another possible element in this persistence of susceptibility to lust is more intangible still. There seems to be a lust-field in the spiritual air about us, with everyone who is captive to and resonating with lust injecting doses of negative energy into that force field. Spiritual contagion. Polluted man polluting Man. It's as though that force field impinges directly on those of us who have been part of it in the past. There's a polarity affinity for it, a susceptibility. Once having been part of that Power, we *know* what it is, even if we can't rationally explain it. We know it, and it "knows" us and seeks our spirit, through sympathetic vibration, to resonate with it. A Darkness trying to overwhelm the fragile ray of Light newly born within us, seeking to reestablish that spiritual connection it once had with us. There almost seems to be an aspect of lust addiction that is demonic, and if not, just as powerful and insidious. (We know so little about the spirit world; perhaps we should be open to learning more.)

Here's a thought from the medical angle. Dr. Jennifer P. Schneider, M.D., Ph.D., brings to our attention what many of us have suspected, that there is something peculiarly potent about sex addiction:

> Milkman and Sunderwirth have divided addictions into three broad categories: arousal, satiation, and fantasy addictions. Sexual addiction is probably best classified as an arousal addiction because its effects on the brain are similar to the effects of cocaine, amphetamines, compulsive gambling, and risk-taking behaviors. In contrast, addiction to alcohol, sedatives or hypnotics, and food are considered by them satiation addictions, whereas marijuana, peyote, and LSD are examples of fantasy addictions. However, Milkman and Sunderwirth (1987) believe that sexual addiction is unique in that it is its "unequaled capacity to profoundly influence each of the three pleasure planes—arousal, satiation, and fantasy—that qualifies it as the *pièce de résistance* among the addictions" (p. 45).[183]

Now add to this what we've just learned about image addiction, the image religion, and the religion of the Self, and we see how our susceptibility problem—and recovery—become immensely complicated.

This is why the solution must penetrate as deeply as the problem and why recovery cannot persist in isolation.

Thus, recovery must begin with physical sexual sobriety, where sex becomes optional instead of addictively necessary, proceeds in victory over lust, and must finally go on to spiritual decoupling from the hard-wiring and *healing of the spirit-to-spirit interface via the real Connection with God and others.* We must find what our lust was really looking for. It has been called "the expulsive power of a new affection."

After all is said and done, regardless of the difficulties, let it be proclaimed joyously that it is possible for the lust-obsessed and addicted to become free not to lust. Thank God!

(Also, see the discussion of "Lust as a Function of the Primordial Warrior Response," in pages 76–78.)

8

RESEARCH SUGGESTIONS

- Check the author's analyses against subjective data from other recovering lust-sex addicts using specially designed questionnaires and interviews.
- Check for the effects of lust (in its various sexual or non-sexual expressions) on the brain. Since science can increasingly detect changes in brain activity corresponding to various thought processes, it might be fruitful to perform such brain scans during actual lust episodes. (A word of caution: for recovering persons to deliberately "drink" reignites the compulsion and can lead to loss of physical sexual sobriety as well.) Also, check and measure physiological manifestations of the lust response. Ref. chapter 4.
- There is much ado about genes and violence lately. Some researchers feel people with low levels of the brain chemical serotonin may be predisposed to violence, and research is looking for "vulnerability genes" that create the serotonin deficit. I suggest testing the relation between *lust* and low serotonin levels, which may be one of the *results* of lust's cumulative inner violence upon the self.
- Plot the rise and types of violence against the culturally evolving expressions of lust. This may reveal linkages between lust and violence hitherto unnoticed.
- Experimental psychologists: Set up some experiments where you can actually detect and perhaps even quantify differences in the subjective reaction to viewing magazine photos, differences between simple perception and Sontag's addictive *consumption*. There's a vast difference between the two kinds of

seeing, and this must be reflected in body/brain chemistry as well. In other words, detect physiological (chemical or neurological) changes induced by lust. I note that there are efferent nerve fibers going from the brain to the retina. What on earth is the brain doing sending signals to the retina?

- Trace how the histories of novels and popular music reflect our evolving pseudosexuality.
- Plot the accelerating incidence of male impotence against the history of lust in the person and the culture.

ACKNOWLEDGMENTS

I want to express my sincere gratitude to the many who have freely given their time and care to read and comment on the manuscript. Your feedback and encouragement helped bring this book into being. Special notes of gratitude are due to two who have passed on: Ron Haynes, my literary agent, who first believed in this book and fearlessly sought its publication, and Edward John Carnell, who taught by example: "Truth, wherever it leads." There is no way I can ever convey my heartfelt gratitude to all those who have been part of the process of my own recovery since April 24, 1974. And no one will ever know, nor can words ever express, what the life, love, and partnership of my wife have meant to me, to this effort, and to the fellowship of recovery. In humble gratitude to the One watching over us all—*sine qua non*.

I am indebted to the following sources for permission to use their material:

20/20 program of January 29, 1993, "Sex with the Unreal Woman." Courtesy of ABC News—*20/20*.

John D'Emilio, *Sexual Politics, Sexual Communities: The Making of a Homosexual Minority in the United States 1940–1970*, University of Chicago Press, 1983.

John D'Emilio and Estelle B. Freedman, *Intimate Matters: A History of Sexuality in America* (2nd ed: Chicago: University of Chicago Press, 1997).

Excerpts from *On Photography*, by Susan Sontag. Copyright © 1977 by Susan Sontag. Reprinted by permission of Farrar, Straus and Giroux, LLC.

Excerpts from *The Film, A Psychological Study*, by Hugo Munsterberg; Dover, 1970; as an exact and unabridged republication of the original edition, which was titled *The Photoplay: A Psychological Study*, D. Appleton and Company, New York, 1916.

NOTES

1　I am dependent here on the study of literary sources in *Solitary Sex—
A Cultural History of Masturbation*, by Thomas W. Laqueur, Zone
Books, New York, 2003, and the review article by Jennifer Frangos in
the *Bryn Mawr Review of Comparative Literature*, Vol. 4, Number 2
(http://www.brynmawr.edu/bmrcl/Summer2004/Laqueur.html).

2　My perception is that there is recently an increasing use of the word
"lust" in the print media. For example, the word shows up twice in the
first two articles I happened to read in *Time* magazine (July 18, 1994):
the family is referred to as "the perfect container for our lusts and loves"
(Barbara Ehrenreich, "Oh, *Those* Family Values," p.62), and America
is "Held Hostage by its own lust for sensation" (Richard Corliss, "It's
Already the TV Movie," p. 36). I note also there's an anthology edited by
John and Kirsten Miller titled LUST (*L.A, Times,* January 8, 1995).

3　John D'Emilio and Estelle Freedman, *Intimate Matters: A History of
Sexuality in America*, 1988, p. 312.

4　*Encyclopedia Britannica*, 14th ed., vol. 17, p. 514.

5　D'Emilio and Freedman, *Intimate Matters*, 1988, pp. 131–132.

6　The photo appeared in the February 1993 issue of *Smithsonian* magazine. The pictures in D'Emilio and Freedman, *Intimate Matters*, give a
sampling of the historical progression of female lustification.

7　Tony Perry, "Mission: Bring Spy Plane in From Cold," *Los Angeles Times*,
August 20, 1994, p. F1.

8　News item from the *Los Angeles Times*, June 3, 1994, dateline Seoul: "Ask
any sixth-graders here about Japanese comic books, and their eyes light
up. . . . Japanese comics deliver the ultimate in thrills, chills and 'interesting stuff with girls, like nakedness,' he said [a Korean boy]. 'We all
like Japanese comics better, because Korean comics are too sissy.'"

9　D'Emilio and Freedman, *Intimate Matters*, p. 280.

10　Kinsey, Pomeroy, and Martin, *Sexual Behavior in the Human Male*,
W. B. Saunders , 1948, Philadelphia, p. 510.

11　ABC News "20/20" program of January 29, 1993. See Chapter 1.

12   See chapter 9 in Masters and Johnson, *Homosexuality in Perspective,*
     1979, for their research on the incidence and comparison of sexual
     fantasy patterns for both homosexuals and heterosexuals.

13   Samuel and Cynthia Janus, *The Janus Report on Sexual Behavior,* Wiley,
     New York, 1993, p. 113.

14   Telecon with *Playboy* corporate offices November 8, 1990.

15   Laumann, Gagnon, Michael, and Michaels, *The Social Organization of
     Sexuality—Sexual Practices in the United States,* University of Chicago
     Press, 1994, and its companion volume *Sex in America,* 1994, Little,
     Brown and Company.

16   According to Larry Flynt, who is at the center of the business, *Los
     Angeles Times,* April 23, 2004; and September 1, 1999.

17   Boardwatch.com, 04/06/04.

18   News Item: "In Guatemala, recently, callers ran up $1 million bills [sic]
     to a sex phone line. Some people, not realizing the cost of the calls, had
     to file for bankruptcy in a nation where only two of every 100 people
     have telephones." *The Daytona Pennysaver,* January 19, 1994, p. 21.

19   *Los Angeles Times,* February 16, 1993, p. D1, 6.

20   Jim Orford, Ph.D. (now Professor of Clinical and Community
     Psychology at the University of Birmingham, UK), "Hypersexuality:
     Implications for a Theory of Dependence," *British Journal of Addiction,*
     73 (1978) 299–310.

21   *The Sexual Addiction,* by psychologist Patrick Carnes, Ph.D., came out
     in 1983 (CompCare Publications). In the psychological community
     there followed considerable debate as to whether the term "addiction"
     was appropriate when referring to sex.

22   The term "sexaholic" first came into usage in 1981 in the literature of the
     recovery program Sexaholics Anonymous, patterned after AA.

23   Some early gay and lesbian magazines originated in the Los Angeles
     area. *Vice Versa,* the first magazine for lesbians, came out in 1947.
     Physique Pictorial came out in 1951 as a magazine for gay men. One
     made the scene in 1953 as "the first widely circulated, explicitly gay
     magazine in the country" (Bettina Boxall, "Fight for Gay Rights Started
     Early in L.A.," *Los Angeles Times,* June 26, 1994, and letter to the editor
     by G. L. Leyner dated June 25, 1994).

24   From *Genesis Interface,* an historical novel of the future, by R. Kuljian.

25   Some authors think this trend is desirable. "Widespread acceptance of
     visual images of lesbian or gay male sex is one of the last frontiers of gay
     liberation." Others claim that "the production by lesbians of sexually

explicit work properly challenges the monopoly on sexual representa-
tion by the heterosexual majority." (Margaret Cruikshank, *The Gay and
Lesbian Liberation Movement*, Routledge, London, 1992, page 54.) If we
would discern what lustification has done to heterosexuality, we might
well have second thoughts about this.

26 Notice how this indicates the man, in ranting against the introduction
of yet another girlie, is unwittingly revealing the destructive effects of
his lifestyle on himself and others. He is powerless to stop, condemning
the very thing to which he is captive. The best anti-porn campaign is
personal recovery.

27 Lawrence Goldstein in the *Los Angeles Times*, July 4, 1993.

28 Quoted in "The Memes of Love, Sex and Marriage" by Leon Felkins,
15 March 2001 (http://www.magnolia.net/~leonf/common/lovesex5.html).

29 Richard Dawkins, *The Selfish Gene*, Oxford University Press, 1976,
p. 192. Sources for the rest of the information on memes come
from F. Heylighen and Glenn Grant in *Principia Cybernetica Web*,
http://pespmcl.vub.ac.be/MEMIN.HTML, "Memes: Introduction,"
"Competition between Memes and Genes," and "Memetic Lexicon,"
as of 3/3/2005; and Leon Felkins, "The Memes of Love, Sex and
Marriage," http://www.magnolia.net/~leonf/common/lovesex5.html,
rev. 15 March 2001.

30 "The C. Everett Koop Papers—Tobacco, Second-Hand Smoke, and the
Campaign for a Smoke-Free America," in Profiles in Science, National
Library of Medicine. http://profiles.nlm.nih.gov/QQ/Views/Exhibit/
narrative/tobacco.html.

31 *Los Angeles Times*, October 24, 1993. Catharine MacKinnon is described
as a feminist legal theorist and anti-pornography crusader.

32 "The Chemistry of Love," in *Time*, February 15, 1993, p. 51.

33 Robert J. Stoller, *Sex and Gender On the Development of Masculinity and
Femininity*, Science House, New York, 1968, p. 23. Dr. Stoller, Professor
of Psychiatry at the UCLA School of Medicine, explains that many species, including the human, apparently are genetically endowed so that
certain systems of the brain will respond to certain stimuli in the outside world so that the animal is receptive to being permanently influenced by these stimuli (page 7).
 Dr. Stoller adds: "The more complex the animal, the more vari-
ability in response is provided by these systems [internal nervous and
chemical systems], until imperceptibly one enters a sphere in which,
first, learned (postnatal) behavior becomes prominent and, finally, in
which conscious choice plays a part." (p. 8)

These descriptions fit exactly my own history of what I am calling sexual imprinting and those of others whose stories I've followed over the years. This imperceptible movement from imprinted responses to conscious choice is the story of sexual mis-orientation in-process.

34   As an example: "Lance's mother bent her son to her wishes, but she did this in a warm, loving, concerned, overprotective atmosphere in which was invisibly mixed her need to ruin his masculinity. So rather than a breach being formed in the protective shield, the shield itself bent him—'imprinted' him." Stoller, *op.cit.*, p. 123

35   *Encyclopedia Britannica*, 1951, vol. 20, p. 420E.

36   Alfred Kinsey, et al, *Sexual Behavior in the Human Male*, 1948, p. 677.

37   Discovery channel special aired the week of July 5, 1993.

38   *Discover* magazine, June 1992.

39   The writings of the late Michael Polanyi are to the point here. See his *Science, Faith, and Society; The Study of Man; Personal Knowledge; and The Tacit Dimension*. This scientist-turned-philosopher should have received a prize for forcing science to think. But his monumental work seems to have had little impact on the sweeping currents of the age which seek only more "advances in science." Polanyi questioned the philosophical and epistemological underpinnings of modern science. Here's to a posthumous Nobel for Polanyi!

40   As reported in *Time*, March 1, 1993, p. 57.

41   Susan Sontag, *On Photography*, The Noonday Press, Farrar, Straus and Giroux, New York, p. 158.

42   _____. *On Photography*, p. 179.

43   Friedman, R. C., *Male Homosexuality: A Contemporary Psychoanalytic Perspective*, p. 3, reported in "Human Sexual Orientation: The Biologic Theories Reappraised," by William Byne and Bruce Parsons, *Archives of General Psychiatry*, vol. 50, March 1993, p. 228. We note that the concept of homosexuality itself, as used in the media, is recent. For example, "The origins of homosexuality have been a subject of intense debate ever since the concept of sexual orientation emerged from reconceptu-alizations of gender that occurred during the 18th century in northern Europe." p. 228.

44   *Sexaholics Anonymous*, p. v.

45   From G. P., used with permission.

46   See *The New Celibacy* by Gabrielle Brown, 1989, a work documenting the remarkable wave of chosen celibacy (including not masturbating) among singles and marrieds alike.

47   I must say that the above scene describes an actual scenario during my morning walks, after years in recovery. The woman was an attractive single mother living on our street. For me to feel the power of that image (usually dressed in shorts) and the temptation to drink, yet not have to do so, is the incredible joy of my life today.

48   In the early 1960s, as a practicing luster, isolated between marriages and living in a dreary ten-dollar-a-week room adjacent to a metropolitan airport, I happened upon the technique of progressively lowering the threshold of my awareness of the subjective antecedents to any memory. This research is documented in my unpublished and unfinished paper "The Microgeny of Recall—The Subjective Analysis of the Mental Process as an Approach to Memory Theory." This work was derived from examining the micro-genesis of hundreds of my own recall specimens.

49   *Discover*, April 2007, p.69, referring to *The Lucifer Effect—Understanding How Good People Turn Evil*, by Philip Zimbardo, Random House, 2007.

50   See Dr. Gerald May's excellent chapter on "The Neurological Nature of Addiction" in his *Addiction and Grace*, Harper San Francisco, 1988. Positron Emission Tomography (PET) is providing revolutionary insights. For example, it is known that "behind every emotion and every piece of behavior there is a change in a molecule." So says Dr. Ira Glick, professor of psychiatry, Stanford University School of Medicine, in "Study Backs Comfort Effect of Music," in Associated Press *Health News*, September 25, 2001, in InteliHealth.com.

51   *The Flight from Woman*, Farrar, Straus and Giroux, New York, 1965, p. 214.

52   See the article "Sex Revolution Triggers National Impotence," by Judith A. Reisman, Ph.D., in WorldNetDaily.com for Friday February 12, 1999.

53   Sigmund Freud, *Observations on "Wild" Psycho-Analysis*, in *Great Books of the Western World*, vol. 54, p. 128.

54   Vance Packard says *Playboy* "dedicated itself to extolling the hedonistic, sensual way of life." *The Sexual Wilderness*, p. 28.

55   August 24, 1972 issue of *Time* magazine, referring to the new magazine *Oui*. (It would be a safe bet to assume that the same type of thing has been happening in same-sex publications.)

56   "As the AIDS Bureaucracy Cashes In, the Prospect of a Cure Dims," by James P. Pinkerton, *Los Angeles Times*, August 6, 2004.

57   The catalyst for this inquiry was hearing Barbara Ehrenreich (Ph.D. in biology) lecture and later reading her book *Blood Rites—Origins and History of the Passions of War* (Metropolitan Books, Henry Holt and

Company, New York, 1997). Application of her ideas to this subject is solely mine.

58   George Chauncey, *Gay New York—Gender, Urban Culture, and the Making of the Gay Male World 1890–1940*, Basic Books, 1994.

59   "Cunning, baffling, and powerful" is the expression used by recovering alcoholics to describe alcohol (*Alcoholics Anonymous*, p. 58).

60   Ehrenreich, *Blood Rites*, p. 80.

61   William H. Masters and Virginia E. Johnson, *Homosexuality in Perspective*, Little, Brown, and Company, Boston, 1979, pp. 186–187.

62   Marybeth Carter, "Speaking Out on a 'Silent Crime,'" *Los Angeles Times*, April 10, 2004.

63   Donna Ferrato was a "wide-eyed photographer shooting the glamorous life in her native America for a Japanese magazine." One night, while shooting a "perfect couple" in their eight-room home outside New York City, she caught the glamorous husband beating the glamorous wife. She snapped the picture and then tried unsuccessfully to stop the heavy-handed blows. That experience broke Donna's heart and changed her focus from romance to abuse, and she began documenting domestic violence, which became her life's calling. In 1991 she opened the non-profit Domestic Abuse Awareness Project in Manhattan to raise funds for battered-women's shelters. (Dennis Romero, "The Ugly Truth," *Los Angeles Times*, July 27, 1994, p. E1.)

64   Many years ago, before anyone started torching churches, I predicted it would have to happen—such the rage against the failure of their advertised ability to save. In an eighteen-month period from January 1995 to June 1996, there were over 100 church burnings in thirty five states. (Jane Gross, "Burning of Churches Condemned by Coalition," *Los Angeles Times*, June 21, 1996, p.A3) I remember church burnings hitting the news in the 1980s. In 1980 there were 1,420 incendiary or suspicious fires involving churches and related property, compared to 520 such fires recorded in 1994, the lowest level in fifteen years, according to the National Fire Protection Association. (Larry Stammer, "Recent Church Fires Run Against Trend," *Los Angeles Times*, June 22, 1996, p. A4)

65   Recent scientific opinion advises that we should look at the gene approach to behavior very critically. We are told genes "are not doing well for 'causing' various behaviors." Thus, even if genes were found to be implicated somehow, they are not the sole determinant of sexual preference. The human organism is "too marvelously complex for such simplistic theories." (Paul Hoffman, editor of *Discover* magazine, on the McNeil-Lehrer News Hour January 4, 1994.)

66 Evidence that we intuitively sense something subversive about the F-word, despite its widespread use in films and printed media, is that the Motion Picture Association of America's Classification and Ratings Administration board will not give a movie a PG-13 rating if it uses the word more than once. (Claudia Eller, "Ratings 'Ain't Broke,' Board Chair Says," *Los Angeles Times*, August 4, 1994, p. F1.)

67 Jeremy Rifkin, "For the Experiences of a Lifetime, Sign on the Dotted Line," *Los Angeles Times,* April 3, 2000.

68 John D'Emilio and Estelle B. Freedman, *Intimate Matters: A History of Sexuality in America*, Harper & Row, New York, 1988, page xx; see also pages xi, xii, xv.

69 *Sexual Politics, Sexual Communities: The Making of a Homosexual Minority in the United States 1940–1970*, John D'Emilio, University of Chicago Press, 1983. In a footnote D'Emilio cites several works bearing on the social sources for human sexuality.

70 Gay historian Dennis Altman says, "The very term 'homosexual' is a product of the nineteenth century...." "If the idea of the homosexual is a product of the nineteenth century, then the idea of seeing her/him in sociological rather than psychological terms, as a member of a minority rather than as an aberrant individual, is largely a product of the 1970s." *The Homosexualization of America, The Americanization of the Homosexual*, St. Martins Press, New York, 1982, pages 42 and 224. See also *The Cultural Construction of Sexuality*, edited by Pat Caplan, Tavistock Publications, London, 1987, where Caplan says "the concept of 'homosexual' is a relatively recent historical construct, which came into use around the turn of the century...." (p. 5) and Jeffry Weeks, in "Questions of Identity" says, "...[W]e now know from a proliferating literature that such identities are historically and culturally specific, that they are selected from a host of possible social identities, that they are not necessary attributes of particular sexual drives or desires, and that they are not, in fact, essential—that is naturally pre-given—aspects of our personality" (p. 31).

71 See Jacques Ellul's *The Technological Society*.

72 Sherlock Holmes makes an interesting observation about London in the 1880s:

> ... [I]ncidents which will happen when you have four million human beings all jostling each other within the space of a few square miles. Amid the action and reaction of so dense a swarm of humanity, every possible combination of events may be expected to take place, and many a little problem will be presented which may be striking and bizarre ("The Adventure of the Blue Carbuncle").

It follows that "every possible combination" of sexualizing will also take place.

73   Michael Walsh, "Gershwin, by George," in *Time*, January 31, 1994.

74   The following piece from the March 25, 1940 issue of *Time* is a case in point:

> Tin Pan Alley's current trend has been called "the double-entendre era" by Eli Oberstein, president of the U.S. Record Corp. Mr. Oberstein's biggest hit (150,000 copies) is *She Had to Go and Lose It at the Astor* . . . Such "blue" songs are naturally not allowed on the radio networks. Last week NBC revealed that 147 songs are on its blacklist. Because their titles are suggestive, 137 may not even be played instrumentally. Among them: *Lavender Cowboy . . . Dirty Lady . . . But in the Morning, No* . . . Many another song has to be laundered before NBC will pass it.

75   *Coming Out Under Fire*, a film by Arthur Dong, Zeitgeist Films, 1994. This film is a documentary about gay men and lesbians in the military during World War II and is based on the book *Coming Out Under Fire: The History of Gay men and Women in World War II* by Allan Berube. A gross disparity in the military reportedly still exists. Whereas cases are pending in which homosexual officers and enlisted men in the Navy are being discharged simply for declaring that they are gay—without having been charged with actual homosexual activity—others found guilty of child molestation, rape, and incest [why don't we add sex addiction, adultery, voyeurism, and exhibitionism?] are allowed to remain in the service. Art Pine, "ACLU Arm Slams Navy's Policy on Gays," *Los Angeles Times*, August 20, 1994, p. A30.

76   "This . . . underscore[s] how little we know of the fantasy patterning of fully functional heterosexual, homosexual, and ambisexual men and women." Masters and Johnson, *Homosexuality in Perspective*, 1979, chapter 9, "Incidence and Comparison of Fantasy Patterns," p. 174.

77   Another gay historian notes, "While homosexual behavior is widespread across both time and place . . . the concept of a homosexual identity is a recent and comparatively restricted one." (Dennis Altman, *The Homosexualization of America, the Americanization of the Homosexual*, St. Martin's Press, New York, 1982, p.47.

78   By the autumn of 1951, members of the early Mattachine Society would continually repledge themselves in ceremony: (The Mattachines were pioneers in the homophile movement of the 1950s and 1960s.)

> ". . . . We are sworn that no boy or girl, approaching the maelstrom of deviation, need make that crossing alone, afraid and in the dark ever again. . . ." Quoted in D'Emilio, *Sexual Politics, Sexual*

Communities, pages 68–69. One cannot help but identify with this soul-searching honesty and concern. I wonder if gays can understand that my crossing the maelstrom of heterosexual deviation was also lonely, dark, and fearful. And I am not alone; many in recovery can identify with this. Oh that we would let down the barriers between us and see how we are really one in this dilemma that was not of our making! Yet is of our making.

79 Rayford Kytle, deputy director of the news office of the U.S. Public Health Service, in the *Los Angeles Times*, January 3, 1994, page B13.

80 Private communication December 5, 1993. This single man was about ten years sexually sober at the time of this statement. Commenting on the difference between fantasy and lust, he made the following note:

> "I remember vividly about a year into [sexual] sobriety having a sexual fantasy (spontaneous) of a woman I had been very close to and still had friendship with. I had been getting deeper and deeper into my same-sex lust at that time. The point is that the image of her came to me—went through me, left me—and left me feeling alive, clean, like water running through me. It was not obsessive, not toxic, not intense, not lust, but an awakening of a sort."

This "awakening" is very instructive. That's exactly what I've been going through in my recovering relation to women, and I come from a background of opposite-sex acting out and lust!

81 Margaret Cruikshank, *The Gay and Lesbian Liberation Movement*, Routledge, New York, 1992, pages 195–196.

82 Sex and Love Addicts Anonymous, Sex Addicts Anonymous, Sex Compulsives Anonymous, and Sexaholics Anonymous. What the world needs is not another sex addiction recovery program but for all of them to see what we're really up against and not to settle for less than full recovery. What is recovery for the lust addicted, for pseudosexuals? There's the real challenge.

83 Quoted in Gabrielle Brown, *The New Celibacy*, Mcgraw-Hill, New York, 1989, p. xii.

84 The umbrella organization for the most visible of these is called Exodus International.

85 Jennifer P. Schneider, M.D., Ph.D., and Richard Irons, M.D., "Differential Diagnosis of Addictive Sexual Disorders Using the DSM-IV," *Journal of Sexual Addiction & Compulsivity*, Vol. 3, No. 1, 1996, pp. 7–21.

86 Philip Elmer-Dewitt, "Making the Case for Abstinence," *Time*, May 24, 1993, p. 64. We note that there is also "a wave of new books" emphasizing

the value of monogamy. Some of these are listed in Elizabeth Mehren's article "Mad About Monogamy," *Los Angeles Times*, February 2, 1994, p. E1. More recently, see the feature essay "Fifteen Cheers for Abstinence," by Lance Morrow, *Time*, October 2, 1995. The trend becomes even more apparent in such articles as "Straight Arrows," *(Los Angeles Times*, May 3, 1996), with the byline "Surely, true, life-enriching happiness lies down the path of monogamy. But how to attain it? Six things you ought to know to begin."

87 Neal Gabler in the *Los Angeles Times*, January 2, 1994.

88 Witness the following ad, appearing January 10, 1994, and subsequently in the *Los Angeles Times*, representing something of a new trend for this urbane metropolitan newspaper.

MEN ONLY
Penile Enlargement
Penile Lengthening
100% Financing Available
Immediate Results
Self-improvement
Self-confidence

Totally Natural. No Implants! Most Patients WILL double in size.
Surgery ONLY Requires 1 hour . . .
with most men returning to work the next day.

DREAMS DO COME TRUE

Dr. R----- is nationally recognized as the leading specialist throughout
the U.S., completing over 100 surgeries per month.

Since surgery is impossible to explain over the phone,
Dr. R----- offers a FREE 20 MIN CONSULTATION.

89 This appears in an advertisement for the new book *Playboy: Forty Years—The Complete Pictorial History*, *Los Angeles Times*, July 31, 1994.

90 Mark Swed, "Lenny the Indispensable," *L. A. Times*, October 10, 2004.

91 Graham Robb, "Monsters, Margeries, and Pooffs," *L. A. Times*, October 11, 2004.

92 *Time*, August 17, 1992, for example.

93 In "Sex and the Brain," by David Nimmons, *Discover*, March, 1994, p. 68.

94 Sharon Bernstein, "Under the Radar, HIV Worsens," *LA Times*, October 16, 2004, an authoritative summary from leading public health experts.

95 George Chauncey, *Gay New York*, Basic Books, 1994, pages 12, 13.

96 America as a Republic of Entertainment is described in Neal Gabler's *Life the Movie—How Entertainment Conquered Reality*, Alfred A. Knopf, New York, 1999.

97 Alfred C. Kinsey, W. B. Pomeroy, C. E. Martin, *Sexual Behavior in the Human Male*, 1948, p. 639.

98 Kinsey, pp. 639 and 641.

99 For a recent formulation of an interactionist model, see "Human Sexual Orientation: The Biologic Theories Reappraised," by William Byne, MD, PhD, and Bruce Parsons, MD, PhD, in *Archives of General Psychiatry*, vol. 50, March 1993, pp. 228–239.

It is interesting to note that gay writers seem to be backing away from their previous focus on biological determinism: "Even if sexual orientation results from what some social scientists call 'cultural formation,' it still presents itself to most lesbian and gay people as a fact rather than a choice." Robert Dawidoff, "Clinton Speaks the Haters' Code Word," *Los Angeles Times*, June 15, 1993. Dawidoff is professor of history at Claremont Graduate School.

"So far no evidence of biological determination has been discovered. . . ." Margaret Cruikshank, *The Gay and Lesbian Liberation Movement*, Routledge, 1992, p. 26.

"While each month brings the announcement of a new gene linked to a specific behavior, it also becomes clearer that these behaviors are strongly modified by culture, environment and chance. . . . This can be seen in an example in which an individual carries a gene linked to alcoholism, but living in a culture that does not use alcohol, might acquire another behavior, or by carrying other modifying genes or being subject to different external influences, might not be affected in any related way." Donald P. Nierlich, Professor, Dept. of Microbiology and Molecular Genetics, UCLA, in *Los Angeles Times*, May 7, 1996.

"A new book, Our Stolen Future, by Theo Colborn, J. P. Myers and Dianne Dumanowski, pulls together a large number of research findings about industrial chemicals that act like hormones. Called 'endocrine disrupters,' they can either block or falsely stimulate cell-wall receptors, turning secretion, metabolism or replication on or off. The evidence suggests that endocrine disrupters are the cause of falling human sperm counts, female birds that act like males, male alligators with shrunken penises and birth defects or reproductive failures in everything from polar bears to Great Lakes fish." Donella H. Meadows, "Can We Avoid a New Silent Spring," *Los Angeles Times*, March 10, 1996.

100 Jeffrey Schwartz and colleagues at the UCLA School of Medicine, as reported by Josie Glausiusz, "The Chemistry of Obsession," *Discover*, June 1996, p. 36.

Of interest here is the recent discovery that certain species of fish can change sexes like chameleons change color, altering their genitalia and behavior to suit the social circumstances. Biologist Matthew Grober of the University of Idaho cites at least three species which can change sex repeatedly when social circumstances require it, restructuring their genitalia and their brain in an average of four days. "Fish Changes Its Sex to Suit the Occasion, Scientists Say," *Los Angeles Times*, November 13, 1995.

When a region of the brain was found to be smaller in gay men than in straight, it was suggested that the brain difference might somehow cause the difference in sexual preference. Marc Breedlove of the University of California at Berkeley looked at neural changes produced by sexual activity in rats. His research showed that having many sexual encounters shrank the rats' neurons. "Differences between brains may be the result, rather than the cause, of differences in behavior." ". . . scientists are more attuned to how the brain affects the body than how the body [and I would say mind] affects the brain!" As reported in *Discover*, February 1998, pp. 32–33.

I remember seeing a man come into the recovery program from the gay lifestyle where pronounced physical changes occurred in sobriety. The newcomer came in with all the body language, speech, mannerisms, facial appearance, and sexual history commonly attributed to gays. After seeing him in meetings a few times, I left town for speaking engagements. When I returned to that meeting five or six weeks later and saw him in a meeting, sexually sober, I actually did not recognize him, such the dramatic and profound change, which seemed to emanate from the inside out and permeate his entire being. That old persona was simply not there. I was amazed. I've also seen dramatic changes some men evince when recovering from heterosexual sex and lust addiction.

101 "When I moved to L.A. 2½ years ago, I was definitely heterosexual," said a British expatriate. "Now I think I should be bisexual, or trisexual or having sex with plants or something." *Los Angeles Times*, August 3, 1993.

102 *Encyclopedia Britannica*, 11th ed., vol. 14, p. 370.

103 *Bowker Annual*, 36th ed., 1991, and *Statistical Abstract of the United States*, 1991, U.S. Department of Commerce.

104 *Los Angeles Times*, June 2, 1993 article on the ABA Convention and the June 24 article on the Book Industry Study Group's report.

105 "Book Industry Trends 2004," a report of the Book Industry Study Group, reported in "Huge Decline in U.S. Book Sales" by Hillel Italie, Associated Press, May 13, 2004.

106 Susan Sontag, *On Photography*, p. 4.

107 Denise Grady in "The Vision Thing: Mainly in the Brain," *Discover*, June, 1993, p. 58.

108 "Susan Sontag gives eloquent expression to many of these common-places [images having a power in our world undreamed of by the ancient idolaters] in *On Photography* . . . a book that would more accurately be titled, 'Against Photography.'" W. J. T. Mitchell, in *Iconology: Image, Text, Ideology*, University of Chicago Press, 1986, p. 8 note 3. Sontag's work was received with the highest critical acclaim.

109 Overheard on radio news around March 1, 1993. The reference was to a report from France.

110 See *The Hidden Persuaders* by Vance Packard.

111 *Encyclopedia Britannica*, 12th edition, vol.31, "Newspapers," p. 1105.

112 Brian Stonehill, "Sex, Lies and Cinematography," *Los Angeles Times*, December 28, 1995.

113 See, for example, the books of Anne Wilson Schaef: *When Society Becomes an Addict, Escape from Intimacy, The Addictive Organization*.

114 Lary May, *Screening Out the Past*, 1980, pages xii, 22, 39, 43, 37, 148, 163–165; Stuart and Elizabeth Ewen, *Channels of Desire*, 1982, p. 86; Hugo Munsterberg, *The Film, A Psychological Study, the Silent Photoplay in 1916*, p. 8; *Encyclopedia Americana*.

115 Richard Griffith in *The Film*, by Munsterberg, p. xiv.

116 Dorcus and Shaffer, *Textbook of Abnormal Psychology*, 4th ed., 1950, p. 583.

117 Quoted by Richard D. Heffner in the *Los Angeles Times*, February 19, 1992, p. B11.

118 "How is it that propaganda is so effective—operating on all levels. . . ? Even its users, for the most part, are unaware not only of their techniques, but of the effects. Propaganda comes so naturally, perhaps there is a common denominator at the personal level. Perhaps there is something in each of us that not only needs it, but is always practicing it. To the one who is painfully aware of himself, there are constant reminders of his automatic efforts to deceive, influence, or persuade; it seems to be part of the very fabric of our daily way of life. I noticed it only yesterday when I went to get my car from the mechanic at the garage. Knowing how unpredictable repair prices were, I was bending every effort to alter his thinking and behavior so he would grant me a special dispensation of grace. I was not walking by faith; I was walking by technique [propaganda]." Author's letter to Jacques Ellul 21 November 1972 commenting on his *Propaganda*, Knopf, 1971.

119 Film critic David Ehrenstein says, "The entire history of the cinema is about the mass audience forging an emotional identification with people whose experiences are not like theirs." Steve Golin, head of Propaganda Films, says, "Nothing takes the taboo off of anything in Hollywood like box office." Both quotes appear in "The Gay Gauntlet," by film critic Richard Corliss in *Time*, February 7, 1994.

120 Robert T. Eberwein, *Film & The Dream Screen, a Sleep and a Forgetting*, 1984, p. 3.

121 Eberwein, pages 4–7.

122 Karl Barth, *The Epistle to the Romans*, translated from the 6th edition by Edwyn C. Hoskyns, Oxford University Press, 1933, p. 45.

123 W. J. T. Mitchell, *Picture Theory*, University of Chicago Press, 1994, p. 2. Mitchell is Gaylord Donnelley Distinguished Service Professor in the Department of English Language and Literature and the Department of Art at the University of Chicago.

124 Donella H. Meadows (adjunct professor of environmental studies at Dartmouth College), "Culture, Behavior: We Are What We Watch," *Los Angeles Times*, September 22, 1994.

125 Barbara Ehrenreich, "Kicking the Big One," *Time*, February 28, 1994.

126 Richard Stayton, "'Night' Delivers Unfocused Message on TV's Influence," *Los Angeles Times*, March 7, 1994.

127 S. Robert Lichter, Linda S. Lichter, and Stanley Rothman, *Prime Time: How TV Portrays American Culture*, quoted in a review by Rick Du Brow, *Los Angeles Times*, November 26, 1994, p. F20.

128 Ian I. Mitroff and Warren Bennis, *The Unreality Industry—The Deliberate Manufacturing of Falsehood and What It Is Doing to Our Lives*, Birch Lane Press, 1989, p. xi.

129 Mitroff and Bennis, p. 178.

130 Listen to an interesting observation from Quincey Jones, world-renowned popular musician, recipient of the prestigious Jean Hersholt humanitarian award from the Academy of Motion Picture Arts and Sciences: "Even today all these changes happening around the world didn't come from armies or government or government agencies; they came from television shows, from seeing how other people live, from movies, music, attitudes, expressions of freedom—that's the real motivating force in the world, because that reflects the soul of every-body, it collects the soul of everybody, it unifies the soul of everybody." (Interview with Janet Clayton, *Los Angeles Times*, March 26, 1995.) Wait a minute here! I want my own soul!

131 Comcast cable television installer Bill, 15 April, 1993.

132 Virtually unknown before television, attention deficit disorder (ADD) is "the most common behavior disorder in American children." Claudia Wallis, "Life in Overdrive," *Time*, July 18, 1994, p. 43.

133 "Inventing Desire" is the column heading of a review in the *Los Angeles Times* of May 9, 1993 on the book *Inside Chiat/Day: The Hottest Shop, the Coolest Players, the Big Business of Advertising,* by Karen Stabiner. "Inventing Lust" anyone?

134 Richard D. Heffner in the *Los Angeles Times*, Wednesday, February 19, 1992, p. B11.

135 *Los Angeles Times*, 26 March, 1992.

136 Oliver Stone's mini-series "Twin Peaks," as reported in *Time*, May 17, 1993.

137 *Los Angeles Times*, March 26, 1995, from an interview by Global Viewpoint editor Nathan Gardels.

138 "The nation lives in a pervasive culture of spin and hype, the agitated, drooling and unembarrassable twin children of publicity. Spin and hype, working mostly through the magic of television, create a sort of virtual reality in which no one is quite accountable and consequences can be annulled by changing the channel—or adducing a childhood trauma. That powerful universe of sensational illusion has increasingly come to determine the moral atmosphere of America." Lance Morrow in *Time*, May 16, 1994, p. 94.

139 Quoted in Richard Corliss, "That Wild Old Woman," a book review of *For Keeps*, in *Time*, November 7, 1994.

140 "I got the idea . . . to try giving up movies. . . . I began to suspect that something was wrong. As far back as five years old, when they cost less than ten cents, I remember them as being a welcome change from the emotionally impoverished family environment in which I lived. For that reason, they had always been an important source of relief.

"Living alone, I really yearn for a 'romantic' movie fix every once in a while. It feeds my fantasy world—the un-reality. But I decided I wanted sobriety more. So, one day at a time, I gave up my weekly sabbatical. One of the most surprising things I learned was that it was not just the visual images that destroyed serenity; it was the sounds. The last few times I went, I noticed how violently my body reacted to the "thrilling" music and startling sounds added to make an impression in certain scenes. I would come out of the theater with my eyes wide open and my head back from the assault of pictures and noise.

"I miss that journey into fantasy occasionally; and every once in a while, I think a movie has come out that would be safe or sufficiently interesting to break my commitment; but as the time to go approaches, I always decide that it's really not worth it after all. I don't want to be assaulted again, and it's not worth it just to look at something that is not real anyway. . . .

"I have found now, after probably a couple of years of not going to movies, that I am much more peaceful. I do not wait eagerly for my weekly fix anymore. I do not look for the same level of excitement in my real life to reproduce what I found so exciting in the theater [a very telling insight]. Life is much more serene and moves at a much slower pace. I am not as eager as many around me and sometimes feel out of step, but I find that the level of sobriety is worth it. I realize now that I never really got that much out of movies in the first place" [interpolation added].

(Private communication April 16, 1993, used with permission,)

The last I heard, this singularly courageous woman—how many will dare to even think about trying this?—had ruefully slipped back into attending the temple of the goddess.

141 See Neal Gabler's *Life the Movie* for a penetrating analysis of America as the Entertainment Republic. Momism is "an excessive popular adoration and oversentimentalizing of mothers that is held to be oedipal in nature and that is thought to allow overprotective or clinging mothers unconsciously to deny their offspring emotional emancipation and thus to set up psychoneuroses." *Webster's Third Unabridged Dictionary*, 1966. The *Random House II Dictionary* (1987) defines momism as "Excessive adulation of the mother and undue dependence on maternal care and protection, resulting in absence or loss of maturity and independence." The term originated with Philip Wylie in his book *A Generation of Vipers*, 1942. The date of its publication is instructive, coinciding as it does with the wave of accelerating social and historical forces. Momism may be but another symptom of the death of father, another term in the pseudosexuality equation.

> *And we are govern'd with our mothers' spirits;*
> *Our yoke and sufferance show us womanish.*
>
> Shakespeare, Julius Caesar, I:III

142 Joseph Campbell, *The Hero with a Thousand Faces*, Bollingen Series XVII, Princeton University Press, second edition 1968, pages 390–391. [It is interesting that the first edition of this work dates from 1949. One wonders how the author would describe the situation today.]

143 Vance Packard, *The Sexual Wilderness*, 1968, p. 72.

144 Peter Gardella, *Innocent Ecstasy: How Christianity Gave America an Ethic of Sexual Pleasure*, 1985, pp. 140–141.

145 John D'Emilio and Estelle B. Freedman, *Intimate Matters: A History of Sexuality in America*, 1988, p. 223.

146 "Cross Currents, Sexuality and the Modern World," in Vance Packard, *The Sexual Wilderness*, p. 72.

147 Freud considered masturbation "the one great habit that is a 'primary addiction'. . . . The other addictions, for alcohol, morphine, tobacco, etc., enter into life only as a substitute for and a withdrawal [symptom] from it." Max Schur, *Freud: Living and Dying*, New York, International Universities Press, 1972, p. 61, as quoted in *Whatever Became of Sin?* by Karl Menninger, M.D., Hawthorn Books, Inc., New York, 1973, pp. 33–34.

148 D'Emilio and Freedman, *Intimate Matters*, p. xiv.

149 From the novel *Genesis Interface*, by R. Kuljian.

150 D'Emilio and Freedman, *Intimate Matters*, p. 285f.

151 D'Emilio and Freedman, *Intimate Matters*, p. 286f.

152 As reported in *Time*, March 1, 1993, p. 57.

153 Neal Gabler's *Life the Movie*, from the jacket.

154 Alexander Mitscherlich, *Society Without the Father, a Contribution to Social Psychology*, Harper Perennial, 1993, first published in German in 1963 under the title *Auf dem Weg zur vaterlosen Gesellschaft*, pp. xiii–xx.

155 Often, when seeing my wife for the first time in the morning, the instant impulse is rejection—to see only the ageing image and not the person. Now, I have another choice: I can take a contrary inner action, break through the negative, and take the second look into her eyes, the look that sees who she really is. It requires faith to take that action against my programmed feelings, because all of the lust-oriented conditioning cries out that the physical image is the reality. The degree to which I take this contrary action is the degree to which I can let not only my wife in but let God in and know Life. And love. It is said that "Adam *knew* his wife. . . ."

156 From "The Problem," used by many in recovery from lust/sex addiction as describing their own experiences. Reprinted with permission of sa Literature.

157 Margaret Cruikshank, *The Gay and Lesbian Liberation Movement*, Routledge, London, 1992, p. 30.

158 Witness the recent trend away from the mega churches to groups of less than fifty who gather anywhere but in churches and extend themselves

to those in need (K. Connie Kang, "These Christians Radically Rethink What a Church Is," *LA Times* August 14, 2004). The last three chapters (23, 24, and 25) of *Impossible Joy—The Good News for Lust and Sex Addicts and Other Sinners*, Libera Publishing, 1999, represent one man's vision.

159 *My Utmost for His Highest*, Barbour, 1963, p. 293. I find it fascinating that this was first published in 1935, the very year AA was born, ushering in the self-help movement—that which began supplying what the institutional church promised but was not delivering. We would do well to be willing to see what is "the spirit of the religious age in which we live." (Oswald Chambers was an influential Bible teacher in England.)

160 Here are the Twelve Steps of Alcoholics Anonymous, from which other 12-step programs make their adaptations: 1. We admitted we were powerless over alcohol—that our lives had become unmanageable. 2. Came to believe that a Power greater than ourselves could restore us to sanity. 3. Made a decision to turn our will and our lives over to the care of God *as we understood Him*. 4. Made a searching and fearless moral inventory of ourselves. 5. Admitted to God, to ourselves, and to another human being the exact nature of our wrongs. 6. Were entirely ready to have God remove all these defects of character. 7. Humbly asked Him to remove our shortcomings. 8. Made a list of all persons we had harmed, and became willing to make amends to them all. 9. Made direct amends to such people wherever possible, except when to do so would injure them or others. 10. Continued to take personal inventory and when we were wrong promptly admitted it. 11. Sought through prayer and meditation to improve our conscious contact with God *as we understood Him*, praying only for knowledge of His will for us and the power to carry that out. 12. Having had a spiritual awakening as the result of these Steps, we tried to carry this message to alcoholics, and to practice these principles in all our affairs (*Alcoholics Anonymous*, 4th ed., 2001, pp. 59–60, Alcoholics Anonymous World Services, Inc., reprinted with permission).

161 In R. Kuljian's novel *Genesis Interface*, the protagonist, Teilhard Mann, runs across those who are wrestling with the issue of how to survive living in the computer-controlled perfection of World-System of the year 2105. There, the challenge for those who were *not* surviving the System-driven utopia, was to *disconnect* from System while still living within it. Survival (recovery) was an "inside job," and they were discovering how to do this *together*. The author must have sensed that the answer to his own life's dilemma would involve disconnecting from the *spirit* of today's World-System and connecting with others who were doing so.

162 Sexaholics Anonymous is a program of recovery for those who want to stop their sexually self-destructive thinking and behavior, where "The only requirement for membership is the desire to stop lusting and become sexually sober." *Sexaholics Anonymous*, 1989–2002, SA Literature, p. 209. Its web site is www.sa.org.

163 Title-page copy from a *Los Angeles Times Magazine* fashion article of August 28, 1994. I was jolted when I saw the cover and other glamour shots accompanying this article. The shock was as though I had unexpectedly opened a nudie magazine, which I had not done for twenty years. Even the typography was highly toxic. This points up the difficulty of recovery from any form of pseudosexuality.

164 Ginia Bellafante, "Lessness," *Time*, November 7, 1944, p. 71.

165 John D'Emilio and Estelle B. Freedman, *Intimate Matters—A History of Sexuality in America*, New York, 1988, pp. 203, 208, 210.

166 Valerie Steele, *Fashion and Eroticism—Ideals of Feminine Beauty from the Victorian Era to the Jazz Age*, Oxford University Press, 1985, p. 5.

167 George Chauncey, *Gay New York—Gender, Urban Culture, and the Making of the Gay Male World 1890–1940*, Basic Books, 1994 pages 299 and 72. See chapter 10 in Chauncey for a detailed account of these balls and their place in the sexual culture of the time.

168 *Gay New York*, p. 96.

169 John Berger, *Ways of Seeing* (1972) cited in Valerie Steele's *Fashion and Eroticism*, p. 247. Does the woman thereby also open a door to same-sex "orientation"?

170 Genesis 3:16. The Hebrew word translated "desire" comes from the word to run, to have a violent craving for a thing, "desire bordering on disease." Keil and Delitzsch, *Biblical Commentary on the Old Testament*, vol. 1, p. 103.

171 E.g., as fictionalized in *The DaVinci Code*, by Dan Brown.

172 In a radio address and speech to the U.S. Conference on Mayors, President Clinton, trying to deal with the sex-offender issue, said, "We have to find a way to change the culture of America." (*Los Angeles Times*, June 23, 1996, "President Backs System to Track Child Molesters.") I dare say the president will not find a way to do that using government alone. The words of George MacDonald are apropos here:

> *There is no way to make three men right but by making right each one of the three; but a cure in one is the beginning of a cure of the whole human race.*

173 Valerie Steele, *Fashion and Eroticism*, p. 214.

174 Cited in Lary May, *Screening Out the Past—The Birth of Mass Culture and the Motion Picture Industry*, Oxford University Press, 1980, p. 234.

175 Estimate received May 18, 1993 from management personnel who preferred to remain anonymous.

176 Daren Fonda, "Zapped! How the Toy Industry Is Being Outplayed by Video Games This Holiday Season," *Time*, December 6, 2004.

177 From *Playland*, by John Gregory Dunne, excerpted in the *Los Angeles Times* article "The Cameras Loved Her," by David Ehrenstein, August 14, 1944, Book Review section, p. 1.

178 John D'Emilio and Estelle B. Freedman, *Intimate Matters*, p. 278.

179 Albert Ellis, *The American Sexual Tragedy*, Lyle Stuart, NY, 2nd ed. rev., copyright 1962. The three quotes are from pp. 16, 17, and 48.

180 I am indebted to George MacDonald for this line of reasoning, especially his Unspoken Sermons—Series One, 1867, "Love Thy Neighbor" and "Love Thine Enemy." All of the quotes are MacDonald's. I am also indebted to a very special editor friend, whose inputs have proven thought-provoking and helpful.

181 George MacDonald, "The Cause of Spiritual Stupidity," in *Unspoken Sermons—Series Two*, London, Longmans, Green, and Co., 1895 (J. Joseph Flynn facsimile reprint, South Pasadena, CA, May 1987), p. 52.

182 When did this mass emergence of the phantom self so typical of our time come on the cultural scene? When God became dead?

183 Jennifer P. Schneider, M.D., Ph.D., "Sex Addiction: Controversy Within Mainstream Addiction Medicine, Diagnosis Based on the DSM-III-R, and Physician Case Histories," in *Sexual Addiction & Compulsivity*, Volume 1, Number 1, 1994, p. 25.